SHAMANISM AND VULNERABILITY ON THE NORTH AND SOUTH AMERICAN GREAT PLAINS

SHAMANISM AND VULNERABILITY

ON THE NORTH AND SOUTH AMERICAN GREAT PLAINS

KATHLEEN BOLLING LOWREY

UNIVERSITY PRESS OF **COLORADO**
Louisville

Published by University Press of Colorado
245 Century Circle, Suite 202
Louisville, Colorado 80027

ASSOCIATION of UNIVERSITY PRESSES   The University Press of Colorado is a proud member of
the Association of University Presses.

The University Press of Colorado is a cooperative publishing enterprise supported, in part, by Adams State University, Colorado State University, Fort Lewis College, Metropolitan State University of Denver, Regis University, University of Colorado, University of Northern Colorado, University of Wyoming, Utah State University, and Western Colorado University.

ISBN: 978-1-64642-034-6 (hardcover)
ISBN: 978-1-64642-035-3 (paperback)
ISBN: 978-1-64642-036-0 (ebook)
https://doi.org/10.5876/9781646420360

Library of Congress Cataloging-in-Publication Data

Names: Lowrey, Kathleen Bolling, author.
Title: Shamanism and vulnerability on the North and South American Great Plains / Kathleen Bolling Lowrey.
Description: Louisville : University Press of Colorado, [2020] | Includes bibliographical references and index.
Identifiers: LCCN 2020026992 (print) | LCCN 2020026993 (ebook) | ISBN 9781646420346 (hardcover) | ISBN 9781646420353 (paperback) | ISBN 9781646420360 (ebook)
Subjects: LCSH: Shamanism—Bolivia—Isoso. | Guarani Indians—Bolivia—Isoso. | Indians of South America—Gran Chaco—History. | Indians of North America—Great Plains—History. | Indigenous peoples—Social conditions.
Classification: LCC GN475.8 .L69 2020 (print) | LCC GN475.8 (ebook) | DDC 299.8/1144—dc23
LC record available at https://lccn.loc.gov/2020026992
LC ebook record available at https://lccn.loc.gov/2020026993

The University Press of Colorado gratefully acknowledges the support provided by the University of Alberta toward the publication of this book.

Cover photograph by the author.

Contents

Acknowledgments   vii

1 No Place Like Home   3

2 The Chaco Prophet   25

3 The Plains Prophet   60

4 Shamans and Wives   80

5 Shamans and Spies   110

6 Wizards and Ghosts   141

7 Vulnerability in American Heartlands   172

   Notes   195
   References   203
   Index   221

Acknowledgments

My first, purest impulse was to preface this book with an enemies list rather than with acknowledgments. I spend almost infinitely more time ruminating over slights than feeling gratitude for favors and therefore am certain to leave out people whom I should remember in this accounting.

To begin with, my deep thanks to the two very kind anonymous reviewers of this book, my editor Charlotte Steinhardt, and the excellent staff at University Press of Colorado.

The peace of mind necessary to writing was provided in considerable measure by skilled childcare providers. Birgit Muschkeit above all, but also Bozena Wojno, Julia Babcock, Erin Wall, and staff members at Students' Union and Community Early Learning Centre at the University of Alberta and Primrose Place Out of School Care in Edmonton.

Teachers and professors who shaped me intellectually in ways that inform all of my thinking and writing include at Jakarta International School, Ranu Dally and Hideh Harger; at the University of North Carolina at Chapel Hill, Patricia Bedinger and Judith Farquhar; at the University of Chicago, my doctoral committee members Nancy Munn, Elizabeth Povinelli, and Alan Kolata and in particular my doctoral dissertation cosupervisors Terence Turner and Manuela Carneiro da Cunha.

During and after my fieldwork, a series of colleagues and acquaintances in Bolivia, Paraguay, Argentina, the United States and Canada provided crucial help at key junctures: Alberto Giménez, Jürgen Riester, Adelina Pusineri, Raquel Salazar, Gundolf Niebuhr, Hedy Penner, Irma Penner, Benjamin Feinberg, José Braunstein, Lorena Córdoba, Laura Graham, Michael Brown, Suzanne Oakdale, William Fisher, Faye Ginsburg, David Price, Augusto Oyuela-Caycedo, Nancy Peluso, Andrew Graybill, Sarah Carter, Robert Smith, and Charles Schweger. A reading course with Alice Lam shaped the cross-cultural consideration of dependency made in this book. Charlene Nielsen generated the map of Guaraní Occidental communities that appears in chapter 7. Liam Wadsworth created the maps of Isoso and the surrounding region that appear in chapters 1. Harvey Friebe digitized many of the book's images, including from the era of slides. A grant from the Social Sciences and Humanities Council of Canada supported my fieldwork in Paraguay, a grant from the Support for the Advancement of Scholarship fund at the University of Alberta enabled follow-up fieldwork in Bolivia, and a subvention from the Faculty of Arts and Office of the Vice President (Research) at the University of Alberta partially supported the publication of this book.

It would be impossible to name everyone to whom I owe something in Isoso. Although the text for the most part uses pseudonyms except in the cases of the already-renowned shamans Miguel Cuellar and Jorge Romero, here I will thank by their real names some of the many Isoseño people, not all of whom are still living, who have offered me kindnesses ranging from loaning me horses, crossing the Parapetí in pitch darkness at night, beautiful handwoven **vökös**, good-natured joking during long bus rides, gossip over mates and meals to places to live and to sleep, dream interpretation in the morning, sincere interest in my life and family, and sincere sharing of their own lives and families: Bonifacio Barrientos Cuellar, Nelson Justiniano, and Walter Ayala of the Capitanía del Alto y Bajo Isoso; Eugenia Lucero, Bonifacio Martínez, Marleni Martínez, Cleotilde Segovia, Martire Curaripe, Martín Segovia, Teodosia Segovia, Luisa Yerema, Dora Cayaguiri, Eulogio Cayaguiri, Justina Pérez, Feliciano Martinez, Rogelia Tercero, Alberto Ramón, Juana Justiniana, Sergio Segundo, Pedro Ortiz, Teolina Velásquez, Eusebio Guacani, Wilson Garcia, Celia Segundo, Jacinta Segundo, Ramona Miguel, Braulia Miguel, Audencio Lucero, Zoila Medina, Fidelia Segovia, Porfirio Guacani, and Katalina Guacani in Ibasiriri; Félix Segundo, Laura Burirú, Carlos Segundo, Norma Segundo, José Luis Segundo, Rudín Segundo, Malvina Segundo, Marquesa Burirú, Francia Sánchez, Secundino Soria, Carmen Soria, Adela Choipa, Acencia Romero, Lidia Romero, Francisco Iti, Ángel Esteban, Xenobia Sitai, Marleni Sánchez, Salome Vaca, Juana Chiku, Custodio, Claver Guarucupi, and Eliceo in Güirampembirenda (the strikethrough indicates nasalization); Guillermo Baldivieso, Hilberto Sánchez, Guido Ortiz, Catalina Montenegro de Ortiz, Eduardo Cuellar, Andrés Cuellar, Elsa Montenegro, Roman Vaca, Venancia Cuellar, Brunhilda Vaca, Benjamin Vaca,

Saulo Vaca, Ismael Vaca, Joel Vaca, Belisaida Vaca, Domiciana Cuellar, Jesús Cuellar, David Cuellar, Petronila Cuellar, Adriana Cuellar, Ana Karen Cuellar, Federico Cuellar, Anastasia Cuellar, Miguel Cuellar, Cristián Cuellar, Eldi Montenegro and Guadalupe Araúz in Aguarati and Aguaratimi. Yasoropai ye ye. Tüpa tomae peretare, ngaraa akañi pegui.

Not all of these friendships have lasted, but what remains are memories of the fun of combining shared sympathies, senses of humor, and interests in anthropology with Isabelle Combès, Diego Villar, Federico Bossert, Silvia Hirsch, and Bret Gustafson. Ever since we met in a dissertation writing group for discouraged Latin Americanists, Michael Reynolds has remained a sharp, funny, and warmhearted interlocutor about life and career. Only Jessica Jerome herself understands what I owe her both personally and professionally, but a lovely passage from Robert Louis Stevenson's *In the South Seas* captures something like it:

> There is no bond so near as a community in that unaffected interest and slightly shamefaced pride which mark the intelligent man enamoured of an art. He sees the limitations of his aim, the defects of his practice; he smiles to be so employed upon the shores of death, yet sees in his own devotion something worthy. (1998 [1896]: 48)

For many years I have relied upon the kindness, wit, and advice of Natasha Sane and Valentina Galvani regarding the larger part of life that falls outside of my work as an anthropologist. They are remarkable women to have as friends and I know how fortunate I am.

Although the closing convention would be to thank my child for her forbearance in putting up with the long absences writing this book required, the fact is that I wrote this book incredibly slowly and mixed up with other forms of absence that I would have engaged in anyway: principally, teaching and noodling around the internet in my office procrastinating about both teaching and writing. So instead I will thank my daughter Rose for the happy home she provides me simply by being in it. Finally, the research and the writing of this book began long before Rose came along. My sister Maegan Lowrey, my mother, Bolling Lowrey, and my father, William Lowrey, were my support—always moral and sometimes financial—across many, many years of study and fieldwork and professional struggle (or at least wriggling). I owe them everything. I only wish my father had lived to see this book published.

SHAMANISM AND
VULNERABILITY
ON THE NORTH AND
SOUTH AMERICAN
GREAT PLAINS

1

No Place Like Home

The place in Isoso, Bolivia, where I can turn up unexpectedly at three in the morning and receive a hug and a bed and leave days later with tears on all sides lost, several years ago, its person of central anthropological interest. This was a shaman, quite a renowned one in the region. He managed to his eventual regret to attract the attention of so many scientists and agents of development that eventually a laboratory was built around him which became, in a way, his sarcophagus.

The people to whom I now go back are women and children: his wife, her mother and sister, his daughters, and their children. Over the years I have experienced a divide between what brings me back to Isoso—these women, and a few others in two other villages and a small nearby town—and what originally brought me to Isoso: men, principally that shaman but also a second shaman in another village and other men who occupied leadership roles in Isoso in externally funded development projects there around the turn of the twenty-first century. For about a decade between 2003 and 2013 I didn't know how to write or even to think about this disjuncture, at least not intellectually, though I knew how it felt emotionally: like a sham. I had profound sentiments about Isoso and people there that did not in any way animate or inform my analytic work as an anthropologist. Visits back felt at once necessary and silly: necessary to fulfill personal pledges and commitments but silly from a research point of view as the questions I most wanted to ask (who had gotten married and who had split up, who had had babies, who was going to school and who was working, who had been ill, who had died) spoke to no problems of

DOI: 10.5876/9781646420360.c001

general anthropological interest as I then conceived it, and addressing problems of general anthropological interest only seemed possible by asking questions I found ever less compelling of people with whom I'd never felt at ease.

The women I go back to in Isoso are the women who cared for me during my fieldwork. They cooked for me, which in Isoso is no small task. Water has to be hauled from hand pumps, firewood gathered, plant food harvested, and animal food butchered. Some of the women made up beds for me, and others found candles so I could see at night or lent buckets so I could bathe and wash my clothes. They made small talk with me, at first just inquiring how I'd slept, what I'd dreamt about, the way I might be feeling (lonesome), but over time asking more detailed questions about my family, my relationships, my house and my work, and sharing with me stories from the offhand (births of puppies, piglets, and chicks) to the richly elaborated (whose marriages were fraught, and why). All of this interaction was in between my "real" work: awkward censuses, stilted interviews, slightly lost wanderings-about.

I was acutely aware that what they were doing for me was hard effort of both the physical and emotional kind. It made my anthropological research possible but would be invisible in the results, aside from the customary lines of gratitude in an acknowledgments section of a doctoral thesis or eventual book. By the end of my fieldwork in the late 1990s, and certainly in the course of the years that have elapsed since, I had spent vastly more time in the company of, and in conversation with, Isoseño women than with the Isoseño men who were the central actors in the traditional medicine and environmental protection projects that had motivated my first fieldwork in Isoso. Those projects themselves, like my fieldwork investigations of them, came by contrast to appear to me as artificial forms of make-believe.

I arrived at the argument of this book circuitously. In the years between my doctoral field research and its writing, I did a bit of ethnohistorical research; I reread all of the fourteen original Oz books and quite a bit of the biographical literature on their author, L. Frank Baum; I attempted new fieldwork in Paraguay. Those disparate efforts all bear conjoined fruit here. But it was reading theory new to me—in disability studies and in feminism—that helped me organize a set of inchoate themes into a case. My first trip to Isoso was in 1997, and my most recent was in 2019. On a visit in 2013 I took with me philosopher Eva Feder Kittay's 1999 book *Love's Labour: Essays on Women, Equality, and Dependency*. She gave a name and a profound theoretical armature to what surrounded me constantly in Isoso and about which I had never been able to write: "dependency work." I began to have an uncomfortable-making understanding of my previous classification of so many of the activities and interactions that made my time in Isoso possible as unworthy of thoughtful note. Most especially, I began to reassess the way in which intellectual judgement was belied by my own daily practice: often finding false and boring the ostensible objects of my investigative interest whilst spending most of my actual time in the field in interactions that felt vital and genuine but not articulable in disciplinary terms.

It is of course the case that anthropology has always cared about kinship, and so the questions about births and deaths, mothers and children and marriages, that compel me in Isoso would doubtless have compelled my colleagues if I'd chosen to write about those questions. There was a time when closely annotated kinship diagrams would have been pored over by anthropologist readers of my work. However, the elegance and aridity of such analyses can serve to paper over vulnerability in the domains where it looms largest. While there has recently been an "affective turn" in anthropology (Rutherford 2016), including lowland South American anthropology (Surralles 2009), it is motivated by theorists like Brian Massumi (2002) and argues over the "ontological turn" inspired by Eduardo Viveiros de Castro (1998) and does not draw, as I do, on feminist scholarship.

PLAN OF BOOK

My original doctoral fieldwork investigated two projects in Isoso that were funded by Western governments during the 1990s. At the time, these projects seemed exciting heralds of the coming of a multicultural postextractive green future. In retrospect, they look like tiny final arabesques of the crumbling Cold War order. For detailed descriptions of these two projects, interested readers are encouraged to consult Lowrey (2003) and Lowrey (2008a). The first was a plan to involve Isoseño people, by virtue of their being indigenous to the land in question, in the management of a very large new Bolivian national park, established in 1995: the Parque Nacional Kaa-Iyaa del Gran Chaco. The second, which was a major focus of my fieldwork, was a plan to involve Isoseño shamans in an attempt to commercialize traditional medicine. Both were explicitly framed as promoting the autonomy and self-sufficiency of Isoseño people. Both did real damage to Isoso. In large part, this book grew out of my efforts to go back in time and sideways in imagination in order to understand why these projects (and projects like them) ever seemed like good ideas.

This first chapter ("No Place Like Home") will introduce my primary field site, Isoso, which is a community of 15,000 Guaraní-speaking people living in twenty-three villages strung along the Parapetí River in the Bolivian Chaco. The South American Gran Chaco shares many geographic, historical, political, and cultural features with the North American Great Plains, something that will be a recurrent theme in the book. While Pan-American and hemispheric indigenous studies often reiterate the important point that the Americas are interrelated, this book draws out some undernoticed parallel histories and geographies in this pair of North and South American heartlands.

Chapter 2 ("The Chaco Prophet") goes back to the late nineteenth century and treats a prophetic movement among Bolivian Guaraní people in the Gran Chaco that ended in a massacre at a site called Kuruyuki in 1892. I systematically go through the authoritative historical account of that movement, which was published in 1972 by Bolivian historian and folklorist Hernando Sanabria Fernández. I show how his version of Guaraní history and particularly his figuring of defiance, autonomy, and masculinity as key features of Guaraníness created certain kinds of opportunities for Guaraní revitalization in the 1980s and 1990s but foreclosed others in ways that have had unfortunate consequences for Guaraní political mobilization. Sanabria's account also seriously misrepresents the historical record of what late nineteenth-century Guaraní people said at the time about their intentions, which his book casts as having been exclusively violent and martial. The fragmentary direct testimony that exists of nineteenth-century Guaraní people articulating their own aims bespeaks concerns for families and relationships: longing for connection with deceased kin and for kinder relations with settler Bolivian authorities.

Chapter 3 ("The Plains Prophet") documents my original research, uncovering how profoundly Sanabria's account was influenced by the scholarly and popular literature on North American Plains Indians, the Old West, the Ghost Dance movement, and the massacre at Wounded Knee. Using disability theory as a theoretical lens, I return to that North American literature and find in it pervasive reference to debility and vulnerability. The historical and anthropological literature on "revitalization movements" looks very different and much less persuasive in light of recent insights from disability scholars. I suggest that much of the twentieth-century analysis of revitalization movements that dwells on fantasized invulnerability in the face of modernity attributed to traditional peoples might be a sort of anxious projection on the part of modern Western analysts. The Ghost Dance and Wounded Knee are the canonical cases for this literature, and so I return to several classic and influential studies to demonstrate exactly how this process has worked and been propagated from that "original." I suggest that in both the Bolivian case discussed in the chapter 2 and the American case discussed in this chapter, settler interlocutors in the past and present have misunderstood or refused to acknowledge indigenous overtures relating to dependence and mutuality, interpreting them instead as deceptive subterfuge masking violent, hostile intent.

Chapter 4 ("Shamans and Wives") focuses on my fieldwork with two Isoseño shamans, both associated with the laboratory of traditional medicine. I describe the families and households I know best in Isoso and argue that the importance of family life has gone underanalyzed in the extent literature on Amerindian shamanism. Much anthropological analysis of shamanism has treated it as directly corollary to traditionally masculinist domains in settler society, supposing shamanism to be either esoteric (akin to a priesthood) or technocratic (akin to science or medicine). Arguing from my own ethnographic evidence, I suggest instead that shamanism is a practice of allyship in the feminist sense, in which shamans commit to long-term solidarity with fellow community members in difficulty, relationships in which their wives and families also play key roles. It is precisely the masculinist misunderstanding of shamanism that led to the externally funded creation of the laboratory of traditional medicine, which was a disappointment to the outside funders and a cataclysmic disaster for the Isoseño people most closely involved with it.

Chapter 5 ("Shamans and Spies") opens with the many dark conspiracy theories the Isoseño people whom I knew best had about the laboratory of traditional medicine—suppositions about which I was for many years dismissive. However, in researching the ethnobotanical justification for its funding and the propositions made in it about what shamanism is and what shamans know and do, I track a path back from South American shamans to a set of North American, Cold War operators. The origins and extant edifice of much work on shamanism and ethnobotany and, especially, that work's combined claims of scientific accomplishment and macho swashbuckling, deserve almost infinitely more critical scrutiny than they have hitherto received in anthropology. By critically examining the backstory of "father of ethnobotany" Richard Evans Schultes and his acolytes and popularizers, I am able to show just how sinister and dishonest is the projection of an infinite power to heal settler ills precisely on to some of global modernity's most vulnerable colonial subjects: indigenous people and, particularly, lowland South American Indians.

Chapter 6 ("Wizards and Ghosts") contrasts two forms of imaginative narrative about power and debility: one drawn from US children's literature, the other from lowland South American myth. In 1891, nearly a decade before Baum began the beloved and heartwarming Oz series, he published a heartless newspaper editorial about, of all things, the massacre at Wounded Knee. It has in recent years become notorious. Baum's defenders suggest it was a clumsy satire. What interests me is its bad-faith attempt to simultaneously lament and glory in Indian vulnerability and the strenuous implicit claims about white power and invulnerability necessary to that stance. From there I look again at the perennially popular Oz books and find in them an astonishing proliferation of themes of disability, vulnerability, disintegration, dismemberment, and radical social dependency. All of this obsessive elaboration of forbidden topics is, I argue, permissible and plausibly deniable because the Oz books are "just pretend" and meant for children. I join to this analysis a contrasting Amerindian case. Here I consider a special class of lowland South American indigenous narratives described in published accounts by renowned French anthropologist Anne-Christine Taylor. Taylor writes about Shuar stories that involve extremely powerful supernatural beings that can be encountered by humans only under unique

circumstances. The outcomes of these encounters sometimes confer dangerous personal power (usually on men) but, more often, produce debilities (usually on women
and children), recuperation from which requires the assistance of close kin. In the
settler case, disability and dependence can only be considered in the safe confines
of children's fantasy; in the Amerindian case, heightened personal power is unusual
(and suspect), and relational vulnerability is the ordinary order of things.

Chapter 7 ("Vulnerability in American Heartlands") concludes by demon-
strating that the issues at play in the book are not inevitably about "settlers versus
Indians" but most fundamentally about the historical self-fashioning of modernity in the Americas. I use the case of Mennonite settler colonies now adjacent
to the indigenous communities with which I have worked in both the Bolivian
and Paraguayan Chaco. Many Mennonite colonies in South America are visually
anachronistic, with women in flowered dresses and men in overalls traveling by
horse-drawn buggies and living in clapboard farmhouses abutted by picturesque
windmills. Mennonites confound any neat categorization that aligns the "West" to
the "Rest" as "settlers" to "Indians" or as "modern" to "traditional." Specifically, they
confound assumptions about settler commitments to autonomy and individualism
as being monolithic. Mennonite theology is marked by its orientation to salvation
in community. Migrations from their origins in the borderlands between Germany
and Holland, first to Prussia, then to Czarist Russia, then to Canada, and later to
Latin America have always been prompted by encroaching modernity. Obligations
to perform military service as a universal duty of citizenship (Mennonites are
pacifist), to enroll their children in national-language schools (Mennonites speak
low German at home, and their schooling is in high German), or to participate
in state-run collectivist agrarian schemes (Mennonites organize their own farming
collectives) have inspired Mennonites to seek out special relationships in a series of
new countries where their special status privileges will be recognized and protected.
Paraguay and Bolivia allowed Mennonites to settle during the twentieth century
under special terms precisely in order to civilize their "savage" hinterlands; they
were permitted their old-fashioned ways as, ironically, agents of modernization.
Now, however, these protections are being stripped away as Bolivia and Paraguay
consolidate their own achieved modernity as states that have no tolerance for vulnerable, dependent citizens, be they indigenous or settler.

THEORETICAL FRAMEWORK

Feminist philosopher Eva Feder Kittay's work on dependency had a profound
influence on the writing of this book, and the analysis offered in it is also indebted
to recent work in disability studies, which is treated in detail in several different

chapters. However, the arguments of the book also draw from a much older scholarly tradition. I have found it useful to employ a distinction first made by legal historian Henry Sumner Maine (1861) between "status" and "contract" societies. Maine described a progressive shift in which Western societies moved "from status to contract," that is, from being organized by status relations toward being organized by contract relations. Non-Western societies, such as Amerindian societies, organized around "status" are treated in his framework as not just different but primitive, archaic. Anthropologists quite rightly find this hierarchized archaicizing untenable. Nevertheless, Maine's typology is useful in other ways.

Status societies are organized around implicit roles assigned by status attributes: sex, race, religion, class. People's recruitment to these roles is involuntary such that "duty" is highly socially valued—in other words, fulfilling the expectations for the role in which one finds oneself, willy-nilly. Contract societies are organized around explicit contracts arrived at by individuals. People's recruitment to these contracts is voluntary such that "choice" is highly socially valued—that is, identifying one's own preferences and proclivities and efficiently forming and severing contractual relations on their basis.

What interests me about Maine's distinction is that societies organized around status recognize (and even enforce) dependence and debility quite explicitly, while societies organized around contract reject, deny, and ignore dependence and debility, being explicit instead (again, often forcibly) on the themes of independence and autonomy. The downsides to status-organized societies are legion and have been exhaustively exemplified in the course of human history (patriarchy, slavery, and feudalism are all status-organized social systems). The downsides to contract-organized societies have only begun to be grasped during the past couple of centuries. One response—in Western and non-Western societies alike—has been what I will call a "flight from contract." This phenomenon (variously described and labeled) has been noted by others, usually disparagingly. I argue that the flight from contract is both inevitable—and inevitably disparaged—because it is a response to the pervasive, inevitable presence of human dependency and debility in societies ever more ill organized to deal with (or, to put it another way, ever more unwilling to even recognize) those features of human existence.

DOMESTIC LANGUAGES OF DOUBT

The book is in some respects predicated on commonplace anthropological formulations of compare and contrast: Western to Amerindian, contract to status. Such pairings can be quite illuminating, but at their most exciting they are almost always overdrawn: primitive versus modern, cold versus hot, multinaturalism versus multiculturalism, purity versus hybridity, to give some of the most familiar examples. The modes of description and argumentation predicated on such contrasts are too often written and spoken in a mode that presumes skepticism only exists for theory-minded analysts while the average Western or Amerindian Joe, the average feudal or modern Jane, has lived and died possessed of no domestic language of doubt.

Paying attention to what people find dubious makes it far more difficult to make confident, overdrawn assertions about them and makes stark cultural and temporal divides begin to look permeable. Dependence and disability, on the one hand, and autonomy and "super-ability," on the other, are subjected to considerable culturally specific questioning while also being present in all the times and places under consideration. Thus this entire project is also animated by an interest in returning anthropology to the consideration of what might be human universals. Disability scholarship has been convincingly insistent about vulnerability, dependency, and frailty counting among these. Claims about human universals have fallen very far out of fashion in sociocultural anthropology in recent decades (while proliferating lamentably in what used to be called sociobiology and what is now known in evolutionary psychology). This fall from fashion—which coincided rather precisely with the emergence of feminist scholarship after the 1960s and the universal challenge it presented to anthropology—relates to, and helps to explain, my own initial experiences as a novice fieldworker setting out at the tail end of the twentieth century and my previous sense that there was nothing of anthropological interest about the dependency work—mostly women's work—that surrounded me in the field and created the conditions of possibility for my being there. Kittay's work on the profound resistance in modern Western ontologies to considering dependency has upended my view of my own society but has also helped me to understand what (and here Freud helps too) was for me coded, in classic dreamwork fashion, as the parts "not worth telling about" when I was living in a society different from my own.

PARTIAL ANTECEDENTS: "DEPENDENCY THEORY" AND THE "ROMANCE OF RESISTANCE"

When describing this book to others as I was writing it, I sometimes was asked if I had thought about the implications of using disability theory when the subjects of my research are indigenous people. The question illuminates perfectly a point disability theorists have made: that disability is an ur-category of stigma. These interlocutors were warily asking if I had realized the insult I was directing at indigenous people by implying they were either themselves disabled or that they had anything significant in common with disabled people.

My interlocutors' question makes clear that the directionality of potential insult in the contemporary context is one-way. In the nineteenth century (which is where the next chapter will begin), this directionality of insult was frequently reversed. People with disabilities were at pains to prove they were not like "savages." Douglas Baynton (1996) has written about how one of the resistances to adopting American Sign Language during the nineteenth century was the fact that Plains Indians had developed a sign language lingua franca for use across Plains indigenous languages.[1] At a time when disability was sometimes supposed to result from archaic biological "survivals" unexpectedly resurfacing in offspring, white American families didn't want their hearing impaired children imitating "primitives."

We don't worry anymore about primitivity but we still do about disability, so the stigma of being charged with the former has mostly disappeared while the stigma of the latter remains strong. If anything, it has become all the stronger for being the rump-stigma against which other categories have proven themselves immune and therefore deserving of deliverance—race, gender, sexuality—as Baynton, again, has shown in a key essay (2001). Liberation movements around these categories have specifically insisted that black people, women, and gay people are not "less able," are not "sick," but are "normal" and "healthy." Similarly, Nancy Fraser and Linda Gordon have documented how across the same late modern period the scope of "dependency" has narrowed and become increasingly stigmatized: many racialized and gendered forms of dependency have been abolished, such that "all dependency is suspect, and independence is enjoined upon everyone" (1994: 324).

What can follow from this discussion is the good and important point that all such categories are social constructions: society "primitivizes," "indigenizes," or "disables" people. You can't be a primitive except relative to a pseudoscientific theory of social evolution; you can't be indigenous without colonialism; you can't be disabled except in a social and infrastructural context constructed to accommodate certain capabilities and exclude others (Oliver 2013). Anthropology has even had a large literature on "dependency theory," understood in this sense: a politicized state of affairs in which some world regions are forced into relations of dependence on other world regions (Gunder Frank 1967; Wallerstein 1979). This sort of critical analysis has been and continues to be important, but it offers only a pejorative understanding of "dependency" as a state of being.

Some feminist anthropologists have offered thoughtful critiques of the way in which autonomy, resistance, and, especially, "agency," variously defined, have been unreflectively posited as universal human desiderata even in anthropological work otherwise leery of universalist ambitions. Lila Abu-Lughod's 1990 article, "The Romance of Resistance: Tracing Transformations of Power through Bedouin women" and Saba Mahmood's 2005 book *Politics of Piety: The Islamic Revival and the Feminist Subject* are perhaps the two most influential such critiques. They draw upon fieldwork in Islamic societies, and their arguments are grounded in cultural difference. However, though the points they make rebut one set of anthropological assumptions about autonomy and agency, they tend to reinforce another set in which assertions about human universals must necessarily be suspect, and according to the lights of which thoroughgoing exposés of hitherto-unnoticed universalisms are supremely laudable.

As a feminist and anthropologist, I feel only partial enthusiasm for these exposés. Disability theory has clarified for me why this is so. In some ways the concerns of disability theorists harmonize well with anthropological critiques of the sort described above, but in other important ways they do not. The work I find most interesting in disability theory is less concerned with the social and cultural construction of disability (though it acknowledges these dynamics) and insists instead upon dependence, debility, and disability as universal features of human experience. This makes the theory, in many ways, an awkward fit for contemporary sociocultural anthropology and in fact aligns it with a previous, now-abandoned (within anthropology) version of feminism (for a cogent rationale by one of the early architects of that abandonment, see Strathern 1987). Research and activism outside of anthropology have given rise to disability theory, which still remains less influential than it might be within the discipline (Rapp and Ginsburg 2010) and present anthropology anew with a familiar challenge about human universals. The last time anthropology faced this challenge—one presented, then, by feminism—it retreated from "master narratives" and "grand theory" in a manner the haste of which was in some ways entirely justifiable and in others deeply suspect (Hartsock 1987). Well, here we are again.

DEPENDENCY

Because Kittay's work is so central to everything I do in the rest of the book and because anthropologist readers may not have encountered her before, I want here not so much to attempt a summary of her arguments as to offer a selection of her ideas. Much of her argumentative heavy lifting is devoted to engaging with influential work in philosophy—particularly that of John Rawls—that needn't detain an anthropological audience. But she makes a series of claims about human universals that have made me fundamentally reconsider my own disciplinary disposition to reject any such claims as either underinformed or overpresumptuous about the nature of humanity in two senses: empirically, as to its real diversity on the ground, and theoretically, as to its difficulty in transcending culture-bound conceptions, such that any convincing assertion about what is universally true is inevitably tethered to conviction-shaping cultural assumptions. I wonder, now, if precisely the universality of what Kittay is talking about is what has caused scholars in the Western tradition to ignore it.

What is this "it"? The dependency that is intrinsic to the human experience. All humans begin life as profoundly dependent beings, and most end life the same way; all of us also experience periods of intense dependency during the life course. This dependence, of course, implicates others: "Whether the work of caring for dependents is viewed as desirable or not . . . it is work that must be done by someone" (Kittay 1999: 16). It is service work that cannot be abolished by movements of liberation.[2]

Kittay notes that "whether or not it is desirable to be a relational, giving self . . . every society must count on certain persons adopting such a moral self" (1999: 51). One of the arguments of the present book is that to the same extent that anthropologists come from societies (and here the key marker is not so much "Western" as "modern") that ignore this fact, such anthropologists ignore it with redoubled steadfastness in the field. They do so especially when the issue of choice—another thorny one for moderns—is involved. Speaking of dependency and dependency work, Kittay says, "Most common and interesting situations . . . are those which are neither coerced . . . nor voluntarily chosen" (62), and she asks,

> How can the partiality exhibited in a caring relation, which might not even have been voluntarily assumed, have a moral character—especially when obligations that are not self-assumed and partiality have so often been the mark of . . . actions which fail to express our moral essence? (54)

Much of living in community with others, in whatever form it takes, involves involuntary care of this kind. We do not have to look for extraordinary, heroic, or exotic examples. Your neighbors have a family bereavement; you'd just as soon not feed and walk their pets while they travel to attend the funeral, but you know money is tight in their household and they can't board the animals and they just moved into town and don't know many people to ask. They can't force you to do it, but are you going to say no? Kittay persuasively makes the case that "if [my] views are correct, then dependency relations are *the* paradigmatic moral relations" (71). The claim she is making is a universal claim—something that sits easily in a philosophical work, less so when borrowed for use in an anthropological one. Nevertheless, many anthropologists will recognize that people in the communities with which they work would agree entirely with Kittay.

Anthropologists do read philosophers, but rarely feminist ones. A major recent anthropological contribution treating dependence and contemporary claims to dependence (Ferguson 2013) manages to not cite any of the feminist literature on these themes—outside of an endnote reference to Nancy Fraser and Linda

Gordon's very famous piece on dependency as a "keyword" for assaults on welfare in the US context (1994). Perhaps unsurprisingly, James Ferguson worries quite a bit about "paternalism" in his essay and seems only to have noticed how theoretically interesting dependence is when it pertains to men (2013: 233, 235), a circumstance that "makes us uneasy" (232). He concludes his piece by telling readers that "Wage labour is not the only way of contributing to the society" though as to desirable forms of dependence, "We still don't know what those are" (237) such that "we still have a great deal of work to do if we are to develop intellectual tools and political strategies adequate to these difficult times" (238). I feel pretty sure I know who the "us" and the "we" are in those sentences, but I also am quite sure they could make their lives a bit easier by reading more feminist theory and also looking again at the available evidence from their diverse field sites around the world. In her response to the piece, Oiara Bonilla goes directly to the Amazonian case she knows best, that of the Paumari of the Purus River. She says subjection can "constitute its own logic, founded on kinship and a relational conception of the person that is at the base of a social and cosmopolitical dynamic which exceeds our ideal of social well-being and autonomy" (247). Just so: in fact, with the lowland South American material I treat in this book I wish to say much the same thing, but at great length, as what Bonilla says with such economy and elegance in this single sentence.

DISABILITY, INDIGENEITY, AND THE FLIGHT FROM CONTRACT

For all that what seem to me obvious omissions in Ferguson's piece, in taking note of the startling proliferation of "declarations of dependence" among hale, hearty, working-age men in his field site in southern Africa, he is indeed on to something. The status categories "disabled" and "indigenous" share a similar recent history of explosive growth. Census reports from throughout the Americas tell us that the self-ascription of Amerindian indigeneity has grown across each decade from the 1970s to the present (Salomon and Schwartz 1999). In the United States and Canada, numbers of claimants to disability assistance have grown tremendously between 1980 and today (Krieger 2003; Reaume 2008).

In both instances, these expansions are simultaneously celebrated and decried. Sometimes they are celebrated, as testaments to social progress, the outcome of successful efforts to combat the stigma that once forced people to hide their status as "disabled" or "Indian." Much more often decried, precisely as so much shameless humbug: baseless claims by large numbers of people to special statuses that when properly defined, could not be growing—only shrinking—in modern contract society. Anthropology by and large has tended toward the first reaction, as it fits well with a disciplinary commitment to the happy proliferation of difference.

In this book, I pay attention to the second reaction, because of its invocation of fakery—a charge to which I think anthropologists always do well to be attentive in any cultural context. We think of anthropology as the study of what people believe, but what people don't believe is at least as illuminating (this theme is expanded upon in chapters 4 and 6 of the book).

Disability theorists have been paying attention. In the United States, a considerable body of literature has grown up around case law associated with the Americans with Disabilities Act of 1990. A bill that generated unusual levels of bipartisan support at its passage, it has suffered a parade of defeats in implementation. In a perceptive analysis of the reasons why, Lennard Davis cites the anxious opinion in one judgment that the ADA creates a legally protected class that is potentially "too large" (2002: 24). Indeed, if disability theorists are right about who is formerly, actually, or potentially disabled and what kinds of people need support and protection, the category becomes universal. In practice, many people do seem to be seeking exactly such support and protection. No doubt the vogue of disability theory in late modern social science is closely related to the proliferation of disability claims in late modern societies.

Claims about disability and indigeneity come in for particular scrutiny because they are status claims, understood to be anachronistic and for that reason, in a modern contract society that makes progress an ordering principle, also anarchic. In many ways they raise the fears discussed by Douglas Baynton (1996) about encouraging "survivals" in a polity shaped by eugenicist social evolutionism. For people to cleave to status designations in a society that insists the good life can and should be built around the expansion of contract capacities is inherently confrontational.

These status claims are also subject to old-fashioned modes of critique: in the case of disability, on the grounds of "malingering," and in the case of indigeneity, on those of "passing." But the motivations of the critique are more confused in contract society than in status society. In a feudal society or a slave society, it is clear why one might wish to "pass" as aristocratic, or white, or—if the opportunity presented itself—to flee it altogether. It is equally clear why its boundaries in all of those respects were strictly patrolled. But in the story of the human story, we are only beginning to understand the brutalities (along with the inducements to loyalty) of contract society.

In its own ideal formulation, contract society is a meritocratic society in which individual people can pursue diverse goods according to their unique proclivities and capabilities. This, of course, creates abyssal, hitherto-unimaginable possibilities for failure: failures of individual imagination and failures of individual achievement. Consider the neglected upsides of status-organized societies: the life of an aristocrat was preferable to the life of a serf, but you couldn't really be fired from either position.[3] Being sexy or charming was surely an advantage in life, but being neither didn't necessarily mean you wouldn't find a life partner when marriages were arranged by families rather than arrived at by individuals and certainly wouldn't mean the gradual disappearance of kinship ties as you aged. You wouldn't be laid off, or left, and then—to add insult to injury—urged to reinvent yourself by "finding your passion" in the aftermath. Being not so good at things—work skills, social skills, "life skills"—is not the same kind of catastrophe in a status society that it is in a contract society.

Status societies are predicated precisely on dependence, debility, and disability. The downside to status societies, of course, is that they make these features obligatory even in circumstances where they are not present. Contract societies are predicated on independence, autonomy, and capability; the downside to contract societies is also that they make these features obligatory even where they are not present. While the "origin stories" of status societies posit a primary dependence (usually supernatural), the "origin stories" of contract societies posit a struggle for independence (both historical and ongoing)—an abolishment of despotism, monarchy, colonialism. For status societies, to reject enforced dependence, debility, and disability is to violate the cosmic order of things; for contract societies, to reject enforced independence, autonomy, and capability is to betray past, present, and future heroic struggles toward the more perfect attainment of those states (usually supposed to be "natural," either a return-to or a realization-of).

For contract societies, disabled people and indigenous people are temporary special exceptions at best; eventually, they ought to disappear: disabilities will be cured, indigenous peoples will become modern. To actively pursue entry into those special, exceptional categories, to expand them, is social treachery. People might be stuck being disabled or indigenous, but no one should expend effort to enter those categories or assert a real desire to stay in them. Davis is right when he says the real fear about disability is that the "protected class" might grow "too large." The secret anxiety here, about which modern contract society is in deep denial, is that it already does include everybody in some way.

Disability—practically and theoretically—is a critique and a betrayal of modernity, and modern society is deeply, deeply anxious about and scornful of it. Disability—abnormality rather than normality, difference rather than equality, dependence rather than independence—makes the politics of disability in the modern context very difficult to negotiate because it presents a fundamental, and transformative, challenge to modernity itself. Reading disability theory makes one look at modern Western society, and its recent history, very differently. So differently, in fact, that historical and contemporary interactions with non-Western societies start to look different, too.

AMERICAN HEARTLANDS, NORTH AND SOUTH

This is where the indigenous—and specifically Amerindian—part of the book comes in. I suggest that anthropology has misrecognized and misinterpreted Amerindian approaches to dependence and debility because it has viewed them through the lens of modern, Western denial and disdain. This view is most sharply the case with late nineteenth- and twentieth-century anthropology, because it was across this time that modern Western attitudes toward disability were themselves sharpening. To put it another way, Americanist anthropology was developing its own theories in this sociohistorical context just as it was systematically applying itself to the empirical study of Amerindian peoples.

The exemplary combined case here is the Ghost Dance movement and the massacre at Wounded Knee. Anthropological treatments of this phenomenon and event are emblems of the misrecognition I describe and document, and they have had a tremendous influence on historical and anthropological study throughout the Americas, as well as on popular conceptions of "Indianness" and even American Indian self-perception. Anthropologists who have read the literature on revitalization movements (and who among us has not read at least some of it?) cannot but feel a jolt of recognition, followed by dizzying defamiliarization, when they read Tobin Siebers on the myriad ways that disability is associated with narcissism: "People with disabilities, it seems, demonstrate a conspicuous resistance to reality, taking flight into an active fantasy life where their disabilities justify special privileges . . . They seek revenge for their disabilities or demand compensation" (45). In an acute analytic turn, Siebers shows how the distress and anxiety of analysts, which arises from the fact that everyone is vulnerable to disablement, are consistently projected onto disabled people themselves: "the threat to the therapist's self-integration becomes an analytic tool used to think about the patient's disability" (46).

Suddenly, a tired old anthropological literature is made strange. It seems at least possible that the standard analysis of movements like the ones in the United States and Bolivia that I treat in chapters 2 and 3—that they are the impotent revenge fantasies of fragile failures—may in fact be hostile projections by anthropologist and ethnohistorian analysts. The avowed intent of anthropology is empathy, but the spectacle of our analysands' vulnerability to politics, economics, technology, modernity, and history—forces from which we are not ourselves at all immune—perhaps instead repels us and excites our anxious disgust. We disavow these discreditable sensations in ourselves by diagnosing fantasy-ridden and revenge-bent impotence and inward-looking narcissism in our interlocutors. The pervasiveness of disability itself, of debility in the face of the world, is what we strive to repress.

The updated version of such analyses is to consider these movements to be expressive of "agency" or "resistance." This position is less pitying and patronizing, to be sure. On the other hand, it flies in the face of many of the observable facts. When one looks at the available historical documentation about these movements, they are replete with calls for succor, avowals of vulnerability, and dependency claims by indigenous people toward modern state agents. It's as if modern anthropologists and historians are embarrassed for nineteenth-century Indians, rushing to explain on their behalf that they didn't mean what they said—that they may have looked and sounded weak and vulnerable but that this was a ruse covering a deeper spirit of indomitability or slow-burning vengeance. Even the modern demographic rebounding of once-declining populations is entered into posthumous evidence that whatever the nineteenth-century Indians may have said about being weak and in need of help, it wasn't really true and they didn't really mean it. It takes a particular kind of habit-forged heartlessness to look at the evidence this way, one that the rest of the book tries to undo—a process that began for me long before its writing, in the lived experience of fieldwork in Isoso.

ISOSO

Isoso is home to some 15,000 people divided among about twenty-three villages (erratically successful colonization schemes to establish new villages closer to the national park territory have made this number fluctuate over the past decade). The villages are strung along the lower reaches of the Parapetí River in southeastern Bolivia, which begins in the Andean foothills and ends in swamps on the northwestern margins of the arable Chaco—the Chaco interior is far too arid for cultivation. Everyone in Isoso speaks Guaraní, the overwhelming majority as a first language, though a few villages are shared with the descendants of white settlers who began arriving at the end of the nineteenth century and who speak Spanish at home. One village, San Silvestre, is majority **karai** ("white"; Guaraní terms will appear in bold when first introduced in the text) and three other villages have significant karai minorities.

Isoso means "water that goes" in Guaraní, and these lower reaches of the Parapetí only run seasonally, when swollen by Andean snowmelt. During half the year, the riverbed turns into a ribbon of sand. Agriculture here depends on elaborate systems of irrigation canals to capture the seasonally available river water and distribute it to fields growing maize, manioc, sweet potatoes, and (in recent decades) rice. This irrigated agriculture has been practiced by Isoseño people for hundreds of years. Since the early twentieth century, Isoseño people have added to their seasonal patterns of agriculture and seasonal migratory wage labor at the sugar-cane harvest: first on plantations in Argentina (still called in Guaraní **Mbaaporenda**, "place of work") and then in plantations established in Bolivia near the lowland city of Santa Cruz de la Sierra (**Karairëta**, "place of white people").

White settlers came not as farmers but as cattlemen, bringing cows and horses. More affluent Guaraní families can own significant herds, but most Guaraní families' pastoral resources are limited to goats, which travel the roads and villages in vast numbers. Many men hunt small game (armadillo, various birds) recreationally, but only a few men are serious and accomplished hunters known for going on extended outings and bagging peccary, brocket deer, and (rarely) tapir, so game meat is a delighted in but not a significant portion of the everyday diet. During two portions of the year (when the river leaves and returns), fishing does provide an important and much-looked-forward to part of the diet. Karai families tend to be marginally more affluent than Guaraní ones, but on the whole settler descendants have not been prosperous here and have adopted the Guaraní way of life with modest modifications (Spanish as a first language, more cattle, more Catholicism).

Isoso was not missionized during the colonial nor early republican era. Its first evangelical encounter was with Anglican missionaries who arrived in the 1920s, just prior to the War of the Chaco between Bolivia and Paraguay (1930–1935). While Catholicism made some inroads in the middle of the twentieth century, many more Isoseño people today are evangelical Protestants (belonging to several, often rival, sects; see Hirsch and Zarzycki 1993) than are Catholics. Every Isoseño village has a state-supported primary school and has had since the 1980s. Beginning in the 1980s, first one village and by now three villages also have boarding high schools, with growing numbers of Isoseño young people completing secondary education, though still as a minority of all children. In the 1980s a minihospital was built in Isoso's central village. It has a small operating theater and is staffed by a Bolivian doctor accompanied by an intern completing his or her medical training. Three other villages have health posts, and one village hosts a military outpost staffed by four or five soldiers: almost always local boys completing their year of mandatory military service.

Isoseño people were known in older accounts as "Chané," defined in part by their subservient relationship to other Bolivian Guaraní speakers known in older accounts as "Chiriguano." Chiriguano call themselves **Ava** ("men"), and they make up the vast majority of the contemporary Bolivian Guaraní people (about 50,000 of 80,000, compared to Isoseño's 15,000; the remaining people are known as **Simba**). **Ava** used to call Isoseño **Tapïi** (the strikethrough indicates nasalization). Isoseño people will explain that this referred to a special sort of small house they traditionally built in their agricultural fields to sleep in during the season when their crops were particularly vulnerable to birds. Ava people say this term meant "slave." I will speak more of these historical dynamics in chapter 4; for now, I will merely also note that one of the leading elite families in Isoso across several nineteenth- and early twentieth-century generations carried the surname **Iyambae**, which means

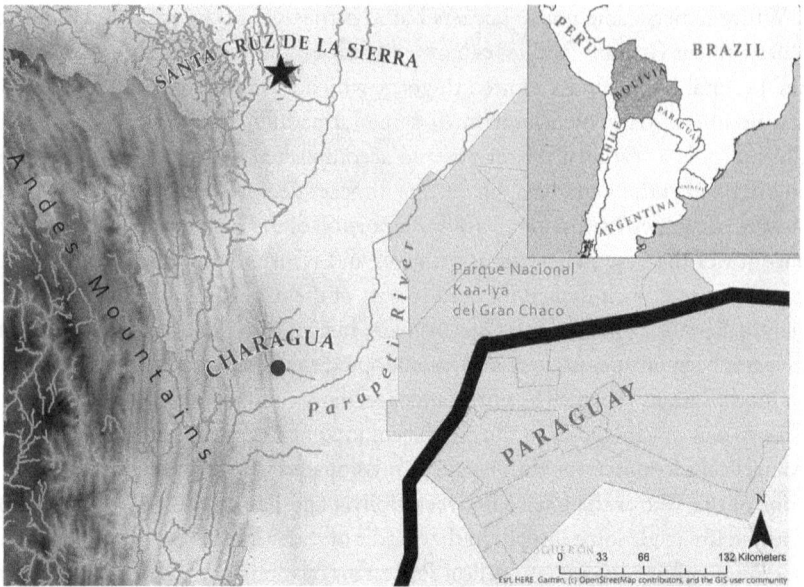

FIGURE 1.1. Locations mentioned in the text: the city of Santa Cruz de la Sierra, the town of Charagua, the Parapetí River, and the Parque Nacional Kaa-Iya del Gran Chaco.

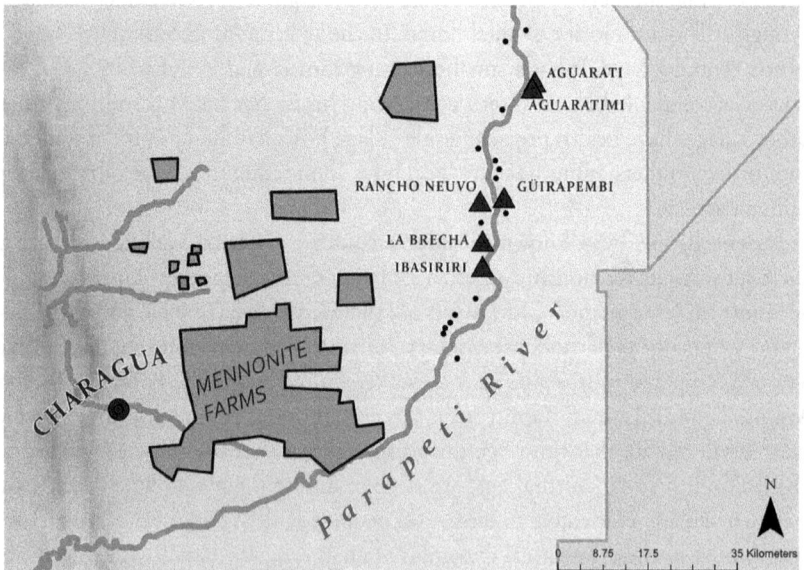

FIGURE 1.2. Location of Isoseño villages along the Parapetí River. Villages mentioned in the text are labeled, and placement of Mennonite colonies (farm) indicated.

FIGURE 1.3. Satellite image of the villages of Güirapembirenda and Rancho Nuevo on facing banks of the Parapetí. The river is impassable at times because of high fast-flowing current and turns into a dry ribbon of sand for a few months. For most of the year, crossing involves wading in water that is knee to waist high.

"without owner" (see Combès 2005a; Combès and Lowrey 2006; Lowrey 2003). Isoso was a particularly good place to learn about what it is to live in a status society rather than a contract one.

PLAINS AND CHACO: TWO AMERICAN HEARTLANDS

As a Chacologist (the moniker trips more easily off the tongue in Spanish, *chacóloga*), I have always felt a bit wistful reading analyses of Andean and Amazonian structural elegance, with their circular and quadratic geometries, their tidy moieties, their lovely formality. I can't pretend to understand all of Thomas Zuidema's arguments about Tawantinsuyu and the Inca zeke system, but I come away from them (and kindred Andeanology) with the sense of a mathematically dazzling lost world, golden khipu threads pinned across a cosmos that connects mountaintops, clouds, rivers, valley bottoms, to velvety dark night skies (Canessa 2012; Orlove et al. 2000;

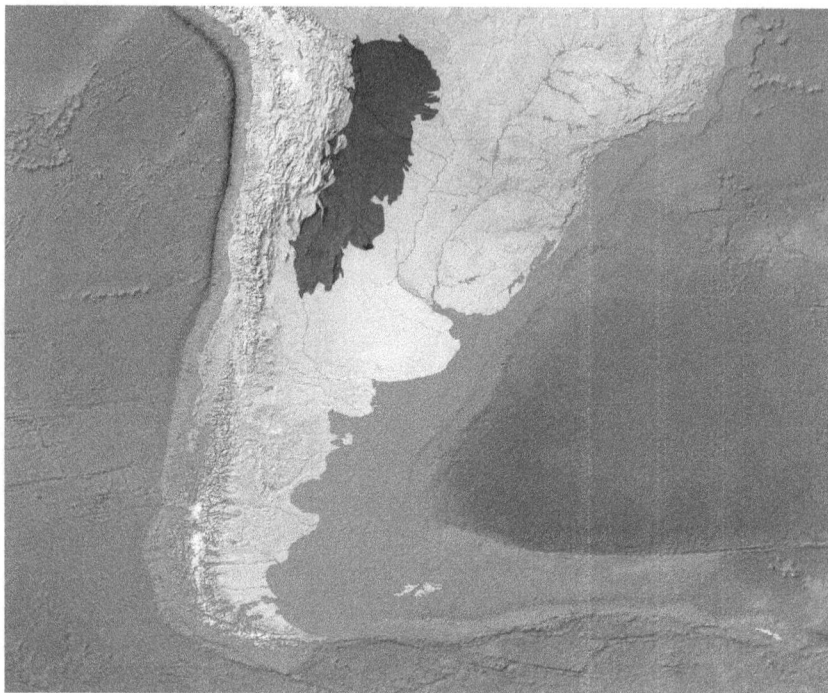

FIGURE 1.4. Approximate boundaries of the Gran Chaco

Salomon 2004; Zuidema 1964, 1977, 1983). I've watched with interest and excitement the emergence of new research in Amazonia suggesting that extant moiety systems were much more elaborate in the past, populations larger, towns and agricultural terrains more extensive (Erickson 2010; Heckenberger 2008), confirming previous suggestions about the continuities between Andean and Amazonian social order and social complexity (Lévi-Strauss 1963; Turner 1984a).

The substrate in question in my own fieldwork is Chacoan sand rather than Amazonian clay or Andean stones. It's not as easily put to the ends of model making (for this argument at greater length, see Lowrey 2006a and Combès et al. 2009). Several of its peoples (Guaraní speakers on the margins, Mataco-maká, Guaycurú, Lulu-Vilela, Lengua-Maskoi, and Zamuco in the interior) are famously anarchic—canonically so in the case of the Guaraní (Clastres [1974] 1977; Viveiros de Castro 1992), quotidianly so in the case of the hunter-gatherer groups of the arid, sparsely populated, inhospitable Chaco proper. However, the societies of the Chaco are not such sports as they seem in the immediate context of the South American family. Expanding the kin diagram to include the rest of the Americas, they share

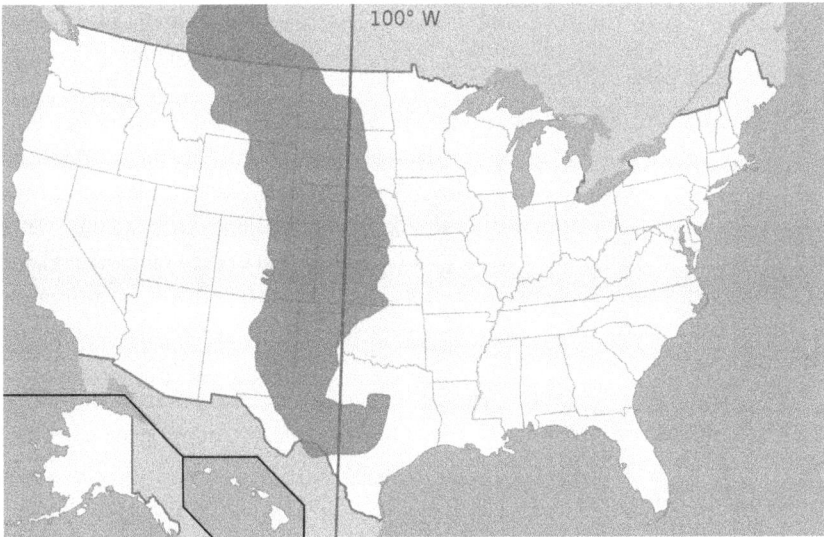

FIGURE 1.5. Approximate boundaries of the Great Plains

many features and characteristics of North America Great Plains societies—among them, the same lonesome swagger and the same secret coziness.

Since 2005, my professional home has been a public university on the Canadian Prairies: the University of Alberta. The parallels between the North American Great Plains (or, as the same geographic region is termed in Canada, the Prairies) and the South American Gran Chaco have long been noted by other observers, and the similarities have been insistently present to my consciousness as I have traveled back and forth for many years now between Alberta, Canada, and the Bolivian and Paraguayan Chaco. While in each case there is much argument as to their limiting margins, their core zones are clear (Rossum and Lavin 2000). These two arid interior regions, each located to the east of a great mountain range and to the west of a great wave of European settlement, were both colonized initially more by cows than people and both have been ecologically pitiless obstacles to settler ambitions. Both have been theaters for an eighteenth- and nineteenth-century florescence of native "horse complexes"—the adoption by some aboriginal groups of an animal introduced by Europeans to much-mythologized native ends (Albers 1993; Albers and James 1986; Métraux 1946a; Mitchell 2015; Nichols 1939; Schindler 1985). Both have given rise to canonical images of "wild Indians" and especially of markedly masculine "Braves," what French ethnohistorian Thierry Saignes described as "indios de abajo" (1980). Both have been home to enormous, nearly feudal land holdings; the King Ranch in Texas compares to the Casado holdings in Paraguay. Estimates of the size of each vary, but hover close to the same number: 1,300,000 square kilometers in area.

What on first sight struck me as the incongruously Midwestern farms of Mennonites plonked down in the heartland of South America are the grafting onto both landscapes, Northern and Southern American, of a "German Russian" cultivation style brought over from the breadbasket of the Ukraine. The religiously separatist diaspora of Mennonites in the Chaco (present also in the Prairies and Plains, and often involving travel between these sites) has parallels in that of the Mormons in Utah (and Alberta, as it happens). Chapter 7, the final chapter, examines the Mennonite case.

But to begin: that the great nineteenth century Ghost Dance movement and the associated massacre at Wounded Knee in 1890 should have a doppelgänger in a prophetic movement in the Bolivian Chaco—and associated massacre at a place called Kuruyuki, in 1892—is an eerie coincidence that makes sense from a dependency logic of everything being related after all. But you may not be as much of a witchyminded conspiracy theorist as I am, yet. I have six chapters left to bring you round.

2

The Chaco Prophet

On January 28, 1892, Bolivian soldiers massacred at least 600 Ava Guaraní people at a place called Kuruyuki. Others were killed in the weeks leading up to this date, and many more (perhaps thousands more) were killed in the weeks after. The name of the site, and the name of a figure supposed to have led the series of confrontations with whites that culminated in the massacre, **Apiaguaiki Tüpa**, are in present-day Bolivian politics deployed regularly as emblems of powerful defiance, proud independence, and indomitable striving for autonomy. In the most flowery of such formulations, these are supposed to be the stuff of the Guaraní "soul," which is also described as aggressively masculine, that of a **kereimba**, a warrior.

In 2008, one of three "Indigenous Universities" founded in Bolivia and the only one to be located in Bolivia's lowlands (the other two are in Bolivia's Andean region) was named for this personage, of whom no photographs exist. The university's website features an artist's rendition of him, shown as a stalwart young man. The long, flowing hair is unlikely for a Chiriguano man of the late nineteenth century; the headdress is approximate, though photos from the period show men with hair cropped to the chin and wearing bands of cloth wound further back round the head. What appears in the drawing—a marked center part, flowing locks with no bangs, and a headband decorated with a design of squares—is instead borrowed iconography: specifically, from famous nineteenth-century photos taken of North American Plains Indian men (the headband, with its narrow style and forehead placement, most closely resembles something sometimes seen in photos of

DOI: 10.5876/9781646420360.c002

FIGURE 2.1. Apiaguaiki Tüpa

Plains Indian women). Although they were not in use among nineteenth-century Chiriguano, the arrow or spear that appears in this drawing slanted at an angle is evidently suspended in a back quiver—another familiar set-piece from historical images of Plains Indians.[1]

As I began to research Kuruyuki and Apiaguaiki Tüpa, I found their historiography persistently haunted by North American Plains Indians, images, and legends—particularly those of Sioux people,[2] and Apache people. The Ghost Dance, Sitting Bull, Wounded Knee, Geronimo—all were mixed up in the telling and retelling of the story of what happened at Kuruyuki and who Apiaguaiki Tüpa really was. The same was the case for the insistence on the masculine ferocity of the Chiriguano themselves and how it echoed North American accounts of the "warrior ethos" of the Sioux and of the Apache. When I first began examining these parallels, I thought of myself as expanding upon prescient observations made by ethnohistorian Saignes, in that 1980 essay in which he pointed out that Plains and Chaco Indians were the canonical "fierce Indians" of their respective continents, the stereotypical "Indian braves," proud, ferocious, untamable (Saignes 1980).

When I first began considering the striking historical coincidence—the Wounded Knee massacre in December 1890, the massacre at Kuruyuki just over a year later, in January 1892—it seemed to offer tragic evidence of the validity of Saignes's insight. Preparing to write about it, I started in on the enormous secondary literature (and some of the primary sources) on the Ghost Dance and Wounded Knee. At the same time, in collaboration with a historian colleague based in Bolivia, Isabelle Combès, I read the main primary sources on Kuruyuki and Apiaguaiki Tüpa for the first time. The standard narrative about the Bolivian case came to appear deeply suspect to both of us on multiple grounds, though Combès had replicated much of its form in her previous work (Combès 2005b). She has since published her revised take on Kuruyuki and Apiaguaiki Tüpa (2014).

For my own part, I found myself pursuing a set of notions and projections (and a few pure inventions) that seemed at first to lead back to North America but eventually seemed nearly as unmoored there as I had found them to be in South America. It's not that Saignes's observations have no basis at all. For example, in both the Plains and the Chaco, the colonial introduction of the horse had transformed many native societies by the advent of the nineteenth century, and in both the Plains and the Chaco the advance of cattle ranching was destructive to many native societies in the latter part of that century. But Saignes's observations partake of an overwhelmingly one-sided traffic in facts and stereotypes as much as they offer original ethnohistorical insight. The consideration of Plains-Chaco parallels is often unconscious and, even when conscious, always imbalanced. Both the production of scholarship and dissemination of popular notions about Plains Indians have always had the preponderant influence—comparisons, when made, are effectively exclusively by South American scholars, scholars working in South America, and by South Americans to the North American case rather than the reverse (Combès et al. 2009). In the next chapter, I will trace some of that influence back to the source. In this chapter I will demonstrate it in action.

HERNANDO SANABRIA FERNÁNDEZ, INDIAN ENTHUSIAST

In 1972, Bolivian historian Hernando Sanabria Fernández published a richly detailed biography of Apiaguaiki Tüpa and account of the events around Kuruyuki, drawing on a combination of previously published material, archival sources, and collected oral histories. *Apiaguaiqui Tumpa: Biografía del Pueblo Chiriguano y de Su último caudillo* (Apiaguaiqui Tumpa: Biography of the Chiriguano People and of their Last Leader[3]), reissued in 2008, has had a tremendous influence on Guaraní cultural revitalization, on regional and national politics, and on academic scholarship. Elaborate in itself, it has been extensively elaborated upon, though it has in recent years been subject to partial critical readings (Combès 2014 and 2005b; Lowrey 2006b; Prudén 2003).

Sanabria (1912—or possibly 1909[4]—1986) was born in the town of Vallegrande, which lies between Bolivia's tropical and Andean regions, and moved to the lowland provincial capital of Santa Cruz while still a teenager. By his own account, he was an amateur enthusiast of all things Indian from his boyhood, and describes his interest in the "tumpa" as having been prompted by two nearly concurrent events while he was just a lad. During the 1920s (Sanabria does not specify the year, though he recalls it was in August), rumors swept the city of Santa Cruz of an "Indian craze" in the countryside. In the resulting flutter of gossip and reports, the specter was raised of a repeat of the sanguinary events of 1892. Just around the time of those rumors, Sanabria's father, a schoolteacher, received a visit from a family friend. This was Santos Aireyu, a Guaraní leader coming into the city from the countryside in order to transact some paperwork. The Aireyu family is an important one among Ava Guaraní people; a lineage of **mburuvichareta** (Spanish, *capitanes*; English, "chiefs") can be traced among them to the nineteenth century and continued into the late twentieth century in Santa Cruz's Kaipependi region.

Sanabria describes sitting, rapt, at the knee of this exotic visitor who conversed with his father in "broken" Spanish ([1972] 2008: 99). According to Sanabria, Aireyu dismissed the present rumor mongering as so much silliness but when asked about the man who led the uprising of thirty years before replied:

> **Tumpa?** He was just a ñeapu (liar)! He that was so-called was no more than an **ava** (Guaraní man) like me and like my people. But what an **ava**, sir! The greatest, the bravest, the most powerful that ever has been! (100)[5]

Sanabria says that Aireyu concluded by saying, "simply," "His own name was Apiaguaiki" (100).

If this passage is read as Sanabria presents it—as dictation from a conversation had when he was a schoolboy, nearly fifty years before the writing of the book in which it is quoted—it would be reasonable to conclude that Sanabria was a man possessed of unusual powers of recall. Taking Sanabria's book as a whole, however, my own conclusion is that Sanabria was something more like a magpie, an assiduous collector and rearranger of diverse bits and pieces of information that interested, excited, and pleased him. The 1972 book was his crowning achievement, the master production of a lifelong connoisseur of Indian lore: firsthand, popular, scholarly; South American, North American, Erewhonian.

This remembered boyhood conversation, for example, resembles rather strikingly one recorded in a 1931 article by anthropologist and historian Alfred Métraux. Métraux, who in his historical researches had come across multiple examples of what he called "god-men" among the Chiriguano from the sixteenth century onward, visited the Bolivian Chaco and sought out living witnesses to the one that had walked the earth in living memory, the Bolivian tumpa of 1892. Métraux records an Ava interviewee telling him dismissively: "Ce *Tunpa* n'était qu'un trompeur" ("That Tunpa was nothing but a cheat") (1931: 86; italics in original).

It is of course possible that the opinion that the tumpa had been a liar, a trickster, was widely shared among Bolivian Guaraní people so that two separate informants, from two entirely different communities, on two separate occasions, would say more or less the same thing about him when asked. However, the rather contradictory judgment about the tumpa's character that Aireyu goes on to relate—the tumpa was at once a "liar" and a fraud and a great, powerful, and brave Ava—is such a favorite theme of Sanabria's 1972 text that it seems to me to be excessively convenient that Aireyu would have described him in exactly that manner in the 1920s. In any event, this theme itself is not original to Sanabria.

BIOGRAPHY OF A GREAT, BRAVE, AND WELL-INTENTIONED HUMBUG

Sanabria was a clear enthusiast of the large English language literature on the Plains Indians of the American frontier and Wild West who were the contemporaries of the late nineteenth-century Chaco Indians of the Bolivian frontier that became the focus of his best-known book. The epigraph to Sanabria's book is a quote (in English) from Sitting Bull, taken from W. Fletcher Johnson's *Life of Sitting Bull and History of the Indian War* (1891):

> I never stood in the white man's country. I never committed depredations in the white man's country. The white man came on to my land and followed me. The white man made me kill him or he would kill my friends, my women, and my children. (qtd. in Sanabria [1972] 2008: 7)

Sitting Bull is here referring to the Battle of Little Bighorn, in 1876, at which a principally Lakota force that included Sitting Bull engaged the Seventh Cavalry regiment under George Custer and effectively annihilated them, leaving 268 dead and 55 wounded. The quote is more probably included, however, to draw a parallel not between this event and Apiaguaiki Tüpa's story but the more apt one that could be made between Sitting Bull's late 1890 murder during the suppression by Indian Police of Ghost Dancing on Standing Rock Reservation that would eventually culminate in the notorious massacre on December 29, 1890, by US soldiers of nearly 200 Lakota men, women, and children at Wounded Knee.

Johnson's account of Sitting Bull is a pastiche of quoted sources, some of which portray him as ludicrous, others as bloodthirsty, and yet others as stalwart and noble. Johnson's commentary endorses all three views. From a letter to a newspaper written by the wife of a civil engineer, describing in the early 1870s how with the help of a "fat old negress" Sitting Bull is dressed in a suit of white men's clothes and invited to dinner:

> I regret to say, however, that in the training of his childhood table manners must have been sadly neglected. The only possible use he could see for a fork was to reach forth with his grimy hands and spear various articles of food which appeared to him desirable[6] . . . For the remainder of the day he strutted about the camp with the most absolute self-satisfaction, his confidence and pleasure in the loveliness of his new attire being unbounded. (qtd. in Johnson 1891: 57–58)

Johnson comments: "Such, then, was the formidable personage around whom the disaffected Sioux rallied, in hope of winning by force redress for their many grievances" (58).

Next, Johnson quotes from an account from a John Finerty, described by Johnson as a "vivid picture" of Sitting Bull:

> His fierce, half-bloodshot eyes gleamed from under brows which displayed large perceptive organs, and as he sat there on his horse regarding me with a look which seemed blended of curiosity and insolence, I did not need to be told that he was Sitting Bull . . . [he] was soon engirdled by a crowd of young warriors with whom he was an especial favorite as representing the unquenchable hostility of the aboriginal savage to the hated pale-faces. (1891: 65)

Johnson concludes the biographical section of his book by quoting at length an "eloquent and impassioned tribute" (1891: 194) by the writer W.H.H. Murray, which ends:

> The spot where this great character was buried—buried like a dog—[ought to be] carefully marked—marked beyond questioning or doubt, for as the Lord liveth and my soul liveth a monument shall be builded on that spot before many years—if I live—inscribed to the memory of the last great Prophet of the Sioux, and of the noble characteristics of the red race, whose virtues, like his own, were many, and whose fate was pathetic. (203)

After this contradictory pastiche of white versions of Sitting Bull's character, the latter part of Johnson's book is an account of relations of the United States military, government, and settlers with the Sioux people that led up to the events at Wounded Knee in 1890. The actual Ghost Dance prophet, Wovoka or Jack Wilson, is described by Johnson in a single chapter using the conflicting information available at the time of writing (anthropologist James Mooney's carefully researched account was not published until 1896). Johnson ends with documents relating to the immediate aftermath and possible consequences for government "Indian policy"; he offers no synthetic conclusion.

In fact the 544-page tome ends very abruptly. Lengthy direct citation of Indian population statistics from the 1890 census is on the final page of text; the facing page is sheet music for the "Dog Dance of the Sioux" and the "Chippewa Scalp Dance." One has the distinct sense, reading Johnson, that he was already (in 1891) slightly overwhelmed by the enormous number of sources (newspaper articles, government documents, military documents, memoirs) relating to Wounded Knee. Johnson's book was intended as a popular, not a scholarly, account and his handling of sources is loose: no footnoting, no bibliography. As we shall see, this casual approach to documentation also characterizes Sanabria's work.

Johnson's suturing of the "story of Sitting Bull" with the "story of Wounded Knee" has in the years since been cemented in the popular understanding of both. It clearly influenced Sanabria's later handling of the comparatively fragmentary documentation available relating to Apiaguaiki Tüpa and Kuruyuki. I will note other examples as they arise, but to begin with, one strikingly peculiar feature of Sanabria's book is its periodic inclusion of lyrics to potted Guaraní songs that appear to be his own inventions (they do not derive from the extensive ethnohistorical and anthropological literature on the Guaraní, and they often feature themes that themselves seem to be borrowings from other ethnographic contexts in North and South America). This is probably an homage—perhaps not even a conscious one—to the model offered by Johnson's text.

Sanabria's book opens with an orientation to the landscape of the "Cordillera Chiriguana" (the foothills and valleys to the east of the Bolivian Andes, extending to the flat landscape of the Chaco), the history of its pre-Columbian settlement, its exploration during the colonial era, and the encroachment upon it across the Republican period (1825 on) by white settlers. Sanabria then turns to the life story of the tumpa. For the tumpa's early years, the only known source is a few lines of a short letter written by one of his followers (Juan Ayemoti) to a Franciscan missionary, Romulado Dambroggi. For many would-be biographers, this absence might present a difficult problem. For Sanabria, Ayemoti's letter becomes a kind of tailor's dummy to be outfitted at will.

Ayemoti writes that the tumpa was the son of a chief (who goes unnamed) who left the tumpa's mother "so that she should marry another man" (Ayemoti, cited in Sanabria Fernández [1972] 2008: 226). Sanabria infers from this terse information that the tumpa's mother must have been one of those Guaraní maidens, who was so extraordinarily attractive that she was taken into a chief's "seraglio" when "scarcely" past her first menstruation and then later handed off to any ordinary village man who would have her, as was the "rite and custom" of the Chiriguano (100). This is ethnographic nonsense, but Sanabria manifests throughout the text an unshakeable attitude that inventive fillips about Indians, sex, and Indian sexuality are his perfect authorial prerogative.

Ayemoti goes on to say that the young tumpa (whom he never calls by a personal name) led an itinerant life with his mother, who sought work on white haciendas "in search of food," and that they ended up in Murucuyati, where the young tumpa "saw the massacre . . . and could escape" ([1972] 2008: 226). Sanabria infers from this, not unreasonably, that the tumpa's mother was killed during a notorious Indian massacre in Murucuyati that took place in 1877. Reckoning back from reports of the tumpa's age at his death in 1892, he would have been about fourteen at the time. According to Ayemoti, the young tumpa was taken from Murucuyati by a "man from Imboche" and "from this suffering has come the rage he has toward whites" (226).

Having used the words of the famous Sioux Sitting Bull as the epigraph to the book, Sanabria here invokes the equally famous Apache warrior Geronimo:

> Twenty years earlier [in 1858] . . . an army detachment made a surprise attack on an encampment of Apache Indians, victimizing around one hundred invalids, women, and children. The very night of the massacre, Geronimo, until then a peaceful youth with no particular tribal prominence, ascertained among the mountain of cadavers the presence of his mother, wife, and three young children . . . 'I was unarmed, nor did have a great desire to fight'—he would later tell a schoolteacher in Oklahoma—I didn't want to think about recovering the bodies of my family members because this would haven't been possible, I didn't ask nor resolve upon anything in particular . . . In the end I followed the tribe, guided by the soft noise of those who marched forward'.
>
> Apiaguaiqui pondered in the same manner, concluding by following, not the tribe, of which there was none, but the man from Imboche, his provident savior.
>
> He who was called Geronimo was to become the bravest chief the Apaches ever had, and the most determined enemy of the whites on both sides of the frontier. What became of Apiaguaiqui is the principal matter treated in this modest book. ([1972] 2008: 110–111)

But of course, Sanabria is already signaling that "what became of Apiaguaiqui" is something very like "what became" of Geronimo, and of Sitting Bull—that is, of "what became" of iconic Amerindians of the North American Great Plains and Old West. Sanabria's insistence on these parallels saturates the book. One of the oddest examples is among the photographs included in the original edition of the book.

There is one photograph of Santos Aireyu, which appears from the hairstyle and clothing to date from the 1940s or 1950s. Most of the others are taken from the archives of the Franciscan missionaries and include several named such missionaries

FIGURE 2.2. "Chiriguano" man included in Sanabria

alongside a few photos taken by missionaries of unnamed Chiriguano. Mixed in with these, and labeled as a nineteenth-century Chiriguano man, is this photo (figure 2.2).

Certainly it is an arresting portrait, of the type that would have appealed to Sanabria's sensibilities about Indians. It is, however, of the Apache leader Victorio (1825–1880) (see Chamberlain 2007 for this and other photos of Victorio).

When I shared my discovery with my historian colleague Combès, I speculated that the photograph ended up among Sanabria's copious notes as an enthusiast of all things Indian and that he simply did not remember its provenance when he included it among the other illustrations to be published in the book. She wryly pointed out that this would not account for the **tembeta** that appears to have been drawn on Victorio's chin in the version that appears in the book, nor the fact that for some reason it is the only photo included in the book for which there is no legend. The tembeta is the labret, or lip plug, that was a traditional facial ornament for Chiriguano men into the twentieth century.

The canny fraudulence displayed here by Sanabria is a quality the biographer repeatedly—and admiringly—attributes to his biographee, the tumpa. To go back to the story of the tumpa's life, Ayemoti says in his letter to Father Dambroggi that the tumpa

> is not a witch, he is a person that god himself sent us to be our lord and liberator, which he only came to realize after the massacre in Murucuyati and an old man of Sipotindi who knows many things and taught him everything had him in his house so that he could use [this knowledge] to serve his people. He was also with the *capitán* Machirope in Mororigua, whose servant he was while still a boy and from the *Capitán* he learned what he knows now about how to treat his people well and how to lead as a good chief when there is nothing and when there is war. (Ayemoti, cited in Sanabria Fernández [1972] 2008: 226).

On the basis of this rich and fascinating—but resistant to definitive chronological interpretation—passage, Sanabria constructs a detailed coming of age for the young tumpa. He has the orphaned youth becoming the errand boy of Machirope, canvasing the entire Cordillera on his behalf. He describes how disillusioned the young man must have become upon realizing that the adherence of chiefly subjects depended not upon loyalty, but the distribution of largesse. An anthropologically informed reader may suspect that this discussion of lowland South American chieftainship as being predicated upon chiefly generosity is Sanabria's again turning of his voracious reading on all things Indian to novelistic ends. Lévi-Strauss, for example, offers such a discussion in *Tristes tropiques*, a book directed toward popular audiences (see, for e.g., Lévi-Strauss [1955] 1961: 304).

According to Sanabria, though disappointed by his people's leaders the dispirited teen was impressed by the credulous respect his compatriots accorded to even the most ordinary of shamans. A plan formed in his mind to learn the shamanic arts in order to realize his destiny as the man who would lead the Chiriguano against the whites. The tumpa then bid a respectful adieu to Machirope and presented himself to the regionally renowned shaman Güirariyu as a prospective apprentice.

To understand how the "old man of Sipotindi" mentioned by Ayemoti becomes, specifically, "Güirariyu" in Sanabria's hands, one must look again to the historical and ethnographic literature with which Sanabria would have been familiar when writing his life of Apiaguaiqui. Güirariyu was a key figure in an 1874 Chiriguano revolt. The Franciscan missionary Alejandro Corrado described him as a witch who enjoyed immense prestige among his people, he made them hear an unknown voice upon the air, which invited them to battle valorously and without fear, assuring them that the bullets of the Christians, their force spent, would fall at their feet without injuring them, and that the walls of their fortresses would melt like wax in their presence. (Corrado 1884: 482)[7]

Combining this information with the biographical possibility that a man in his prime in 1874 would have been of an age to act as a mentor nearly twenty years later, it seems that Sanabria turned these events into a certainty. He spends several pages detailing how Güirariyu

> as a senior enchanter and like the shamans of the ancient Asian cults, was united, or attempted to be, with his ancestors in the same tribal practices, by way of subtle threads of ritual evocation. Of these he preserved the memory of their deeds, conceiving of them as an essential part of the "Avaísta" tradition and most deserving paradigms of presentation to his fellows, for being exemplary and for being a reason for pride. ([1972] 2008: 120)

Sanabria not only knows for sure that the "old man of Sipotindi" mentioned by Ayemoti was Güirariyu, he knows exactly what he talked about to the young tumpa. Sanabria has the older man regaling the younger with the histories of previous celebrated tumpas in the history of the Chiriguanos, who inspired messianic revolts against the whites during the Spanish colonial period.

The list, sequence, and details of these putative conversations between two nineteenth-century Indians are all in fact taken from a twentieth-century source: Métraux's 1931 article again, "God-men of the Chiriguano." As a closing flourish, Sanabria speculates as to how the last example in the series, that of the eighteenth-century "prophet of Masavi," who had been accompanied in his peregrinations by his mother, "Maria Tambora," and is said to have died obscurely after the capture of her rebel son, "must have agitated in the most touching fashion his [that is, Apiaguaiqui's] memory of his own mother, how he traveled with her through the land, until her death at the hands of [white] soldiers" ([1972] 2008: 121). We have now moved in Sanabria's account from certainty about the mode of the tumpa's mother's death to mind reading about how the young tumpa must have felt about it.

To go back to the tumpa's (putative) relationship with Güirariyu, Sanabria details how when first approached by the bold youth this "senior enchanter" was taken aback, later becoming so convinced by the boy's confidence and insistence that he ended up not only taking him under his wing but, before dying, declaring in confidence to a Guaraní chief that the young fellow was the savior whose arrival he, Güirariyu, had long anticipated:

The announcement was first circulated primarily with caution and only among the leaders of Ivo and its immediate surroundings, so that the missionary fathers would not learn of it:

"The tumpa redeemer has arrived. He is among us. It is he who began as Güirariyu's disciple. Güirariyu knew it, but did not want to reveal it until the hour had come." ([1972] 2008: 124)

Ayemoti's letter, which is the only source cited by Sanabria for all of this, says only,

If our tumpa has emerged and been put above his people it is not because he has wanted this but instead because the Avas took him when they knew him to be the best of them all and sent by god, they brought him here to Ivo and made him a house, an altar, and an office, afterward everyone has come behind him and are with him so that he directs them and so that they may know what he commands this is what suits all of us. (Ayemoti, cited in Sanabria [1972] 2008: 227)

Sanabria's source-free identification of Güirariyu as the young tumpa's mentor is consistent with his cramming of information and ideas from diverse sources into this story of this singular figure. However, I think it was also specifically motivated. Sanabria describes the young tumpa as learning ventriloquism from Güirariyu, at which Corrado said this latter excelled (this skill is often mentioned for Tupí-Guaraní shamans in the ethnohistorical literature). In a public talk given some years after the publication of the book, Sanabria assured his audience:

He [Apiaguaiqui] didn't do this for fiction, he didn't do it to trick his people, he didn't do it to make a spectacle, he did it to attract his fellow Guaraní, to call their attention to him and to make them all consent to a single ideal: to liberate his people. (1992: 17–18)

This description is in accord with one of Sanabria's central contentions in the book, about the tradition he has this fledgling young tumpa joining:

The Tumpa, for his part, in order to obtain the fervent adhesion and the blind mystic following of his people, that is to say the unreserved acceptance of his tumpaist mission, has to appeal to certain reserves of magic existent in the cultural heritage of the tribe. He thus becomes the actor in a drama whose apparatus is mounted with the rigging of the old tradition of sorcery and whose success depends on the best possible montage and the highest quality of actor. ([1972] 2008: 130)

This invocation of masquerade and loftily motivated fakery is something I ask the reader to keep in mind. Here it is a projection by a white author onto an Indian subject, but it will reappear (pardon the irresistible play on words) in many guises in chapters to come.

DIAGNOSING VENGEANCE

In Sanabria's version of events, once the tumpa was "revealed" to his people and began working his magical arts of high-minded duplicity upon them, he attracted an enormous following to his redoubt in Ivo. Local settlers, missionaries, and government authorities grew concerned. Rumors circulated, preparations for conflict were made on both sides, trouble brewed. According to Sanabria, the event that finally drove Apiaguaiki and his followers to violence was the murder of a "young Guaraní girl" by a white settler around the turn of the 1892 new year, an event, he speculates, that was probably preceded by her actual or attempted rape ([1972] 2008: 143).

This speculation is now widely repeated as fact, not only in relatively popular literature but even in the work of serious scholars (Combès 2005b: 223; Gustafson 2009: 36; Langer 2009: 190; Saignes 1990: 193). My own careful examination of the available sources revealed a single reference to a Guaraní woman (age unspecified) being whipped to death by a white settler around this time (Chavarría 1892: 29; Combès 2014 notes this without crediting me for having pointed it out to her). I will show further on that there are good reasons to suppose this terrible death bore no causal relation to the violence that followed it. It is typical of Sanabria, though, to turn an event about which almost nothing is known into something luridly eroticized (a woman of unknown age becomes a "young girl," a death by whipping is turned into a rape-murder).

In any event, now supposedly bent on vengeance, Apiaguaiki and his followers began to fall upon isolated white ranches and settlements to bloody purpose. Sanabria describes their nocturnal preparations for one such operation:

> The women, always encouragers and exhorters of the courage of their men, after stimulating in private the exaltation of the masculine qualities of the warriors, broke into an ululating chorus to sing the ancient invocation to their tutelary deities, put into a sort of high-pitched and nasal monotone:
> *May they be defeated, my Father Sun, the evil enemies.*
> *May the perfidious ones be defeated, completely defeated!* ([1972] 2008: 154)

Although he gives the text of this ditty in Guaraní, which he then translates, its provenance is dubious—"father Sun" is more of an Andean than Guaraní religious notion. Guaraní phrases are scattered throughout the book. To many readers, they no doubt lend it considerable authenticity. I find them ever more Fennimore Cooperesque with each reading.[8] Sanabria, who did not himself speak Guaraní, never specifies where he got these songs nor (as is far more likely) who translated fanciful phrases of his own invention into Guaraní. Nor does he reveal a documentary or testimonial source for the detail about the "stimulation in private" of the "masculine qualities" of the warriors, and the collective distaff agreement to follow it up with a group singalong.

Sanabria felt free to take these sorts of narrative liberties because he was sure he understood both the consciousness and subconscious of Chiriguano people. He confidently declares in the introduction to the 1972 book:

> Savagely harassed, expelled from his land and humiliated to baseness, the Chiriguano nourishes still the hope of returning to what he was, with a fiery expulsion of the invading white . . . Needless to say, most of those [messianic leaders] proceeded and proceed conscious of the fictitious and luring advocates of action. Nevertheless, there has been no lack of those convinced of themselves, those so taken in by their own sug-gestiveness as to arrive at firm belief in their own messianic destiny. ([1972] 2008: 45)[9]

Sanabria kept elaborating upon the tumpa's story even after the 1972 publication of Apiaguaiki's "biography." Shortly before his death in 1986, Sanabria spoke to an audience of underprivileged boys attending a boarding and agricultural train-ing school outside Santa Cruz. This talk was later reprinted as a monograph in the watershed year of 1992 (the Columbian quincentennial, and the centenary of the massacre at Kuruyuki). In the talk, he handles the parallels between the Chiriguano case of Apiaguaiki Tüpa and North American instances as not simply positive resemblances, but negative contrasts to cases closer to home.

Sanabria is at pains to emphasize, before this young Santa Cruz audience, the distinctiveness of Apiaguaiki *as against* much better-known Andean indigenous leaders who had by that time entered the national canon: "Tupac Katarí, Willca, and others of the Andes" (1992: 10). He says that in contrast to these men, who led only a portion of their people, Apiaguaiki was the "universal chief of his people. All of the Guaraní people . . . obeyed him, all ran behind him" (10; Combès 2005b demonstrates this was far from the case). Sanabria goes on to elaborate the contrast:

> It is known that the Chiriguano people have been the most valiant people in the
> Americas. One could perhaps compare to them the Apaches of North America . . .
> They never submitted to the Spanish . . . All other indigenous groups that exist today
> in Bolivia, all submitted to the Spaniards. Some under force of arms, others voluntarily.
> For example, if we speak of the indigenous peoples of the Andean mountains, of the
> West [in the sense of a Bolivia-internal contrast to the tropical lowland east], upon
> the mere arrival of the Spanish they ran to deliver themselves tamely, submissively to
> the Spaniards. They never protested, never complained of that condition. Instead they
> went spontaneously, they presented themselves voluntarily to submit to the Spaniards.
>
> The Chiriguano, quite the reverse; they never submitted to the Spanish. They lived
> for centuries in continuous struggles, in continuous back and forth. (1992: 11)

I have discussed elsewhere how this focus on generating a mythologized lowland Bolivian history in contention with that of the Andes has to do with regional rivalries of long historical standing (Lowrey 2006b). What interests me here is something else: Sanabria's increasingly free interpretive hand. By 1986, he describes the 1877 massacre at Murucuyati in gruesome detail and appends to it a dramatic account of the bloody demise of Apiaguaiki's mother:

> Among the dead was a poor woman who had with her her little son, and the boy saw his mother dead; when he was just seven years old, he realized that his mother had died murdered by soldiers. He was recovered in a bloody ditch, the blood of his mother and the other victims of the attack; there was a compassionate person among those who managed to flee, those who were not within reach of the attackers and so this child found someone to seize hold of him, who carried him into the bush, and this person delivered him to a shaman. (1992: 16)[10]

The audience to whom Sanabria was speaking was composed of school-aged and adolescent boys, who almost surely would find the story of a smaller and more helpless version of themselves rescued under such tragic and dramatic circumstances deeply compelling. This plea to the audience is perhaps why Sanabria chooses here to shave about seven years off what he had previously given (and which other sources suggest would have been) as the age of the young hero in 1877. But this dramatic license also speaks to the degree to which Sanabria treated Apiaguaiki as his own authorial creation, to edit and embellish at will and according to circumstances.

In an analysis of a famous speech supposed to have been delivered by Chief Joseph of the nineteenth-century Nez Perce, Thomas Guthrie says, "*the written text is the one and only original*" (2007: 520; italics in original), and "the text is indeed originary, though for the opposite reasons it claims for itself and that others have claimed for it" (520). Similarly, Sanabria's writing is the source, not the record, of almost every known element of Apiaguaiki Tüpa's now-renowned biography.

As the success of the book and the fame of Apiaguaiki grew, Sanabria's account of his own authorial methods shifted. In the 1972 text, he emphasizes his thorough review of archival sources and lists nine interviews with informants to gather oral histories. In the 1986 talk he says instead that though he researched the archives, he wrote his book relying "principally" on oral tradition (1992: 22).[11] Finally, shortly before his death in 1986, he was interviewed by a group of students and told them:

> To write this biography, there were no archival documents to consult. It was simply penetrating the Chiriguano soul, that of their leaders, conversing with them, discovering their traditions. Later I completed the biography with an archival document that was in the departmental prefecture. (Pérez Fernández 1995: 3)

This method is, of course, very dubious on the historical merits. At the same time, as an anthropologist I can't mock too mercilessly the notion of the conversational palpitation of others' souls—it is one way to describe ethnographic fieldwork, after all. But there is no record that Sanabria really did any such systematic ethnographic palpitation. It's hard to imagine he would have supposed he needed to because he knew, already, what he would find there: a mix of nobly intended humbug, thirst for vengeance, and proud independence, in doses rather exactly equivalent to those other white writers found among North American Indians of the Plains and Old West, specifically fabled "braves" such as Sitting Bull and Geronimo. In the next chapter I will trace those doses to their "origins" in North America—there, too, they are mostly textual—but first I want to turn to the powerful appeal Sanabria's account has had for Bolivian Guaraní political leaders in recent decades.

MASCULINITY AND REVITALIZATION

Even as close to the events in question as the late 1920s, Métraux did not find it easy to find informants about the tumpa of 1892. By the time of the 1972 publication of Sanabria's book, the tumpa had fallen into near oblivion. Of the nine "oral histories" listed among the sources for Sanabria's book, eight are from whites, one of whom is said to have relayed information given to him by a deceased Guaraní family servant; the ninth is the only Guaraní informant and was originally interviewed by Métraux. My private and unprovable supposition is that Sanabria never met this person (Taruiri) but included him in his listing to give the impression of having had direct contact with his oral testimony rather than simply reading it in Métraux.

Even if Sanabria began working on this book within the living memory of the tumpa period (very elderly eyewitnesses could have been found into the 1960s), it would have been difficult for Sanabria to locate direct informants. The region involved was impacted by the 1932–1935 Chaco War between Bolivia and Paraguay, with many Guaraní people displaced into Paraguay (some of whom will be discussed in chapter 7), and Argentina and those still in the region having had to reorder their communities. The missions were abolished and turned into normal parishes in the years after the war (Langer 2009: 266). Thus the already-tenuous historical memory encountered by Métraux on the eve of the war was obliterated by the war and its aftermath. Between Métraux 1931 and Sanabria 1972, the story of the tumpa did not attract the attention of historians or folklorists, either. I will suggest toward the end of the chapter what I speculate to have been the immediate prompt to Sanabria for the writing of his biography.

In any event, obscurity was not the fate of Sanabria's book. It was soon seized upon by Catholic scholar-missionaries building a new model for engaging Bolivian indigenous peoples in the wake of the 1971 Barbados Declaration. Missionary scholar-activists such as Xavier Albó, Bartomeu Meliá, and Francisco Pifarré cited Sanabria's work and expanded upon it (Albó 1990; Meliá 1988; Pifarré 1989) as they worked with Guaraní peoples to develop a sense of their own political history and contemporary rights. In 1987, the Catholic Church assisted in the foundation of the Ava-dominated (because long-missionized) Asamblea de Pueblos Guaraní (APG) in Bolivia. The APG is the central coordinating organization for Bolivian Guaraní peoples: the Ava, the Simba, and (to a lesser extent), the Isoseño. The Ava and Simba are the people who were formerly known as the Chiriguano; the Isoseño were known as Chané, as noted in chapter 1. During the 1970s and 1980s, the work of Catholic clergy in indigenous communities in Bolivia (and, relatedly, Paraguay) was influenced by liberation theology and aimed at consciousness raising on class, ethnic, and spiritual fronts. The figure of a "Guaraní messiah" who combined elements of Christian theology realized in Guaraní flesh (Sanabria himself made several allusions of this sort, e.g., calling Güirariyu John the Baptist to Apiaguaiki's Christ: 2008: 128), while also being a rebel against usurping landowners, and (if one believes Sanabria's version of events, which many people do) a model "race man," was tailor made to the needs of the era.

The 1992 publication of Sanabria's 1986 talk was under the auspices of a Catholic Church–supported NGO, and in 1992 the story of Apiaguaiki Tüpa and Kuruyuki became a multiply charged one for the then-five-year-old APG. Celebrations commemorated "500 years of resistance" (since Columbus arrived to the Americas in 1492), "100 years of resistance" (since the massacre at Kuruyuki, Bolivia), and the notion that the Chiriguano people who had fallen in the flesh in 1892 were resurrected in institutional form by 1992. Their spirit had not been defeated. The cultural resonance of this in a context so influenced by (and materially dependent upon) the Catholic Church is obvious; and of course, the pathos of the story is powerful on its own. But this attention would only explain the "promotion" of Apiaguaiki Tüpa between 1972 and 1992 by allies to the Bolivian Guaraní.

As is well known, between 1992 and the present indigenous peoples throughout the Americas have taken over their own political agendas and the business of image making and choosing. In the specific context of Bolivia, the material support provided by the Catholic Church has shrunk across that time; its material support is much less important than it once was, and the "grand old men" (Xavier Albó, Bartomeu Melía, Gabriel Siquier) of the church of the 1970s, 1980s, and 1990s are aging and dying and not being replaced. But the hold of the story of Apiaguaiki Tüpa is only growing. Guaraní people themselves have taken over its promotion.

Paying close attention to post-1992 contention over the name of the tumpa can help to explain this. Let us go back to the putative conversation with Santos Aireyu with which Sanabria opened his book, a conversation Sanabria reports Aireyu closed by saying, "simply," "His own name was Apiaguaiki." A similar name, rendered as "Apiaiqui," appears in the 1892 report by Coronel Melchor Chavarría to the Bolivian federal government on how the events in Kuruyuki developed and their aftermath (Chavarría 1892: 4). Métraux reports a Chiriguano informant, Pedro Ignacio Taruiri, speaking in 1929 of "Apiawaikí" (Métraux 1931: 86). Note the way Sanabria's rendering sutures together two earlier spellings: "Apiaiqui" and "Apiawaikí" into the single (and more Spanish-orthography-friendly) "Apiaguaiqui."

The portmanteau word "Apiaguaiqui" is not recognized as meaningful by Guaraní speakers (nor is "Apiaiqui," recorded earlier). Jesuit scholar and ethnographer Francisco Pifarré gathered oral testimony relating to the tumpa during the 1980s:

> Mr. Arnulfo Camargo, of Alto Parapetí, gave us the true name of the Tumpa. As
> a youth he was called "Chapiaguasu."[12] It was only in Kuruyuki that he was called
> Hapia-oeki. According to Mr. Camargo, it was he who gave this name to the
> writer Hernando Sanabria, who transcribed it erroneously in denominating him
> "Apiaguaiqui" (personal communication). Cecilia Tejerina, from Ivo, remembered
> that her grandmother who died in 1950 spoke to her grandchildren of Chapiaguasu-
> Tumpa (personal communication). (1989: 388n3)

Mr. Camargo does not appear in the list of interviewees given by Sanabria himself at the end of his book. In any event, Pifarré used Mr. Camargo's assertion to argue that "Hapia-oeki Tumpa" might best be translated as "testicles taken away by God" or "eunuch of god." Pifarré asserts that the tumpa was "celibate" (1989: 388n5). Although he does not provide a source, perhaps he was thinking of testimony that Sanabria attributes to "Taruiri" that the tumpa "never knew a woman" (Sanabria [1972] 2008: 131).

"Taruiri," recall, is the only Guaraní informant listed among the persons from whom Sanabria says he collected oral histories in the course of researching his book; also, Sanabria does not mention that this person is named as an informant in the 1931 article by Métraux, upon which he so heavily draws. It is possible that he sought this person out, having read Métraux's article, and found him alive and talkative more than thirty years on from Métraux's 1929 visit. The passage in question, however, is not reassuring on that point for a reader familiar with Sanabria's favored themes:

> The informant Taruiri, of whom it is said that he knew the tumpa, took pleasure
> in affirming, dragging out the words with a certain penetrating emphasis, that "the
> Tumpa never knew a woman." Such an assertion leads one to suppose that he was
> chaste by temperament or abstemious by presumed obligation, as have been certain

leaders of peoples, that gave everything to their cause, up to and including [or leading to] the inhibition of their virile faculties. (Sanabria Fernández [1972] 2008: 131)

Later, historian Saignes suggested that Pifarré's casting of "Hapia-oeki Tumpa" as "eunuch of god" was rather too obvious a projection on the part of an analyst who formed part of a celibate clergy himself and suggested "japia vae ko" tumpa instead: the tumpa who has testicles, or, prosaically, the very ballsy tumpa (1990: 189–190). The anthropological linguist Bret Gustafson, an accomplished speaker of Guaraní who has helped to write both a dictionary and a grammar with Guaraní coauthors under the auspices of the APG, reports this interpretation from his own informants in the field during the 1990s (2009: 287n6). This interpretation, though, is not on the basis of the "sense" of the word in Guaraní but is offered in specific refutation of the "castrated" interpretation that Ava indigenous leaders are now perfectly aware has appeared in print (rather like Mr. Camargo's testimony, which was also a critique of "official" knowledge rather than a naive observation).

Both readings require the appearance of an initial aspirated "h" sound (rendered with "j" in contemporary Guaraní orthography) and certain other deformations of the written forms recorded in 1892 and 1931. Whatever their incompatibilities, what they both share, of course, is the way they make their meanings out of Indian masculinity. This trait, at least, is very much in accord with the tradition laid down by Sanabria. In the introduction of his book he is at great pains to establish the centrality of aggressive, preening masculinity to the Chiriguano ethos. In typical fashion, he offers an unsourced anecdote,[13] which is about a contemporary Chiriguano man whose resistance to receiving an enema as part of a necessary course of medical treatment had to be overcome by force, and who—though he was cured as a result—was afterward so ashamed of having experienced the "passive" sexual role that he ran away from his home and village, never to be heard from again ([1972] 2008: 44). Sanabria introduces this anecdote in his inimitable fashion: "This concatenation of concepts in the trinomial man-value-sex goes to extremes of proof as unexpected as they are conclusive" (44).

But while it is easy (sometimes irresistibly, overwhelmingly so) to poke fun at Sanabria, the adoption of certain aspects of the character he has created as an indigenous hero by Guaraní people themselves merits sober consideration. Sanabria's portrayal of Apiaguaiki Tüpa as a noble humbug has found no purchase, and in any event Sanabria's flowery, showily archaic prose means his book would have been unreadable by the 1980s generation of Bolivian Guaraní political leaders who first and most strongly identified with Apaiguaiki Tüpa. These were almost exclusively men with primary school educations. It is only since the early 1990s that a few women have moved into indigenous politics in Guaraní country (in striking contrast to the situation in the Andes) and only since the late 1990s that large numbers of Guaraní young people have finished high school (more each year go on to university as well).

What resonated early on, with lasting consequences into the present, was the notion of Apiaguaiki as a **kereimba**, a warrior. Guaraní political leadership in the 1980s and 1990s was almost exclusively male, and the leaders' aim was precisely to combat a situation in which Guaraní indigenous people were vulnerable, helpless, weak, defenseless, and dependent on *patrones* (bosses, but the cognate "patron" actually captures the sense better). Their accomplishments along those lines have been tremendous, though I will turn in chapters 4 and 7 to the ways the limitations and contradictions of that political approach are becoming ever more clear, not least to Guaraní people themselves.

Be that as it may, the "indigenous" discourse around Apiaguaiki Tüpa that began in the 1990s is that there is nothing so quintessentially Guaraní as to be an aggressive male warrior. Across the course of this book I hope to show that this framing is in fact doubly alien to Bolivian Guaraní people and particularly so to Isoseño people; that it comes, first, from (also mythologized) North American exemplars and, second, from the instilling of a Western set of values that disdains vulnerability and dependence.

However, one must always be wary of anthropological modes of argumentation that posit too-tidy contrasts between the culture under study and culture of the anthropologist. In fact this claim may be equally staked and equally countered in entirely "local," that is, Bolivian Guaraní cultural and historical, terms. Guaraní speakers did come as warrior-conquerors to the Andean foothills along the western margins of the Bolivian Chaco. They arrived from the east, in several waves, and found a population of sedentary Arawakan agriculturalists, the Chané. Guaraní men took Chané wives and Chané vassals; the language of the resulting "Chiriguano" population became Guaraní, but much of its social organization remained Arawakan (Combès 2005a; Combès and Lowrey 2006; Combès and Villar 2004; Combès and Villar 2007; Lowrey 2003). Guaraníness was figured as maleness to Chané feminine subjugation; these ideas were explicitly expressed in Guaraní, but at a more "implicit" level the structure of society was one of dependency relations that remained Arawakan. One cannot speak of mere imposition, however. The explicit championing of "Guaraníness" and, with it, maleness and aggressive dominance as supreme cultural values was entirely adopted by Chiriguano people while, at the level of daily practice, relations of mutual dependence and the Chané scaffolding of life remained constant.

It would seem that at least part of the impetus for Guaraní migrations was a "throwing off" of status relationships: religious movements inspired by prophets who urged (among other things) followers to "give their daughters to whomever they wish" (Clastres [1975] 1995: 38). The work of Hélène and Pierre Clastres, suggesting Tupí-Guaraní peoples of the pre-Columbian era as "societies against the state," has drawn renewed interest in recent years, as an ethnographic example of anarchist principles in lived practice (Graeber 2004). Male prerogative, however, seems not to have been among the social mores thrown off among these ancient Guaraní.

Isoso, where I did my fieldwork, was known into the twentieth century as a "Chané" redoubt. The evidence is that Chané people pushed off more desirable agricultural land by the new Chiriguano society ended up cultivating that inhospitable portion of the arid Chaco proper, along the lower Parapetí river (Combès 2005a; Lowrey 2003). These Isoseño Chané were historically treated by the Ava with considerable disdain and called by them **tapii**, "slaves." What is interesting is that as one moves downriver—corresponding to the direction of historical displacement—the population was historically "more Chané" and the swamps into which the river finally disappears are called **Yande Yari**: "our grandmothers." The contemporary explanation for this, very much inflected by eco-sensibilities, is that the swamps are a reservoir of ancestral riches in the form of fish spawning grounds. But this is also a term for Chané ancestors, collectively gendered as female relations; indeed Chané slaves were sometimes called **yari**, grandmothers. The way in which relationality (including the relationship of dependent subjugation) is figured as female, and independence and domination are figured as male, has a deep cultural history in the Chiriguanía. It has created a "structure of the conjuncture" (Sahlins 1985) whereby the creation of a hypermasculinized culture hero such as Apiaguaiki Tüpa by a white author such as Sanabria has been adopted as part of the revitalization of Guaraní values by Guaraní people themselves. This latter-day revitalization is articulated explicitly as a manifestation of sturdy virility, and in fact many contemporary Guaraní indignantly reject the possibility that their ancestry could be partially Chané (Combès and Lowrey 2006; Combès and Villar 2007). This position has consequences for contemporary Guaraní political leadership. Not only is the leadership overwhelmingly male dominated, but those women who do become involved are frequently derided as "unrepresentative" women because they are either never married or divorced, that is to say, not in a relation of direct dependency as a "proper" woman should be, which is not merely an imposed Western cultural value but a Chiriguano one. On the other hand, in Isoso—one of the more historically Chané communities—women leaders were not unknown in the historical past (Combès 1999: 26; Nordenskiöld [1912] 2002: 212). These intriguing "deep historical" possibilities will be returned to in chapter 4. For now, it remains for this chapter to finish the immediate history of what happened in 1892.

THE "BATTLE" OF KURUYUKI

The account of Kuruyuki in Sanabria's book is as dubious as the biography he weaves for Apiaguaiki Tüpa, but here Sanabria is not the only unreliable narrator. There are two principle sources of information, both of which Sanabria drew upon: an 1892 report by a military officer, Coronel Melchor Chavarría, who had been sent by the federal government to visit the region where the events unfolded a few months before there was any sign of trouble and who returned in the immediate aftermath of Kuruyuki; and an account published also in 1892 by a Franciscan missionary, Angélico Martarelli, who was living at the mission located closest to the events and who was himself closely involved in the lead-up and aftermath. Much of Martarelli's account was reproduced, with some telling additions and embellishments, in a mission history published in 1918 by his fellow Franciscan missionary Bernardo de Nino.

In September 1891, a delegation from the central government (then located in Sucre) that included Coronel M. Chavarría and Lieutenant T. Frías visited the Franciscan Mission of Santa Rosa (established four years previously, in 1887) near Cuevo, where they were welcomed by Father Martarelli and his colleagues including Father Romualdo Dambroggi. They heard a presentation by "the most influential Capitanes" among the Chiriguano, pleading for government support for the establishment of a new Franciscan mission in Ivo. According to the missionaries, the Chiriguano believed such an establishment would help to protect them from settler abuses and usurpations of land. Persuaded, Chavarría and Frías agreed to make a favorable recommendation to the government in Sucre.

By December 1891 a growing number of Indians were gathering at Kuruyuki, near Ivo (site of the proposed new mission), located about seventeen kilometers from Santa Rosa Mission. Martarelli writes,

> The plot began to manifest in early December, but being fearful of having their
> machinations discovered, the barbarians simulated a GENERAL PRAYER, with
> the specious pretext of having a bountiful harvest. For this, the Capitanes enclosed
> in a hut an Indian *hipaya* witch, giving him the name *Dios Tunpa*, who immediately
> began predicting the prosperity of his tribesmen, if they presented themselves to him.
> (1892: 5; boldface mine)

The word **hipaya** is a rendering of the Guaraní **ipaye** or **paye**, now usually translated as "shaman" rather than "witch."

According to Martarelli, whose explanation is echoed by Chavarría, the motive for this Indian gathering was growing unrest at settler abuses combined with anxiety that the settlers might prevent the establishment of the requested mission. Later scholars have accepted this explanation (Gustafson 2009; Langer 2009). Given that settler abuses were continuous in time and regionally ubiquitous, there is something odd about the fact that this gathering followed almost immediately upon the prospect of another mission being established in the region and occurred precisely at the site of the proposed new mission.

In his 1918 version, Nino does not mention the "prayers for a bountiful harvest" explanation of which Martarelli was so dismissive and supplies considerable new detail, including an estimate of the age of the tumpa, which has since been repeated (including by Sanabria) as established fact:

> There they adopted the project of a general uprising against the Christian usurpers of their lands. For the resolution taken to stimulate the desired effect it was desirable to lend to it the necessary authority and prestige capable of impressing the superstitious nature of the Indian. To this end they chose a brave and astute youth of 28, to whom they gave the name Tunpa (superior being). This fictitious divinity placed into a hut the interior of which they adorned with linen hangings and brightly colored cloth, was kept under guard and no one was allowed to come near without the prescribed ceremonies which obliged the supplicant to speak to him on his knees and via the intermediation of his associates and advisors. (Nino and Martarelli [1918] 2006: 134)

The 1918 version goes on to say that these preparations had the desired effect, and via the tumpa's agents, word of him spread throughout the neighboring provinces such that "a multitude of savages flooded Curuyuqui, whose number was calculated at 5000 fighting men without counting women and children . . . aside from the customary weapons of the savage they had various rifles and revolvers" (134).

Nino in 1918 is supplying one number ("5,000 fighting men") that appears—as we shall see—rather differently in Martarelli's 1892 original, while editing out another: "Along with counting upon the customary weapons of the savage, prepared with the patience that characterizes them, they had some 10 rifles and various revolvers that they handled with singular dexterity" (1892: 1). Like the tumpa's age, the number of "warriors" at Kuruyuki is now widely repeated as "five thousand," but this ferociously large figure (along with prudent silence as to their paucity of firearms: only ten all told) is Nino's post hoc doing, a quarter of a century later.[14]

Martarelli mentions a more modest figure when recounting a visit in December by one of the mission fathers,

> Romualdo Dambrogi [sic], competent in the Guaraní language, accompanied by the Mayor of the canton and other neighbors, personally visited the Tumpa to discover, if possible, his barbarous intent: said Father made every effort to get the Tumpa to come out of his hut, and there were moments in which he threatened in the name of the authorities the *three hundred Indians* who guarded him, but seeing their intransigence, he admonished them with flattering words until he was able to speak to him.

> The Indian emerged from his hut and before the Missionary appeared humble and submissive, saying to him: 'this meeting is completely peaceful, we are merely trying to make a plea according to our ancient customs, with the aim of having an abundant year in which we can enjoy something, after some years of scarcity. (1892: 5; italics mine).

This smaller number of 300 appears nowhere in Nino's later version. Nino leaves out the specific content of the tumpa's response to Dambroggi, saying only that while the tumpa did claim the gathering was religious in nature this "was a stratagem to trick him and gain time in order to prepare for war" (Nino and Martarelli [1918] 2006: 135).

Sanabria, as we have seen, goes much further than Nino in constructing a version of events in which the tumpa is a wily manipulator bent on bloody confrontation. Sanabria's tone is admiring rather than aghast at the tumpa's audacity, but he shares with Nino (and Martarelli before him) total certitude that all of the talk of prayer, harvests, and peaceful intentions is a bunch of humbug. They are sure they know what the Indians really want: violent revenge.

When I read back through these documents, it's difficult for me to feel the same certitude. It seems clear that the issue of the mission provoked the gathering, but whether this was due to Guaraní people's intense desire for a mission—an explanation given by the missionaries—seems to me insufficient on its own. It does not strike me as implausible that the poorly armed Guaraní people who gathered around the tumpa at the site of the prospective mission were hoping to avoid violent conflict. Ayemoti says as much in his letter:

> Leave us here with our captain, a child of god like yourselves, we are many who are here and we will be here come what may, if the whites do nothing we will do nothing that Tumpa doesn't want, but if they come we will defend ourselves. (Sanabria Fernández [1972] 2008: 227)

I am curious about the fact that the closest associate of the tumpa, Ayemoti ("I have made myself white"), was a Christian convert and former acolyte of Father Dambroggi himself. In a letter sent to a local newspaper in the aftermath, a settler reports that the tumpa promised "resurrection in Paraguay" to his followers (May 3, 1892 *Estrella del Oriente* [for which reference I am indebted to Isabelle Combès]; Saignes 1990: 194 also notes a reference to resurrection in Paraguay in another of Martarelli's accounts).

It's difficult to know how much credence to give this report, but it is intriguing because on the first day of the Chiriguano harvest festival, the **Arete Guasu** ("Great Festival"; literally, "Exemplary Time") masked guests arrive representing the dead. They are tenderly welcomed, stay for the several days of celebration, and depart on the last day amid tears. They are said to come from (and return to) the east, from "Paraguay." December is months before the harvest season, so it would be strange to choose "harvest" themes if all the Indians were doing was making up excuses for their behavior to deceive white interlocutors. It seems to me that the extant literature has followed Sanabria's lead (and Martarelli's and Nino's before his) much too closely in paying little to no attention to the symbolic, spiritual, and religious aspects of this situation outside of treating them as cover-up of, and motivated by, plans for violent revenge. It may well be that given the documentation available, even a partial understanding of those aspects will be forever elusive. That is not a license to dismiss them out of hand.

Martarelli 1892 and Nino 1918 give the same account of what happened next. Father Dambroggi orders the Indians at Ivo to disperse, but he returns to Santa Rosa Mission convinced that they will not. In both versions, his visit is followed up by one from a loyal mission Indian dispatched by the Fathers to emphasize to the Indians gathered in Kuruyuki that they were now at risk of incurring the wrath of the regional subprefect, who was prepared to send armed men against them. Both versions repeat the same answer from the tumpa and his captains: "Well, we are not afraid of the sub-prefect nor of a thousand armed Christians." Both versions repeat a very similar formula at this point—that war was now declared, though the hostilities broke out later (Martarelli 1892: 6; Nino and Martarelli [1918] 2006: 135). This puts the "declaration of war" in an Indian mouth. Sanabria (typically) goes further, and in his book has Chiriguano stalking through the countryside, passing the word from one Chiriguano to another that "war is again being made" ([1972] 2008: 139, for another example of his potted Guaraní) but close reading suggests the absolute reverse.

Nino carefully repeats Martarelli's exact phrasing in the passive voice:

> The Sub-Prefect was immediately informed of all that had happened with the savages of Ivo, who without delay sent Lieutenant Simon Sanz with a guard of 12 rifles and 100 cartridges. (Martarelli 1892: 6; Nino and Martarelli [1918] 2006: 135)

Now, who was it that "immediately informed" the subprefect of the failure to convince the Ivo Indians to disperse? Who was it that escalated what had been a peaceful standoff into a military encounter?

It can only have been the missionaries themselves, though given the ultimate consequences, one can understand their reluctance to say so forthrightly. According to both versions, Sanz made initial contact with the rebel Indians and arranged a date for negotiations to take place in Ñumbite January 4. The Indians did not appear on the appointed day, but on the January 6 began attacking Christian settlements in the environs of Ivo.

On the January 7, Sanz made an excursion from Ñumbite to Santa Rosa to bring reinforcements to it. He and his men were attacked on the return journey; between this attack and a simultaneous assault on Ñumbite a total of five named criollos (including Sanz himself) and five *aliados* (allied Indians, unnamed) were killed. The rebel Indians were, ultimately, repelled and in Nino's 1918 version retreated to Kuruyuki "with many losses" (Nino and Martarelli [1918] 2006: 137).

Both versions agree that after this the rebel Indians went rampaging across the region, "killing every Christian they encountered" (Martarelli 1892: 8; Nino and Martarelli [1918]: 137)—though no deaths are recorded by name—and stealing live-stock. Martarelli's 1892 version says, "anticipating death at any moment, the mortal anguish of the [criollo] asylum-seekers in Santa Rosa lasted three days" (8). Nino's 1918 version elaborates this at much greater length, describing how any little rumor spread panic among the people gathered at Santa Rosa, especially the women and children, and that the "Mission Fathers had offered to God the sacrifice of their lives, and were ready to die together with all the people sheltering there, if that were His will" (Nino and Martarelli [1918] 2006: 137).

On January 10, having received en route the alarmed notice sent by the Mission Fathers together with the Mayor of Ñumbite and having redoubled the pace of his march in consequence, Lieutenant Coronel Tomás Frías arrived in Santa Rosa with 50 men, 30 rifles, and 500 cartridges along with 400 allied Indians armed with bows and arrows. On the January 13, a party under his command went out on a recon-naissance mission to visit the rebel redoubt in Kuruyuki, burning down the homes of rebel Indians encountered en route. On this outing, they were attacked twice by the rebels resulting in the deaths of the "assistant of Coronel Frias and three allied Indians"; Frías and the rest of his men returned to Santa Rosa in the late afternoon, having run short of ammunition (Martarelli 1892: 10; Nino and Martarelli [1918] 2006: 138), suggesting they spent the day shooting Indians.

Here the two versions differ significantly. Nino's 1918 version includes a section describing the incredible anguish experienced by those left behind in Santa Rosa that day, their worry over the fate of Frías's expedition, their terror when a few "cow-ards" returned early from the expedition reporting on the attack on Frías and his men, and speculation as to what would have happened if the rebel Indians had gone on to still worse depredations following that attack:

> Who could have calculated the damages, the blood that would have been spilled, the deaths, the destruction of communities produced by the ferocity of the savage who had decided upon the extermination of all the Christian populace of the frontier, if divine Providence by unexpected means had not saved them? (Nino and Martarelli [1918] 2006: 138)

The 1918 version then adds that Coronel Frías at that point wrote to the central government to send backing.

Martarelli's contemporary 1892 account does not describe sentiments in Santa Rosa at all, but at this juncture inserts a communication sent from the subprefect of Lagunillas to Tomás Frías on January 15, recounting events elsewhere in the region. This letter declares, the "uprising of the savages is almost general and it seems that they have proposed to exterminate us" (1892: 10). It says criollos are organizing self-defense forces and that a notable Chiriguano chief has been taken into preventive custody. It declares that while Indian rebels at Huaraca have been "suffocated" (10), elsewhere Indians have "slit the throats of various [inhabitants] . . . and burned the houses and establishments of Sra. Teresa Franco and of Don Salustiano Chavez" (11).

This formulation is peculiar, to say the least. Somehow the names of (or even numbers of) Christians killed went unrecorded, while those whose property was damaged can be accounted for by name. It would not be so notable except that it recurs in the documentation. Many more Christian deaths are alluded to than are enumerated by name. One might put this down to general confusion except that the presumably less dramatic events of damage to property do often come with names attached. It suggests—as do other elements, which will be recounted below—an atmosphere thicker with rumors of Indian savagery than with attested instances of the same.

The letter goes on to tell of the death of "thirteen" Christians and "various" allied Indians in Tacuarandi on January 11. Named as among the dead were "the foreigner Mr. Lelarge and the two brothers, Pedro and Teodosio Barba" (1892: 11). The events in Tacuarandi are featured in Sanabria's book as part of a regional outbreak of Indian fury following that precipitating "rape and murder" in Ñumbite. But, as we have seen, neither of the mission-produced accounts allude in any way to such a "rape and murder." Instead, the obvious motive for the attack on Ñumbite would have been that Sanz's men, the first outside armed forces to arrive, at the express request of the missionaries at Santa Rosa, were quartered there.

What is clear in the letter from Lagunillas is that by mid-January 1892 criollo settlers were either themselves convinced—or wanted to convince the Bolivian military recipient of the letter, Tomás Frías—that all of the Indians in the region were engaged upon a violent collective rampage. The letter goes on to describe the organization of committees of defense and collection of arms and ammunition by white authorities across the region and the inscription of "volunteers" along with considerable numbers of "allied Indians" to these efforts. Martarelli quotes from another letter from another regional official, "of the same date," describing the efforts made in that region and recounting that as a result "the enemies have suffered various losses and injuries; we have taken some captives and rescued some horses" (1892: 12). Very much in the vein of the foregoing, Martarelli goes on to say, "In those days we knew that the rebels had sacked . . . the house and establishment of Mr. Vanuchi, and slit the throats of all the Christian colonists of the place" (1892: 12). Note, again, that Mr. Vanuchi of the damaged house is noted by name. Those many Christians with putatively slit throats are not.

By mid-January, then, white attacks on Indians were being fomented and organized across the region. Sanabria's very different account in his book describes coordinated *Indian* attacks on whites throughout the region. Of course, Indians were not writing each other letters that have been left to history, as the whites were, but when compared to the available documentation Sanabria's version begins to look suspect indeed.

To go back to Martarelli, he says of the conditions at Santa Rosa Mission in mid-January: "How sad and afflicting was our situation! We scarcely counted upon 200 cartridges, confronting five thousand savages with various weapons" (1892: 13). Here, surely, is the number that Nino turns into "five thousand fighting men"; Martarelli seems instead to be referring to the *total* number of Indians gathered at Ivo. Even so, as we shall see, the estimate is surely much too high.

The next event in the 1892 narrative is the appearance, at 6 AM on January 21, of

> the enemy before the Mission in a decided attitude of readiness to burn the town and its residents . . . the sudden appearance of the bloodthirsty savage host, occasioned for a moment a terrifying confusion among us . . . The serenity and energy of the brave Coronel Frias knew how to impose itself upon the circumstances, and in a few brief moments all of our force, composed of nationals and allied Indians, occupied the most weak and threatened positions on the town; the combat began on both sides, a rain of arrows crossed with our bullets and after a short hail of gunfire sustained by our riflemen, the enemies were disconcerted and retreated . . . While this was taking place, a considerable force of the enemy was descending the hill in front of the Mission in order to take part in the action, but upon seeing the havoc wrought by our bullets and arrows upon their lines, they lost courage and retreated toward Ivo; seeing them flee, our forces chased them for a long distance, from whence they retreated overwhelmed by exhaustion, the heat, and *a lack of ammunition*. If in those moments our lancers had horses at their disposition, the victory would have been complete.
>
> The combat that day lasted three hours, leaving 40 dead and various injured and captured on the enemy side, among whom fell the Indian traitor to the Mission, Capitán Chabuco, who was subjected to justice. On our part we only had to lament some 15 lightly wounded allied Indians. (1892: 13–14; italics mine)

Note that as at Ñumbite what brought an end to this "combat" was the white side running short of ammunition.

Nino, in 1918, adds quite a bit of new detail to Martarelli's 1892 account:

> They were divided into two wings, one on foot, composed of 1000 Indians and the other mounted, of some 300 under the command of the Tunpa in a decided attitude of burning the Mission, the town, and its inhabitants. The number, the bravery, and the happy omens of the Tunpa were the sure guarantee of triumph. (Nino and Martarelli [1918] 2006: 139)

The picture presented here, of a huge Indian force—1,300 strong, drawn up in military formation, and divided into infantry and cavalry—is very striking. So very striking, in fact, that one cannot help but wonder why Martarelli's eyewitness account of 1892 failed to note any of it.

Both versions, by their separate routes, now come to the dramatic, final confrontation. As usual, Nino writing in 1918 offers the more dramatic build-up:

> The state ... of uncertainty in which we lived facing these barbarians resolved to die drowning in their own blood sooner than retreat a handsbreadth ... and the news that, while the uprising was growing immeasurably in neighboring regions, the pitiless hosts of Curuyuqui, along with becoming more numerous each day, were redoubling their ferocious efforts to become invincible against even a well-seasoned army, all powerfully confirmed that our situation was becoming graver and more dangerous each day, like that of a flock in the midst of a storm trapped by the bank of an impetuous torrent. (Nino and Martarelli [1918] 2006: 141–142)

Martarelli's 1892 version merely reports, directly on the heels of the events of January 21, that on the January 26 the happy news arrived that the central government had named Melchor Chavarría as its delegate and that he was on the march with 50 infantrymen, 30 rifles, and 1,000 bullets; and on January 27, in heavy rain, General Gonzáles arrived with his forces. He reviewed the situation, the position and forces of the enemy, and the combined forces at his disposal, given in both versions as follows:

- 1500 allied Indians, armed with bows, arrows, and knives
- 100 riflemen
- 40 "nationals" (criollo volunteers) armed with shotguns

This makes for a total of 1,640 men and considerable force of arms under the joint command of General Gonzáles and Lieutenant Coronel Tomás Frías. Early on the morning of the 28th, the combined force set out. After a two-hour march they arrived at Kuruyuki, finding it "surprisingly" well defended by an elaborate set of trenches. Here Nino repeats Martarelli very faithfully:

> . . . the savage fought with truly surprising valor, resolved it seemed to triumph or die; they fell dead from bullet and arrow, but did not lose heart and though they suc-cumbed, gravely wounded, they didn't let go of their bows and arrows and knives, but still waylaid our forces to victimize them . . . Why not say it? There were moments of trepidation and doubt among our forces, the savage horde charged with incredible resolve, and despite the heavy fire from our infantrymen, our forces had to retreat for an instant, until the serenity of General Gonzáles, and the rapid maneuvers of the forces commanded by Frías, dislodged the enemy completely from the first set of trenches, leaving a multitude of dead. In this first attack, General Gonzáles was lightly wounded in the arm and his horse received 7 arrow-wounds.
>
> More bloody and tenacious yet was the attack on the second set of trenches, where many *families of savages* sheltered: the entrance was disputed hand to hand, until the trenches were filled with cadavers and they penetrated at last the final set of trenches and burned the village, killing the few who offered resistance. After the enemy was dislodged from their trenches, it was thought that they would flee, but on the con-trary they kept fighting bravely until General Gonzáles, seeing that the resistance was now much reduced *and that the supply of munitions of his forces was exhausted*, called the retreat, such that by 6 pm the government forces returned to their headquarters in Santa Rosa.
>
> *The numbers of savages dead in this action was calculated at 600*, without counting the many wounded who disappeared. On our part, *4 allied Indians died* and 30 were hurt; among our infantrymen there were 5 injured including one officer, and among the nationals a few were lightly injured. In this action about 1000 animals were recov-ered, that the savages had carried off from the Christians. (Martarelli 1892: 16–17; Nino and Martarelli [1918] 2006, essentially identical, p. 143; italics mine)

The narrative conjures up a battle that the numbers belie: on the rebel side, 600 dead, including "families"; on the military side, 4 dead—all "allied Indians." One does not have to be a military historian to suppose that those four dead Indians were quite probably killed by friendly fire. The military forces, for a third time in a little over two weeks, only withdrew from the field once they ran short of ammu-nition. The number of dead they left behind—600, including many women and children—suggest that the estimates of "five thousand fighting men" were com-pletely fantastical and that even 5,000 as an inclusive total for "followers surround-ing the tumpa" would probably be too high.[15]

In his book, Sanabria amplifies this portrayal of a military massacre, principally brought about by settler and missionary calls for intervention, as a "battle." The term "battle" is repeated in the literature produced since (Combès 2005b; Langer 2009; Pifarré 1989). It is only recently that the term "massacre" has begun to be used instead (Gustafson 2009: 36). One begins to guess the reasons for Nino's modifications to Martarelli's account in the following long defensive paragraph, which does not appear in the 1892 original:

> Judging by the attitude and decisiveness of which the rebels had offered so many proofs in the last combat, it was to be supposed that the war would not terminate immediately and that a lot of blood would have yet to be spilt on order to return peace to the frontier. Events nevertheless proved otherwise. With the defeat of Curuyuqui its populace put aside their arms and possessed by panic dispersed in the forest, fleeing from the Christians. What had been the powerful motive that obliged them to disband, terrified, to the benefit of the rule of law? It was no doubt the horrible hecatomb that they had just contemplated in their destroyed stronghold, and above all the eloquent and total unmasking that it thereby manifested to them of the false promises and hollow predictions and grotesque impostures of their adored Tunpa. Notwithstanding all this, given our uncertainty as to his whereabouts and his hidden intentions, we had good reason to fear that they would continue hostilities against the Christians, eternal target of their distilled ire, and that the complete pacification of the anarchized regions would perhaps cost other bloody sacrifices and other days of mourning and horrific tragedies. This is how we were forced to judge and fear the treacherous and extremely vengeful character of the Chiriguano, clearly manifested on earlier occasions. (Nino and Martarelli [1918] 2006: 144)

According to both accounts, an expeditionary force returned to Kuruyuki (presumably resupplied with ammunition) but found it effectively deserted; Frías and another commander managed to find and kill a little over thirty more Indians in the area before rendezvousing back in Santa Rosa on the February 1. On February 2, Gonzáles returned with his infantrymen and the volunteers to Sucre. Frías awaited the arrival of Chavarría. On February 3, the mayor of Ñacaroinza sent word that one of the most important *capitanes* involved in the uprising, Chaparilla, had surrendered with his followers. Frías went to Ñacaroinza to take custody of Chaparilla, who convinced his followers to return with Frías to Santa Rosa. Along the way, "no doubt because they were trying to escape or revolt" (Martarelli 1892: 18), "Coronel Frias [was obliged] to shoot a few to control them" (Nino and Martarelli [1918] 2006: 144). Upon their return to Santa Rosa, about 100 Guaraní persons, including the capitanes of several communities, were "executed in the same way in the plaza of Santa Rosa"; their "wives and children, numbering about 400, were distributed among the nationals and Christians of the area" (1892: 18). In Martarelli 1892, one has the clear impression that Frías and his soldiers executed the rebels on the grounds of the mission with no protest from the Mission Fathers. Nino, writing twenty-six years afterward, feels the need to explain:

> The fear of increasing the discontent among the Christians, exacerbated by the dangers and sufferings they had undergone, caused the Sub-prefect to commit the error of leaving the unhappy surrendered Indians to their discretion, who in the presence of their wives and children barbarously slit their throats . . . *The opinion of the Nation reproved such excess but the deed had no remedy.* This bloody measure produced, nevertheless, a salutary effect infusing among the savages such terror and shuddering that only with difficulty would they again dare to try another uprising against the Christians. (Nino and Martarelli [1918] 2006: 144; italics mine)

The proposed mission at Ivo was finally established in October 1892. Readers will not be surprised to learn that it was for several years unable to attract much in the way of an Indian population (Nino and Martarelli [1918] 2006: 147).

Both the 1892 and 1918 versions describe the arrival on February 10 of Melchor Chavarría, to whose account we will now turn. The text has two short prefaces, the first of which contains the realization that when he began a military career, as he put it, "I was not going to traipse a flowery path, I knew, to the contrary, that a distinguished position and the mere exercise of military power would excite suspicions and hatreds that would surround me with their rancor" (1892: 2) and the second of which notes,

> A certain anonymous publication has attempted to belittle the merit, whatever it may be, of the work of the Delegation. I will not descend to the terrain which honor forbids: to that terrain of recriminations to which I am called, and in which truth and reason cannot battle with disguised calumny, with anonymous accusation. No . . . For the anonymous, there is nothing but sovereign disdain and silence. (3)

To my knowledge no one has discovered the anonymous text to which Chavarría refers, but clearly his efforts came under some sort of contemporary criticism, and the strenuousness with which he refuses to engage those criticisms at the outset gives the entire text a feeling of being the response that he has declared he will not offer.

Chavarría's arrival on February 10, 1892, was of course not his first visit to Santa Rosa. He had been there several months before, in September 1891, in order to hear the case for the establishment of a new mission precisely in the location that became the focus of so much fear and violence in the intervening months. Like Martarelli and Nino before him and Sanabria years later, Chavarría in talking about his own violence emphasizes that the tumpa was a fraud bent on havoc:

The principal objective of my mission was a bloody one. I was going to destroy a savage mob which, to the natural depravity of its instincts, united the ferocities of fanaticism, excited by the ascendancy of a savage caudillo, an impostor, who, making himself adored like a god and feared like a king, managed to inflame the courage of his subjects to such a degree that they launched themselves into combat with extraordinary valor and abandon. (1892: 4).

Now, by the time Chavarría arrived on the scene in February the "savage mob" had already been quite effectively destroyed by Gonzáles and Frías at the end of January. After describing his journey toward the troubled region, Chavarría acknowledges this backhandedly:

Even while sincerely applauding the deed, for which, and in extraordinary measure, I congratulated the victor, I did not suppose the victory to be decisive. It was my opinion that the surroundings of the region, given the character of the rebels and the theater of action, would, because of features of the terrain and the dense mountains cloaking it, give secure refuge to the rebels and facilities for their strategic operations. We felt, then, that the insurrection was not crushed. (1892: 6)

What follows are several paragraphs describing skirmishes in which groups of Indians were killed or captured by Chavarría in his progress toward Santa Rosa. He entered the mission with "250 prisoners and more than 100 families" (1892: 7). Upon arriving, he heard from Lieutenant Coronel Frías that Capitán Chaparilla remained alive and imprisoned at Ñacaroinza (having promised to help capture the missing tumpa, who had managed to escape Kuruyuki alive). His first order was for Frías to bring Chaparilla to Santa Rosa, whereupon Chavarría organized a military trial that duly condemned Chaparilla to death. Executed with him was the tumpa's secretary, "the ferocious Ayemonte the Great [this would be Ayemoti], terrible savage, active cooperator in the atrocities of his God (Tumpa)" (7).

One becomes somewhat inured to tragedy reading these documents, but it is still possible to feel a flesh-crawling horror at this passage in Chavarría:

Chaparilla left an orphaned and penniless family. My duty fulfilled, with respect to the law and military orders, which imposed upon me the bloody punishment of that caudillo, it was necessary to give succor to the natural sentiments of the heart. From the Father who gave Christian assistance to the prisoner, I learned that he left in Santa Rosa, among the captives, a daughter and a son … Wanting to lighten their misfortune, I took charge of their fate, to which I have attended since then with great care, along with that of other unfortunates who are also the beneficiaries of my efforts.

It seems that nothing is so compatible with mercy as is the soldier's mission. (1892: 8)

THE BIOGRAPHY OF THE CHIRIGUANO
PEOPLE AND OF THEIR LAST LEADER

It's easy to understand why the missionaries who called in troops, and the military officers who were sent out, would in the aftermath construct accounts that turned an ugly massacre and a subsequent vicious mop-up operation into the "Battle of Kuruyuki." Writing in 1972, Sanabria had no guilty conscience to expunge, no "opinion of the Nation" to contest. Why did he take the scanty available information about Apiaguaiki Tüpa, and the damning documentation relating to Kuruyuki, and turn them so forcibly into something that they almost certainly were not?

I've begun to answer that question with respect to the tumpa, suggesting that much of Sanabria's inspiration came from already-mythologized stories of North American Plains Indians: Sitting Bull and Geronimo. When it comes to the story of Kuruyuki, however, I believe Sanabria was working with an even more exact model in mind: one more influential on his text, even, than the W. Fletcher Johnson from which he draws his opening epigraph. Although he cites it nowhere in his 1972 text (though citation, with Sanabria, is an inexact science), I think it probable that Robert Utley's 1963 book *The Last Days of the Sioux Nation* prompted the writing of *Apiaguaiqui Tumpa: The Biography of the Chiriguano People and of Their Last Leader*. The titles are obviously similar, but more important, the elegiac attitude toward an entire indigenous society is the same. Utley says the Sioux Nation "died" at Wounded Knee (1963: 5); Sanabria says that after Kuruyuki "the Ava, as a nation, had ended forever" ([1972] 2008: 217).

The chapter organization of both books is strikingly similar, as are the organization of the bibliographical references and the presentation of photos. Utley's discussion of the Sun Dance may even help to explain the otherwise ethnographically inexplicable song Sanabria has Chiriguano women singing about "Father Sun." Utley's book has fifteen chapters, Sanabria's, thirteen. Utley ends his chapter 11 with a condemnation of the conduct of a US military officer who, having acted differently, could have in Utley's view prevented the events at Wounded Knee; the next chapter is called, "Wounded Knee" and spares no narrative effort to frame the story of the massacre there as an account of a battle.[16] Sanabria ends his chapter 10 with a condemnation of the conduct of a Bolivian military officer who, having acted differently, could have in Sanabria's view prevented the events at Kuruyuki; the next chapter is called "Curuyuqui" and spares no narrative effort to frame the story of the massacre there as an account of a battle.

Like Sanabria's, Utley's book has been extremely popular and influential. One treatment calls it the "definitive modern historical study" of Wounded Knee (DeMallie 1982: 386), and like Sanabria's book it has been reissued in a second edition (in 2004). Unlike Sanabria's book, Utley's book has been sharply criticized in the years since its publication. Utley has conceded certain of his critics' points, but ends the preface to the second edition with a self-defense that is thoroughly Sanabrian in spirit (and sourcing):

> A warm memory lingers with me. At some point in the late 1960s, I gave a speech on an unrelated topic at the historic old hotel in Hot Springs, South Dakota, near the Pine Ridge Reservation. Afterward, a Sioux elder, braided and in traditional garb, introduced himself and, telling me he had read *Last Days*, said, "All the old people at Pine Ridge, they say that's just how it happened." (Utley 2004: xv)

I might be the only person in the world able to form an opinion on the matter, but my sense is that Sanabria and Utley would have gotten along very well together. Be that as it may, I am also probably the only person on the planet (aside from Sanabria himself, who is no longer with us) who has read both Utley's and Sanabria's books. Unless readers wish to do the same, they will have to take my word for it that they are uncannily similar. What I can demonstrate, though, is how while there are empirical historical similarities (which surely drew Sanabria's attention) between the processes that produced Kuruyuki in South America and those that produced Wounded Knee in North America, the most striking parallel—as I will demonstrate in the next chapter—is in the narrative and analytic modes that have been applied by non-Indians (and sometimes taken up, in part, by Indians themselves) to both.

FAMOUS LAST WORDS

What of the escaped tumpa? He was eventually captured and executed on March 29, 1892. His body was displayed in the plaza of Sauces (present-day Monteagudo) for a day. His burial place is unknown. According to Sanabria, his last words were uttered in Guaraní to a Father Quiroga: **A chengapini ma**, "Now I am satisfied." Sanabria asserts that this is recorded in a letter, that along with the letter from Ayemoti he claims to have seen in the archives of the Apostolic Vicarage of Cuevo. They have not been located by others.

Coincidentally enough, a young Sioux man—Plenty Horses—who was tried and acquitted for killing an army officer on January 7, 1891, offered the following explanation for his actions, which appeared in a popular account published in 1941 by Julia McGillycuddy, Indian agent Valentine McGillycuddy's widow:

> I am an Indian. Five years I attended Carlisle and was educated in the ways of the white man. When I returned to my people, I was an outcast among them. I was not a white man. I was lonely. I shot the lieutenant so I might make a place for myself among my people. Now I am one of them. I shall be hung, and the Indians will bury me as a warrior. I am satisfied. (McGillycuddy 1941: 272)

3

The Plains Prophet

Along with their chronological proximity (the massacre at Wounded Knee took place on December 29, 1890, and that at Kuruyuki just over a year later, on January 28, 1892), many parallels between Kuruyuki and Wounded Knee are undeniable, even eerie. It is not known what became of the children of Chaparilla, taken under the buzzard wing of Chavarría. We do know heartrending biographical details about one of the little survivors of the massacre at Wounded Knee, described here by anthropologist James Mooney:

> A baby girl of only three or four months was found under the snow, carefully wrapped up in a shawl, beside her dead mother, whose body was pierced by two bullets. On her head was a little cap of buckskin, upon which the American flag was embroidered in bright beadwork. She had lived through all the exposure, being only slightly frozen, and soon recovered after being brought in to the agency. Her mother being killed, and, in all probability, her father also, she was adopted by General Colby, commanding the Nebraska state troops. The Indian women in camp gave her the poetic name of Zitkala-noni, "Lost Bird," and by the family of her adoption she was baptized under the name of Marguerite. (1896: 879)[1]

Marguerite's later fate was not happy. General Colby eventually left the wife with whom he had adopted the little "Lost Bird." In straitened circumstances, this adoptive mother raised the girl into a troubled adolescence, during which she was briefly sent to live with her adoptive father, who soon placed her in a reformatory.

DOI: 10.5876/9781646420360.c003

Attempts to reconnect with Lakota relatives were not successful and after the death of her adoptive mother she suffered terrible poverty, dying in an influenza epidemic in 1920 (Flood 1995).

The snow to which Mooney refers fell after the killings at Wounded Knee, but before burial parties went out to the site, producing the dramatic and tragic photographs, such as the one of Big Foot's frozen corpse, that became infamous in the immediate aftermath of the confrontation and retain their power to horrify into the present. This photographic record (and an enormous written accompaniment) distinguishes Wounded Knee quite strongly from Kuruyuki, for which documentation is scanty and photographic records nonexistent. Wounded Knee has had such tremendous resonance and influence in part because it was so exhaustively documented at the time and has as a result been extensively revisited (including, of course, here). In many ways, the "literature" on Kuruyuki consists of iterations (and often direct repetitions) of Sanabria's 1972 book. The literature on Wounded Knee, on the other hand, is vast. Given Sanabria's interest in North American (and especially Plains) Indians, it would have been difficult for him not to have been influenced by it. Even if I am correct that Utley's 1962 book was the immediate impetus for Sanabria to write his own history of events in the Chiriguanía, heavily influenced also by older popular literature such as Johnson (1891) and McGillycuddy (1941), it probably only suggested a handy template for structuring a diffuse set of suggestive parallels and received notions that had been percolating in Sanabria's mind for many years.

Here I can confess my own sympathy and even perverse fondness for Sanabria, which in an odd way only grew the more egregious the inventions I turned up in his work. He was himself an ambitious humbug, creating a fantastical account that ultimately did help to unite Bolivian Guaraní people for ends of self-renewal in the early 1990s in much the manner Sanabria credits with having been the original aim of Apiaguaiki Tüpa himself in the early 1890s. When I began work on this project, I initially thought of myself as noticing the commonalities between Kuruyuki and Wounded Knee that Sanabria seemed only glancingly to touch upon. It was only as I read Sanabria more closely, and his sources more closely, and as I began to familiarize myself with the secondary literature on Wounded Knee (and to grasp how much of it Sanabria had read half a century before me) that I realized how many of the parallels I congratulated myself for noticing had been put in place, without attribution, by Sanabria's own hand. At the same time, however, it was clear that many aspects were really shared between the two histories, such that Sanabria's book could be called a "fake fake," a notion expanded upon in chapter 6.

WOVOKA

As an American and as an anthropologist, before I began reading systematically about the Ghost Dance and Wounded Knee I thought I knew much more about both than I did. I must apologize, then, to better-informed readers for repeating information familiar to them. Much of this section is for readers like me, who may also be surprised to learn that much of what they thought they knew about Wounded Knee is in fact fuzzy and incomplete. The Ghost Dance, so closely associated with the Lakota, did not begin among them. Its principal prophet was Wovoka, a Paiute shaman living in Utah. Although the content of his message in good part regarded traditional Indian lifeways, it was spread by modern developments: letters and messages written, carried, and shared by Indian young people from many different tribal backgrounds who had attended white-run boarding schools and who used the growing network of western railways to travel between aboriginal communities. While many Indian communities in the Plains and the western United States that heard it accepted some form of the Ghost Dance message (see Kehoe 1989 for an example of a version perduring into the 1970s), others such as the Navajo rejected it altogether (Mooney [1896] 1973: 809–811). Wovoka hosted Indian seekers at his home but also was also visited by delegations of white Mormons in whose eschatology Amerindians play a privileged role and for whom his message of impending cataclysm and renewal was deeply persuasive.

While Wovoka welcomed Mormon visitors, he was far more interested in reaching fellow Indian people. Between 1889 and 1890, Wovoka kept up a correspondence with other Indian tribes, warmly inviting them to come by rail to visit his home and hear his prophecy. Individual mission-educated Indian people were also writing to one another: "Boarding school alumni among the Northern and Southern Arapaho wrote letters to each other, so the Southern Arapaho learned about the Ghost Dance" (Fowler 2003: 97). Wovoka hosted various delegations; whites and Indians alike were permitted to attend the Ghost Dance rituals held near his home, though Indians made up by far the largest part of the visitors. All the while, he also sent ritual paraphernalia (white feathers, red ochre paint, and occasionally a black hat worn by him and imbued with his force) to epistolary supplicants from a local white trading post and using the US postal service.

Michael Hittman (1990) estimates that Wovoka was born between 1856 and 1863, which would have made him quite close in age to the estimates we have for Apiaguaiki Tüpa. There are other parallels. According to Mooney, Wovoka was the son of a "prophet" who participated in—and perhaps even led—a predecessor version of the Ghost Dance message and who died in 1870. Paul Bailey (1957) asserts that Wovoka's mother also died when he was young (of course, given the 1957 publication date, Sanabria could have borrowed this detail about Wovoka and applied it to Apiaguaiki Tüpa). Mooney and Hittman agree that by his early teens if not before, "Jack Wilson" was living as something like an adopted servant at the home of white ranchers (and devout Presbyterians) David and Abigail Wilson. According to Hittman, as a young man Wovoka traveled to the Pacific Northwest to pick hops, where he learned of the Smohalla movement that attracted thousands of followers from Indian tribes along the Columbia River. Smohalla's immediate concerns were resisting encroachment on Indian lands by white settlers, and avoiding removal to reservations. Upon his return to Nevada, Wovoka experienced a powerful vision and began to preach a message that may have combined elements of the 1870 Ghost Dance prophecy, evangelical Protestantism, Mormonism, and the Smohalla vision and practice.[2]

Here there are many genuine parallels to what we know about Apiaguaiki's life from Ayemoti's letter. I have no reason to believe that Sanabria made a careful study of Wovoka (though of course, with Sanabria, one never knows). The North American sources on which Sanabria seems to have relied do not treat the Ghost Dance prophet himself at any length (indeed, Wovoka is not clearly identified in many popular accounts of the Ghost Dance prophecy and its relation to the massacre at Wounded Knee). Like Wovoka, Apiaguaiki was orphaned as a youth and spent a large part of his childhood living and working among white cattle ranchers. Like Wovoka, Apiaguaiki may have had a "white name," though if he did we don't know what it was. As in the case of Wovoka, Apiaguaiki was reputed to be the son of a powerful father and later analysts have found in Wovoka's prophecy similarities to earlier Indian prophetic movements, as have many analysts of Apiaguaiki Tüpa (most notably and influentially, Métraux 1931). Wovoka has probably not attracted the same kind of mythologizing as the kinds of figures with whom Sanabria identified Apiaguaiki (Sitting Bull, Geronimo) because he didn't suffer a martyr's end. He was never present at Wounded Knee, he lived for many years after that tragedy (he died in 1932), and he generated his own extensive correspondence and gave interviews relatively readily throughout his life—including the one with James Mooney, who wrote the first scholarly account of his life and prophecy ([1896] 1973).

Wovoka's sturdy longevity and his readiness to pose for photos and to speak to interested visitors all seem perversely to have contributed to his erasure from the popular memory of the Ghost Dance and Wounded Knee. Wovoka was canny rather than tragic. He continued to press claims on whites, asking for compensation for pictures and interviews, unlike Sitting Bull, who went down in a hail of bullets and could be written about at length without contradiction (or charge).

THE GHOST DANCE AND WOUNDED KNEE

While interest in the Ghost Dance message was widespread in indigenous communities in the Plains and western United States in the late 1880s, the excitement of the so-called Messiah Craze specifically among the Lakota was outmatched by settler frenzy in the Dakota Territory about what those Sioux might be up to, and capable of. This, of course, is very much like the nearly contemporary situation in the Bolivian Chaco regarding the "tumpa." By contrast, in Wovoka's home territory in Nevada his message seems to have raised nothing in the way of white alarm (and very little even of notice—see Mooney [1896] 1973: 767n1, for a letter from the US Indian Service agent in the area saying, "There are neither ghost songs, dances, nor ceremonials among them about my agencies. Would not be allowed" and Mooney's scathing reaction to this obliviousness). In fact, until the anthropologist Mooney tracked Wovoka down in the course of researching his Smithsonian Institution–underwritten 1896 account, several misidentifications of the prophet were made in journalistic accounts published by whites.

Lakota delegations had paid visits to Wovoka in Nevada and returned persuaded that his message and prophecy were important ones (Mooney [1896] 1973: 817–820). As the practice of Ghost Dancing spread on Dakota reservations, the Indian Service agent Daniel Royer, recently appointed to Pine Ridge Agency—a man whom the Lakota nicknamed "Young Man Afraid of Indians" (Mooney [1896] 1973: 848), became panicked and demanded troops be sent from the eastern United States to suppress it. But settler demands for troops had begun long before he arrived:

> On May 29, 1890 a citizen of Pierre, South Dakota, wrote what was probably the first letter to the Department of the Interior expressing this fear [of the Ghost Dance as a prelude to war or outbreak]. Although the fear was unjustified, it grew to epidemic proportions after newspapers began publishing unverified stories about Indian "depredations." (Jensen, in Jensen et al. 1991:6)

According to the testimony of the Jesuit Father Craft, who had managed a Catholic mission for many years at Pine Ridge, "interested whites took advantage of this state of affairs and howled for troops" (Johnson 1891: 470–471). Charles Eastman, a Lakota medical doctor then working at Pine Ridge Agency, advised Royer that he didn't think there was a plot to make war on whites and didn't think it was yet time to bring in troops, which would be regarded as provocative. To no avail: "The agent had telegraphed to Fort Robinson for troops before he made a pretense of consulting us Indians, and they were already on their way to Pine Ridge" (Eastman [1916] 1977: 97–98).

Detachments began arriving on November 18, 1890. The eventual troop presence in the region was the largest military mobilization on US soil since the Civil War (Utley 1963: 260), finally involving some 3,500 military personnel in the field (Utley 1963: 251). With the troops came a press contingent to match:

Altogether, there were at one time or another no fewer than twenty-five journalists (using the term in its broadest sense) on the scene ... It was the largest number of correspondents that had ever been sent to cover an Indian war ... The Ghost Dance "outbreak" was also the most photographed Indian war in history ... Among [the] favorite subjects, incidentally, were the "war correspondents," invariably draped with lethal weapons to provide pictorial evidence of their stout-hearted courage in defying death to get the news. (Watson 1943: 210)

In the words of Charles Eastman, the Lakota physician:

The press seized upon the opportunity to enlarge upon the strained situation and predict an "Indian uprising." The reporters were among us, and managed to secure much "news" that one else ever heard of. Border towns were fortified and cowboys and militia gather in readiness to protect them against the "red devils." Certain classes of the frontier population industriously fomented the excitement for what there was in it for them, *since much money is apt to be spent at such times.* As for the poor Indians, they were quite as badly scared as the whites and perhaps with more reason. ([1916] 1977: 102–103; italics mine)

On December 1, a Judge Burns of Deadwood reported on a visit to "the hostile camp" (which is not specified): he "corroborated fully the previous reports as to the abundance of food and ammunition which they had, and said, they were making up a big supply of a new pattern of tomahawk, more ugly than the old style" (Johnson 1891: 411). This fearsome description of a stone tool brings to mind Father Martarelli's insistence on the "dexterity" with which the Chiriguano handled their arrows, never mind the possession by the Chiriguano around Apiaguaiki of a mere ten firearms all told. In the same vein, Johnson (1891) reports a series of detailed accounts of damages to property in early December, all charged to Indians (412–413). However, in the aftermath Indian agent Valentine McGillycuddy, who was Agent Royer's far more experienced predecessor in the position, insisted:

Up to date there has been neither a Sioux outbreak nor war. No citizen in Nebraska or Dakota has been killed, molested, or can show the scratch of a pin, and no property has been destroyed off the reservation. (January 15, 1891; qtd. in Mooney [1896] 1973: 833).

Several Indians were nevertheless killed in white ambushes in the first weeks of December (Utley 1963: 141, 143).

In early December 1890, the order went out that all Indians on the reservation were to come in to Pine Ridge Agency or be declared "hostiles" (Jensen et al. 1991: 85). Most complied, but there were at least three holdouts: a group around Sitting Bull, a group in a place called the "Stronghold" accompanying Short Bull and Kicking Bear, and a group accompanying Big Foot (Utley 1963: 142–143). The agency became very overcrowded, surrounded by tents of Indians and military. Various plans were made to induce the remaining holdouts, now termed "hostiles," to come in. On December 15, a detachment of Indian police were sent to arrest Sitting Bull. It is difficult to know how to credit the stories of what happened at Sitting Bull's camp, but what is certain is that Sitting Bull was roused from sleep and ended up shot to death, along with his young son; six Indian policemen and six other people in Sitting Bull's camp also died. The Indian police went in first, but a cavalry squadron waited in the offing and also entered the camp after shooting broke out (Utley 1963: 158–165).

Because Sitting Bull was a well-known figure from his time working with Buffalo Bill Cody's Wild West Show, his killing drew national attention and its circumstances considerable condemnation. A probably apocryphal story associated with the death is that amid the flying bullets, Sitting Bull's horse began to perform tricks he had been trained to do in the Wild West Show when he heard gunfire (Utley repeats this story; one can track it to Stanley Vestal's 1932 [p. 300] popular biography of Sitting Bull, on which Utley relies, but not beyond: Vestal does not cite sources). Both its appearance and its endurance may have to do with the fact that it rehearses themes of performance, trickery, and pathos that by 1932 were already linked tightly to the conventional wisdom about the Ghost Dance.

After Sitting Bull's murder, some of his followers came in to the Standing Rock Agency while others joined Big Foot's group (Utley 1963: 169). Big Foot and his followers were on the move to Pine Ridge Agency with military permission and at the express invitation of Indians there, because he was known as a negotiator who might help calm things down. The arrival of Sitting Bull's followers with news of Sitting Bull's murder seems to have frightened Big Foot's group, understandably, and put them off continuing to Pine Ridge. During this time of uncertainty, they encountered a Colonel Sumner, who accompanied them back to their own homes, now with thirty-eight of Sitting Bull's people added to their numbers. The total number in the group was reported as 333 (Utley 1963:179–181).

In the meantime, however, the military forces at Pine Ridge declared Big Foot "escaped" and began to track him down (Utley 1963: 176–178). Sumner received an order to bring Big Foot's people in to the Cheyenne Agency, which he passed along to them. Big Foot, suffering from fever, wished to stay put but his group decided to resume traveling to Pine Ridge Agency responding to the original invitation of fellow Indians there (185). General Miles interpreted this response as defiant hostility. The military and the Indians met on December 28; Big Foot surrendered, and his followers were marched to Wounded Knee Creek to make camp (196).

Colonel Forsythe arrived the next day, and supervised the setting up of Hotchkiss artillery pieces in a semicircular array around the Indian camp. Convinced the arms that Big Foot's group surrendered represented only a poor fraction of the guns in their possession, on December 29 the soldiers began a systematic search for hidden weaponry. Utley's attribution of causality warrants direct citation:

> The Miniconjous could not shake the fear that if they gave up their guns they would be slaughtered by the troops. It was an unreasonable and unjustified fear, but a very real one. *It explains what was soon to happen.* (1963: 205–206; italics mine)

For Utley, then, Miniconjou (a subgroup of the Lakota people) fear was the ultimately to blame for white violence. During the search for weapons, gunfire broke out (accounts differ as to who fired the first shot, and why), and the Hotchkiss guns were put into action. Utley's account of the firefight beggars belief (212–220). A representative sample of his approach appears in a footnote, regarding the bodies of a woman and three children found shot—one in the back of the head—three miles away from the Wounded Knee Creek site:

> These bodies were found some days after the battle by Capt. Frank D. Baldwin of General Miles' staff. Miles, then in the midst of his attempt to discredit Forsyth, made much of the incident. Baldwin declared that there were no leaves on the brush and that the troops could therefore clearly see and identify their target, leaving the implication, which Miles reinforced, that Godfrey's men had deliberately killed the women and children. Many years later Godfrey stated that on December 29th the brush was covered with dead leaves and pointed out that the blizzard that swept this locale on December 31st stripped the vegetation. The limbs were thus in fact bare when Baldwin visited the scene. Godfrey was, as he said, "shocked by the tragedy," although it seems clear that he himself had been a trifle hasty in giving the order to fire. (224n43)

Utley also tenderly explains how, in the flight from the Creek site, after firing into a ravine in which a group of Indians including women and children were sheltering, upon their surrender "Captain Edgerly himself bandaged [an] injured child" (226).

Many contemporary accounts were less impressed by the soldiers' conduct. Charles Eastman, the Pine Ridge doctor, recalled,

> Fully three miles from the scene of the massacre we found the body of a woman completely covered with a blanket of snow, and from this point on we found them scattered along as they had been relentlessly hunted down and slaughtered while fleeing for their lives ... [at the camp itself] I counted eighty bodies of men who had been in the council and who were almost as helpless as the women and babes when the deadly fire began, for nearly all their guns had been taken from them. ([1916] 1977: 111–112)

Accounts agree as to the number of soldiers killed at Wounded Knee: twenty-five. They differ regarding numbers of Indian dead. One hundred and forty-six bodies were buried in a mass grave on January 3, 1891, of whom eighty-four were "men and boys," forty-four women, and eighteen children (probably higher, depending on the ages of those "boys" included in the eighty-four). Indians had retrieved some bodies before January 3, and some wounded carried away from the site later died; it is now supposed that for Indian deaths, a "total in excess of 250 is almost certain" (Jensen, in Jensen et al. 1991:20).

As early as December 30 "the first accounts of the incident at Wounded Knee appeared nationwide in the daily newspapers" (Paul, in Jensen et al. 1991:36). Photographers rushed to the scene in the aftermath, photographing corpses frozen in the snow. On December 31, General Miles arrived at Pine Ridge Agency. On January 2 he telegraphed to Washington:

> It is stated that the dispositions of the 400 soldiers and 4 pieces of artillery were fatally defective; large number of troops were killed and wounded by fire from their own ranks, and a very large number of women and children were killed in addition to the Indian men. (Utley 1963: 244)

On January 4, Miles relieved Forsyth of command; Agent Royer was dismissed soon after. The findings of a Court of Inquiry convened by Miles, who suspected many soldiers were killed by friendly fire because of the poor positioning of the Hotchkiss guns, were later dismissed. Surviving members of the Seventh Cavalry under Forsyth's command denied this possibility and further testified that Indians themselves had killed many of the women and children who died at Wounded Knee (Johnson 1891: 478).[3] Twenty members of the Seventh Cavalry were eventually awarded Medals of Honor for their conduct on December 29. Efforts to rescind these medals have failed repeatedly but are ongoing (Lone Hill 2013). In later life, General Miles repeatedly raised before the US Congress the issue of compensation to the Lakota for what he clearly considered a military atrocity.

In the aftermath, Dr. Charles Eastman said of the Lakota at the agency:

> They had necessarily left their homes, their live stock, and the most of their household belongings unguarded ... The "war" being over, these loyal Indians found that their houses had been entered and pillaged, and many of their cattle and horses had disappeared. ([1916] 1977: 116)

In fact, despite settler anxieties, the great losses to life and property out of the "Ghost Dance Craze" were borne by Indians. The same, by the by, was true among the Chiriguano in 1892: repeated criollo reports speak of horses and cattle "liberated" from Indian hands, with the implication that all of it had previously been stolen by "rebels," though many Chiriguano leaders and communities possessed their own large herds by the late nineteenth century (Langer 2009).

DAMNED GOVERNMENT PETS

In the aftermath of Wounded Knee, in mid-January 1891, white settlers ambushed a group of two Indian families out hunting, killing a man. One said of the incident, "I have shot one of those damned Government pets, and if any more of them want to be fixed, let them come this way" (Utley 1963: 264). The settlers were brought to trial (partially due to the insistence of ex-agent McGillycuddy), but were acquitted by a jury in Sturgis (267).

Before and after Wounded Knee, local settler sentiment was strong that the US government was far too indulgent of Indians, that they were treated, as this killer had it, as "pets," given rations and assistance to which white pioneers were not entitled, and that—generally—their status treatment was incompatible with the expanding frontier of a nation founded on contract and, after the liberation effected by the Civil War, busy realizing its promise. The Lakota doctor Charles Eastman noted at the time, and later commentators have documented since, that the "Messiah Craze" was the pretext for the outpouring of considerable government largesse in the Dakota Territories (Jensen et al. 1991). The troops sent out had to be billeted, fed, and entertained; the press following them did, too. Settlers who were finding farming and ranching in the arid Plains hard going were loath to see the "excitement" die down because when it did, the financial boomlet it brought would disappear with it.

The plucky pioneers whose attributes are so central to Plains modernity—grit, independence, self-reliance—in 1890 leapt flying at the opportunity to declare themselves vulnerable, to make a case for their own "protected" status at time and in a place that was supposed to be the apotheosis of hard-bitten contract. With the Homestead Act of 1862 and the Mining Act of 1872, the government offered its free white citizens a square property deal: take it and make something of it, or die trying.

The Bolivian Chaco context of the massacre at Kuruyuki was not identical but was shaped by some of the same world-historical currents of republican American modernity. The independent Latin American nation-state had thrown off the shackles of aristocratic European imperialism at the beginning of the nineteenth century; named for the Great Liberator, Bolívar, the 1851 Bolivian national anthem—like so many throughout the Americas—gives a full-throated endorsement of "freedom." Like the Plains in North America, the Chaco in South America was the heartland frontier, the zone where you could move into the temporal future and physically away from the decadent metropole (for the United States, the imperial-era cities of the eastern seaboard, for Bolivia, the imperial-era cities of the Andes). The protected status of Indians—however fragile in practice—was resented by settlers in both contexts who were themselves ostensibly aspiring to pure plucky independent contract society modernity. And yet, given half a chance, both settlers in both places and at very nearly the same late nineteenth-century modern republican American nation-state moment insisted they (not "the damned Indian pets") needed—just temporarily, of course, but really really urgently—protection and help.

NATIVE NEUROSIS, OR, SPOT THE LOONEY

Michael Taussig's notion of "*the colonial mirror* which reflects back onto the colonists the barbarity of their own social relations, but as imputed to the savage or evil figures they wish to colonize" (1984: 495; italics in original) pertains here. Certainly with respect to the figuring of Indian intentions of violence, in both the cases of Kuruyuki and Wounded Knee one can find hostile projections by whites everywhere. A problem that arises for latter-day analysis of these events is that the counterproposition is discomfiting in other ways. If instead of being strong and menacing, the Indians were weak and vulnerable, this tends to make them simply contemptible in a different way.

Sympathetic modes of analysis notice this problem. One historian puts it this way:

> As Wounded Knee became a marker for the end of the Indian wars and, indeed, for the end of the frontier . . . "ghost dancing" became a metaphor for the desperate and illusory attempt of a people to recover the unrecoverable. (Smoak 2006: 2)

Gregory Smoak argues that this is misguided, because "viewing the Ghost Dances simply as a heartbreaking delusion ignores both the survival of the religion . . . and the far more complex issues of ethnic and racial identity raised by such movements" (2). His own study concludes that the Ghost Dance was part of a process in which "American Indians . . . used common experiences and the common discourse of prophecy to declare and enact their survival as a people" (205). A slightly older reexamination says, similarly, "Although privation undoubtedly contributed to the spread of the religion, a more fundamental cause lay in the Lakotas' desire to reclaim control of their own destiny" (Jensen et al. 1991: 64).

These framings salvage the Ghost Dance and American Indians, too, making them "agentive" rather than passive, canny rather than deluded, and they point out that after all, the Sioux (like the Chiriguano) have hardly died as a people since the late nineteenth century. Quite the reverse: their populations and their regard for their own cultural values are now booming (Thornton 1986). It follows, then, that they weren't weak and mad then, and they aren't weak and mad now.

This kind of analysis is attractive, not least because popular deployments of notions such as "messianic movements" and "revitalization movements" are so hazy, inexact, and breezily condescending. My own favorite example is from an undergraduate essay about cargo cults in the Pacific in which one of my students wrote that Pacific Islanders had lived happily until the whites came and killed all the buffalo. The student in question actually knew better and was embarrassed to have made such a silly blunder once I pointed it out, but the fluidity with which that misdirected parcel of geohistorical notions made it on to the page is telling.

The contextualized investigation of what people were doing in place of the generalized invocation of what was done to them is surely a good thing, in scholarship and popular culture alike. That being said, the particular rejoinders to the generalization are uncannily rote in their emphasis on agency and something like the will to power: Smoak 2006 on the Ghost Dance, or—to take an example from the nascent restudy of Kuruyuki—Combès 2005b, which analyzes the many ways in which internal factions among Chiriguano and Chané people and the participation of allied Indians as troops shaped the outcome of the so-called battle there. It's as if to notice debility playing a role in the outcome is to pay a terrible insult to indigenous dignity. It creates a situation in which the obvious (Kuruyuki was not a battle; the Ghost Dance was not a long-term stratagem directed at twenty-first-century outcomes) becomes the unmentionable.

How did this come about? The first anthropological, as opposed to popular, treatment of the events at Wounded Knee was published five years after the events there: anthropologist James Mooney's *The Ghost-Dance Religion and the Sioux Outbreak of 1890* (1896). Much of the text is empirically meticulous, studded with bitter wit, and bristling with a lively sense of outraged justice. But the legacy this warm, human book has left to American anthropology has been of its driest aspects: a classificatory scheme, described in the introductory and concluding sections, that places the Ghost Dance as a single token of a universal type of religious impulse. In the introductory sections Mooney locates it as the most recent in a sequence of North American Indian religious movements he sees as having responded to the experience of European colonization. In the concluding section, he broadens the comparison to include the Judeo-Christian tradition, Islam, Joan of Arc, and various Christian revival movements of the modern period (Methodism, Quakerism, Shakers), among others. Ecumenical and admirably "culturally relativist" as this is, its broad-brush comparative analytical style could not be more at odds with the keenly observed, idiosyncratic, and passionately engaged mood of the interior chapters that treat the specifics of the Ghost Dance movement and lead-up, events, and aftermath of the killings at Wounded Knee. These sections of the book ought to be required reading in US history and civics courses at the high school level—Mooney has a sardonic magpie's eye for details that beggar belief but are illustrative Americana. An experience often promised is one that these chapters of Mooney delivers: readers will cry; they will also laugh and laugh.[4] One comes to like and admire the Mooney of the middle chapters; one has no personal sense of the scholar writing the framing ones.

The parts of Mooney's book that are based on his own direct observation are alive with a sense of justice. The parts that purport to "place it in perspective" are morally lifeless (and, not incidentally, excruciatingly boring).

It was this latter mode of Mooney's, though, that propagated in the twentieth-century scholarly literature on the Ghost Dance and Wounded Knee. Anthony F.C. Wallace's 1956 treatment—equipped with the full psychoanalytic armature of the time—has become particularly influential, having been cited in the anthropological literature well over a thousand times. Wallace, like Mooney, places Ghost Dance as a token first of a North American type and then expands the field of comparison to include European, African, Asian, Melanesian, and South American exemplars. However, Wallace's essay, unlike Mooney's book, employs an "organismic analogy" (1956: 256) and on its basis is scientifically, indeed medically, diagnostic where Mooney was merely ecumenical (that is, noting parallels but proposing no explanatory formulas). To do this, Wallace invokes the notion of "stress," "defined as a condition in which some part, or whole, of the social organism is threatened with more or less serious damage" (265). On the basis of this "organismic analogy" Wallace treats, quite explicitly, societies as patients and certain societies as psychologically damaged patients. The essay describes the stages through which these "stressed" patients move: from anxiety to regression, which

> empirically exhibits itself in increasing incidences of things such as alcoholism, extreme passivity and indolence, the development of highly ambivalent dependency relationships, intragroup violence, disregard of kinship and sexual mores, irresponsibility in public officials, states of depression and self-reproach, and probably a variety of psychosomatic and neurotic disorders. Some of these regressive action systems become, in effect, new cultural patterns. (269)

Wallace says that "'Regressive' behavior, as defined by the society, will arouse considerable guilt and hence increase stress level" (1956: 269). If the stressed society-patient does not simply collapse in the face of this, it may enter a "period of revitalization" in response. These are typically prompted by "hallucinatory visions by a single individual" (), "dreams" that

> express (1) the dreamer's wish for a satisfying parental figure . . . ; (2) world-destruction fantasies . . . ; (3) feelings of guilt and anxiety . . . ; and (4) longings for the establishment of an ideal state of stable and satisfying human and supernatural relations (the restitution fantasy . . .). (270)

Wallace, of course, is inspired in this mode of analysis "by psychoanalytic dream theory" (271) and, with reference to shamanism generally, suggests that "the relevance of psychopathology to the vision experience needs to be explored" (272). However, he concludes that "the religious vision experience per se is not psychopathological but rather the reverse, being a synthesizing and often therapeutic process performed under extreme stress by individuals already sick" (273). Wallace argues that under the right (stressful) circumstances, when these hallucinatory fantasies are communicated by a charismatic individual to others, "followers achieve similar satisfaction of dependency needs in the charismatic relationship" (279); the conditions under which this can occur—and a "revitalization movement" result—include "high stress for individual members of the society, and disillusionment with a distorted cultural *Gestalt*" (279).[5]

The most exuberant example of the comparative psychoanalytic approach, published in 1970, is anthropologist Weston LaBarre's *Ghost Dance: The Origins of Religion*. LaBarre's application of the medicopsychoanalytic method to anthropological problems is breathtakingly confident. The distancing of the analyst, who has a firm grasp on reality, from the analysand, who lamentably does not, could not be more starkly drawn. I ask the reader to pardon the extended quotations, as lengthy passages really make the case:

> What strikes the observer of nativistic cults is this same helpless autism in (cultural) reality-deprived people under stress—deprived, that is, both of their own traditional explanatory myths and also of appropriate information about the cultural workings of the new economic myths. Stress, trauma, and wounded narcissism invariably thrust both individuals and societies back on to autistic preoccupation with the old and intimate. Autism is the state of preoccupation with subjective thoughts or fantasies, and ranges from brief indulgent revery in healthy persons to completely self-referent ideas and magic ritual behavior without reference to any immediate outside reality. (305)

and

> The paranoid fantasy of invulnerability is found many places in the world, and is especially interesting psychologically. (307)

and

> With inside and outside, self and not-self poorly discriminated, the narcissist feels the whole world threatened, literally, to the degree that he *is* the world. To the narcissistic paranoid his mind, and to the schizoid with feeble ego-boundaries his body, is the world. World-destruction, then, can be seen as a projection of fears of body disintegration, and *fear for oneself* the pattern of fears for the world. (313)

and

> There is no reason to suppose that primitive persons under stress cannot be paranoid or schizophrenic too, simply because many other people in the society join in their

> beliefs—and even enthusiastically, for the same psychologically defensive reasons . . .
> In a mob state, people can as easily abandon their intelligence as their morality. (313)

So far so clear: movements like the Ghost Dance are a kind of stress-induced collective mental sickness, definitely narcissistic, perhaps paranoid, perhaps schizophrenic. Anticipating objections to the application of such stigmatizing descriptions, LaBarre extends his diagnosis of reality impairment yet further:

> Some [anthropologists] demonstrate repeatedly that they cannot discern evidence
> right in front of them . . . They lack the experienced clinician's awareness of continu-
> ous gradation . . . as individuals, prophets and shamans run the full gamut from
> self-convinced and sincere psychotics to epileptics and suggestible hysterics, and from
> calculating psychopaths (more rare than commonly believed) to plodding naifs only
> following the cultural ropes. (318–319)

Some gamut. But though the piling-on of pejorative descriptors of native analysands can hardly be missed, what might be is the brief portrayal of the markers of the competent analyst. He is an "experienced clinician," surveying a wide array across time and space of human frailty, admitting only to a sort of homeopathic minimal dose of it in himself ("however fleetingly, all of us share the identical defense mechanisms of the most dilapidated patient"; 318).

There are, of course, anthropologists who don't make the mark: the ones, for example, who might object to LaBarre's analysis. But the ones who do can be recognized by their objectivity (no "autistic" immersion in "subjective" "self-revery" for them) and actual, as opposed to fantasized, relative invulnerability. They are the ones who have a good grasp on reality. In short, they are the ones who are not themselves sick.

An edited volume published in recent years (Harkin 2004) returns to Wallace's 1956 essay on "Revitalization Movements" and argues for its continued relevance to anthropological scholarship. The centrality of the notion of "stress" to Wallace, his organismic metaphor, and his medicopsychoanalytic emphasis are all put to the side. Instead, the rationale for the return is a championing of the virtues of abstraction: "Although such abstract theoretical models have generally fallen out of favor in most quarters of professional anthropology, this is a pity, because without them we lack the ability to address cross-cultural data in a comparative context" (Harkin 2004: xvii). With this, we are back to the drearier chapters of Mooney, the ones, perversely in my view, for which he is most lastingly known in the anthropological literature. The edited volume to which Harkin's essay makes an introduction casts a wide cross-cultural net, assembling a series of North American Indian and Melanesian case studies. The generalizations possible on their basis turn out to be limited; Harkin ventures that revitalization movements, which may apparently isolate (in the case of nativistic movements) or connect cultures and groups, are simply one of the most obvious and obviously transcultural mechanisms by which groups attempt to articulate with the outside world. At the same time, such articulations have profound resonance on the individual, who feels threatened and insecure in a changing world . . . This is particularly the case of the prophets, such as Wovoka. (Harkin 2004: xxxiv)

Why is it that this framing: abstract, objective, "realist" on the one hand; and confidently diagnostic of fear and insecurity in the analysand on the other, so recurrently attractive to anthropologists? Why, at the same time, have we not in fact generated interesting and compelling "transcultural" ways to talk about the vulnerability we keep identifying everywhere but in ourselves?

DEPENDENCY AND DISABILITY

It is difficult to read any of the literature on Ghost Dance, or Apiaguaiki Tüpa, or revitalization movements generally in quite the same way after having dipped even a toe into the emerging literature in disability theory. Tobin Siebers's essay "Tender Organs, Narcissism, and Identity Politics" offers an explanation as to why this analytic mode is perennially compelling to anthropologists and reappears again and again despite otherwise profound transformations to the discipline. Siebers demonstrates the consistent link made in the medical and particularly the psychoanalytic literature between disability and narcissism. Sigmund Freud suggested that sick, wounded, or injured people were unlikely to become neurotics: neurosis is a pathological response to the multiple uncertainties life presents to everyone. By contrast,

People with disabilities, according to this theory, have one good reason for all their failures—the tender organ—and so the radical uncertainty of human existence disappears or at least becomes more manageable . . . The fortunate fall of people with disabilities does not really guarantee a healthy mental existence. There are worse things in life than neurosis, according to Freud, and these are the narcissistic disorders. Bodily scars may serve as a protection against neurosis, but the sufferer's extreme investment in the body produces a parallel exaltation of the ego. (Siebers 2002: 44–45)

Far from being an idiosyncratic position of Freud's, Siebers shows how pervasive this thesis about disability and narcissism is in the subsequent medical and psychoanalytic literature, that once one is mindful of it one repeatedly encounters the contention that

people with disabilities, it seems, demonstrate a conspicuous resistance to reality, taking flight into an active fantasy life where their disabilities justify special privileges . . .

> The narcissism of patients with disabilities supposedly inhibits the . . . efficacy of therapy. They seek revenge for their disabilities or demand compensation. (45–46)

Anthropologists will have no difficulty recognizing these formulas, so frequent is their application to movements such as the Ghost Dance or Apiaguaiki Tüpa's: a wounded population, taking refuge in fantasy, perhaps not unable but definitely unwilling to cope with reality, bent on revenge or compensation for the injuries they have suffered. LaBarre's pseudodiagnostic invocation of "autism" is a particularly acute example of this attribution of pathological egotism to collectivities undergoing (willy-nilly) anthropological analysis. Siebers notes that Freud himself compared "narcissists to 'primitive peoples,' in addition to people with disabilities" (2002: 54n7). As Sean Kicummah Teuton recently noted, there is a corrosively dismissive intellectual history to the contemporary idea that "the disabled Indigene cannot escape the narcissism that blinds her to see beyond her own group" (2014: 573).

What is truly revelatory about Siebers's argument, however, is not the way one can find familiar resonances between the medicopsychoanalytic handling of disability and the anthropological handling of Ghost Dance and kindred phenomena. It is what he notes about the way that

> studies of face-to-face interaction between able-bodied and dis-able-bodied individuals . . . show that able-bodied people focus in face-to-face encounters more on their own anxiety than on the feelings of the person with the disability and that their acceptance of disability lessens as narcissistic regression increases. (2002: 47).

Siebers suggests that in effect, "the threat to the therapist's self-integration become an analytic tool used to think about the patient's disability" (2002: 46). The attribution of narcissism to disabled patients projects the therapist's reaction and thus insulates her from its damning import. Siebers goes on to say that the "accusation of narcissism rages just below the surface in current debates about disability . . . in American culture" (47).

Siebers makes this assertion in the context of an argument about attacks on the emergence of disability studies in the academy. But as an Americanist anthropologist, it struck me as profoundly familiar. The analytic distancing, the attribution of profound dis-ease to analysands, the repetitive insistence that because *they* are vulnerable and wounded, *they* are liable to fantasize about invulnerability and compensation, and *they* are narcissistically fixated upon their weak and injured state—this is much of the traditional anthropological handling of prophetic movements and cargo cults in a nutshell (much of which, in its turn, drew upon psychoanalysis). The analyst is contrastively figured as "abled," that is, as relatively objective, relatively invulnerable, relatively whole and unimpaired, relatively realistic, and relatively capable of appropriate empathy. In a more recent and less stigmatizing mode, it is the literature of what Abu-Lughod calls the "romance of resistance" (1990) in which the tone is sympathetic rather than accusatory but treads its weary way round the same set of assumptions. Here, the charge of weakness is vigorously refuted on behalf of the analysands; they are not weak at all but "agentive" in all that they do. The seeming assumption: it is simply not possible to actually be weak, vulnerable, and dependent without being supposed to be contemptible too.

The most repeated stories about both Wounded Knee and Kuruyuki involve fantasies of invulnerability. Putatively, Ghost Dancers were supposed to believe their Ghost shirts made them bulletproof, immune to the death-dealing reach of modern technology. Followers of Apiaguaiki Tüpa were believed to have supposed the same, that the guns of settlers and soldiers would shoot "only water" when turned against his faithful. These are so often repeated in white accounts about Indian collective madness ("and on top of being so vulnerable, they imagined themselves to be invulnerable, poor saps!") that they must offer some kind of lurid attraction. What could it be?

Here, Taussig's notion of the "colonial mirror" is helpful but shouldn't be where we stop. Playing a game of "who's the real narcissist fantasist after all" is, in this context, to simply reverse the charge of disability: to say that the analyst rather than the analysand is, really, the "sick" one, the "crazy" one, the "weak" one; that the "dependent variable" is not the one usually charged with dependency. Much of the literature of "resistance" and "agency" does this, but to dubious effect.

Dubious because it treats the state of disability and vulnerability itself as a hot potato, an insult to be leveled in some direction, a charge to be made to devastating effect. What would it look like not to do that? Siebers closes with an offer, regarding the context with which he is concerned:

> Narcissism is profoundly incompatible with the reality of disability because we ... have to rely so often on other people ... People who rely on caregivers have to be diplomats ... People with disabilities ... are at risk when they are alone ... We need a community to support us ... We do not love only our own kind or ourselves. You others are our caregivers—and we can be yours, if you let us. (2002: 53)

As L. Davis puts it, "the notion of an undamaged observer who is part of an undamaged society is certainly one that needs to be questioned" (1995: 14). Yes! Universally so. It's not that certain vantage points don't offer privileged views of certain processes; of course they do. The problem is finding it necessary to insist upon some perspective (whether the "white" or the "Amerindian") as the nonsick, noncrazy, nonweak, nonvulnerable, nondependent, absolutely autonomous agentive one before listening to it. Finally, to go back to points made in the introduction, about the kinds of anthropological investigations that compel interest and the kinds that are, well, boring: the analytic abstractions, the comparative schemas, the "here is a token of a type" sorts of analyses are all designed to ignore or eliminate tangled interrelations, the way people's lives and contexts lean up against one another and bleed into one another. What would it look like not to do that?

TO "CONSIDER SERIOUSLY THE SYMBOLIC CONTENT OF INDIAN CULTURES"

In 1982, anthropologist Raymond J. DeMallie roundly criticized what he called Utley's overattribution of hostility to the Lakota (and discounting of white violence) in precipitating the events at Wounded Knee and more generally Utley's reliance on the notion that "the ghost dance was a political movement merely masquerading as a religion" (DeMallie 1982: 388) such that Utley (like other white analysts of the same events) failed to "consider seriously the symbolic content of Indian cultures" (388). De Mallie emphasizes in particular the relational aspects of the Lakota worldview, in which human conduct and the natural order are mutually dependent and reciprocally vulnerable:

> The Indians themselves recorded testimony which showed dramatically that the Lakotas thought of the land, the animals, and the people as a single system, no part of which could change without affecting the others . . . The ghost dance Messiah's promise of a new earth, well stocked with buffalo, was completely consistent with the old Lakota system of cause and effect by which they comprehended the ecology. (391)

DeMallie also cites the testimony of a ghost dancer, reflecting years after the fact: "I suppose the authorities did think they were crazy—but they weren't. They were only terribly unhappy" (399). Somehow this admission of softness, of weakness, has been recast by a series of overtly hostile and then putatively sympathetic observers over the years as treacherous sleight of hand, as vengeful narcissism, or as crafty secret "agency"—never just sadness and a longing for connection, full stop.

Recalling the previous chapter, I would like to point out that no scholars have considered with any seriousness the testimony of the Chiriguano people themselves who gathered round Apiaguaiki Tüpa that they hoped in so doing to better their collective situation by calling upon a range of potential allies, influences, and circumstances—the harvest to come, the benevolent return of the ancestral dead associated with that season, any friendly possibilities at the missions (they were very seriously disappointed in this last, if so). Most often—first by the mission authorities who called down military force upon them, later by settler historians, still later by indigenous leaders responding to the political possibilities of the latter part of the twentieth century—these tantalizing hints are dismissed as fabrications to cover true martial strategizing and plans for aggressive violence. But what if this is all wrong?

There is, to my knowledge, simply not enough historical documentation from the Chiriguano side to know very surely or very clearly. But I still wonder about Kuruyuki and the lead-up to it. This is because of what I know about everyday life in Isoso.

4

Shamans and Wives

The literature on Amerindian shamanism, like the literature on the Ghost Dance and Wounded Knee, is large. The literature on Amerindian shamanism and on Ghost Dance and Wounded Knee are at many points mutually referential and keyed to the encounter of whites and Indians, to colonial history, and to global power structures. Taken together, these two literatures conjure clashes of male titans: vicious or heroic, doomed or gloatingly triumphant, wily or ham-fisted.

I followed these leads in my first forays into the field, finding two important male shamans of renown to study. In the many years that have passed since, both of these men have died. When I go back to Isoso now, the people I visit are their families and their friends and are mostly women. Because of this, how I understand "shamanism in Isoso" is now informed by homely dynamics of everyday life that are neglected in much—though certainly not all—other writing on shamanism. In Amazonian anthropology one tradition of analysis has emphasized continuities among shamanism, hunting, aggression, wildness, antisociality, and predation (Chagnon 1968; P. Clastres [1974] 1977; Fausto 2000, 2007; Taussig 1987; Viveiros de Castro 1992) while another has concerned itself with shamanism in the context of kinship, healing, and domestic care (H. Clastres [1975] 1995; Gow 1996; Oakdale 2005; Overing 1975; Surralles 2009). The former tradition shaped my initial fieldwork, while the latter has helped me to make sense of my findings.

DOI: 10.5876/9781646420360.c004

"THERE IS SOMETHING"

In 1997, I first visited Isoso and presented my research proposal at a community-wide **Ñemboati Guasu** ("Grand Assembly"; for more on this feature of Guaraní political life, see Lowrey 2006c, 2011). There I met the shaman Don Miguel Cuellar Vaca, next to whose home an ethnobotanical "laboratory" was being built with funds from the French government and technical cooperation from the Bolivian Universidad Mayor de San Andrés. My connection to the project was via a meeting in La Paz in 1996 with a Bolivian biochemist, Alberto Giménez, who had returned home after earning a doctorate from an Australian university. Professor Giménez was eager to expand investigative laboratory science in Bolivia, working within the constraints of scarce research funding and limited laboratory infrastructure, and to do good at the same time: to train ambitious students and provide social benefits to the population at large. Ethnopharmaceutical research seemed to offer the perfect vehicle. Collecting and assays were not particularly expensive but provided ample training opportunities, international funding was available to support research into low-cost alternative medicine, and the social benefits were potentially enormous. As Giménez liked to joke, if he and his team found a cure for AIDS or cancer that was great, but they were specifically interested in developing treatments for diseases that plagued poor rural Bolivians but did not interest commercial pharmaceutical giants at all: Chagas disease and leishmaniasis in particular.

An assay of a plant collected in Isoso that was not traditionally used medicinally but that was occasionally eaten as a food suggested it had powerful antifungal properties. In Guaraní the plant is called **guirakillo**. The idea of the laboratory, then, was to collect and process guirakillo in order to locally produce a humble remedy for athlete's foot and jock itch and to generate some income from its sales. The (eventual) profits were to be split between the community and reinvestment in the larger project of assaying Bolivia's ethnobotanical resources for potential drug development (UMSA, CABI, ORSTOM 1996). The project is exactly the sort of big-eyed puppy that one wishes to see lead a happy life on a bucolic farm but that readers will probably not be surprised to learn will be squashed by a truck in a subsequent reel. I have written about this at length elsewhere (Lowrey 2003, 2008a) and return to the international side of the story in the next chapter.

During my first visit to Isoso in 1997, after the ñemboati I spent a night at the new laboratory built next to Don Miguel's home ("Aguarati-mi" or "little Aguarati") outside of Isoso's most remote village, Aguarati. This visit was not a success (interested readers can find many photos of places and people described in this chapter in Lowrey 2016, available online). Therefore, when I began fieldwork in 1998 I leapt flying at an offer from an NGO, APCOB,[1] run by a German anthropologist to live in the house they maintained in a village in central Isoso called Ibasiriri.

Another shaman lived in Ibasiriri: Don Jorge Romero, junior to Don Miguel but also involved in the traditional medicine project to some extent.

Soon after I settled in Ibasiriri I found a woman willing to tutor me in Guaraní, Doña Beatriz. Doña Beatriz's father had been an unusually accomplished hunter, who on several occasions narrowly escaped being lured forever by the wife he had among the **iyaareta** ("owners" of the forest and its game animals) and whom he visited in dreams. About a decade before I began my fieldwork he had been murdered by another Ibasiriri man, an evangelical pastor (I came also to know this man well in time) who denounced Dona Beatriz's father as an **mbaekuaa** (witch; literally "thing-knower"). Doña Beatriz's husband was a skilled and hardworking carpenter who suffered terribly from headaches and malaise brought about by witchcraft persecution. He had recently stepped into the role of principal advisor to the shaman who lived in Ibasiriri, Don Jorge. About five years before, Don Jorge's advisor of many years had died suddenly. He had been struck down by witchcraft. That previous advisor's son told me Don Jorge himself had confirmed this about the cause of death by saying: "there is something."

VISITING

Time with Doña Beatriz became, little by little, relaxed and chatty. I also invented for myself a task that turned out to be rather more interesting than I had supposed it would be—carrying out a household-by-household survey of medicinal plant use in Ibasiriri. By some decision-making process to which I was not privy, a young woman named Marta was deputized to help me with it. She both translated my queries from Spanish to Guaraní and helped me find all of the households in Ibasiriri. These homes were tucked away down meandering paths spreading out in several directions from an inexactly central "plaza," which was itself irregular in shape: a sort of long oval clearing with raggedy edges. A few tall trees stood about in the clearing, useful for providing nice shade for meetings, and the village itself was, essentially, forested—low trees located near individual households doubled as storage, with all kinds of useful items hanging from lower branches; tall trees provided plenty of shade. I got lost constantly and found particularly excruciating the process of following up invitations on my own—people would tell me to come by, and I could never remember how to get to their homes; sometimes, after a visit, I had the very embarrassing experience of traveling in a meandering forested circle back to the very house I'd left ten minutes previously. Because people found their own village layout with its kin-based districts and family groupings so clear, it did not occur to them that I was lost (usually within a five-minute radius from the village center, obscured to me by trees and houses but obvious to everyone else from habit), and they would look friendly but nonplussed by my unanticipated return.

My pattern was to spend half of the day with Marta, doing the survey, and then the other half paying follow-up thank you visits on my own, delivering a package of sugar and one of yerba mate to each home at which we had done an interview. Because I made these visits by day, the interviewees were almost always women, occasionally accompanied by elderly husbands or fathers. At the time men were busy doing the heavy work preparing irrigation canals and agricultural fields, and later, when the river began to "arrive," fishing.

Marta had a high school education and was in her early twenties and unmarried. She lived with a married older brother because both of her parents had passed away. She had a sort of horsey, sporty friendliness that made her unusually outgoing for an Isoseño woman her age. Marta evidently enjoyed the survey work quite a lot. I later learned that her family had for several years been ostracized due to witchcraft accusations: her parents' deaths were sometimes attributed to their own witchery "falling back" upon them. Although I wondered, under the circumstances, if it were wise for her to accompany an outsider with an unseemly interest in health-related information, she seemed merely pleased to have an opportunity for so much sociability. Her views on the matter were, of course, better informed than my own: when I last visited Isoso, in 2019, she had been the **mburuvicha kuña**, or "women's captain," of Ibasiriri for nearly a decade.

I think, now, what Marta enjoyed was simply visiting everybody. This is not a novel observation about village or small-town life, but it still came as a surprise to me how everyone could live in what seemed to me such a tiny place and yet lay down yet tinier patterns of sociability within it. Older people lamented that as evangelical Christianity made ever more converts in Isoso (to rival sects, which sometimes fought very bitterly amongst themselves), traditional villagewide festivals had lapsed. Catholic saints' day festivals sponsored by **karai** (white) settlers were no longer attended by evangelical converts (and more and more karai themselves converted each year), but above all the annual **Arete Guasu**[2]—with its singing, dancing, and drinking, and its visit from the masked ancestral dead—had gradually but entirely disappeared since the early 1980s. One last village had maintained the festival in its old style as long as its elderly, Catholic *capitán* was alive, but since his death in the early 1990s it too had ceased to celebrate it (see Hirsch 1991). In the years since my original fieldwork, there has been a revival of its celebration in this village, initially prompted by an agreement with a documentarian for a Bolivian television show about rural folklore but then with more enthusiasm from a generation of younger people who have gone through the bilingual education program and are self-conscious about revitalization (about this process generally in

Guaraní-speaking Bolivia, see Gustafson 2009). Witchcraft was supposed to have increased in the same interval, a measure I am in no position to assess, but certainly belief in witchcraft is entirely compatible with evangelical Christianity (the Bible mentions witches and sorcery many times, quotations readily invoked by evangelical Isoseño pastors preaching from Guaraní Bibles: see Hirsch and Zarzycki 1993) while drinking, dancing, and visits from dead ancestors are not.

A GENTLE MAN

Ultimately I carried out the same medicinal plant usage survey in each of the three villages in which I was to live in Isoso. The results were roughly the same in each. People named an average of three or four medicinal plants, with a high degree of replication between households. A vast pharmacopeia was not in play. Isoso is a community of settled agriculturalists, not of hunter-gatherers, but Isoseño people have lived in Isoso for hundreds of years and the larger region, probably, for thousands, so presumably they have had ample opportunity to become familiar and avail themselves of the local medicinal plant possibilities. This result flew in the face of many claims that were made about indigenous plant knowledge and that underpinned the establishment of the laboratory of traditional medicine in Isoso (Gallo Toro 1996). One unexpected outcome of the survey was the startling frequency with which people mentioned wild animal fats as having curative properties: jaguar, in particular, but also lizard and fox.[3] Needless to say, these sorts of observations never made it into the "healing forest" discourse about ethnobiological lore that I'd encountered before starting fieldwork and that is treated at considerable length in the next chapter.

Just as time in Ibasiriri allowed me to avoid Aguarati-mi, time doing survey work with Marta and practicing Guaraní with Doña Beatriz allowed me to avoid visiting Ibasiriri's shaman, Don Jorge. Jorge accepted my visits to his home as I had officially been approved the year before as somebody "studying shamanism" at the meeting attended by Don Miguel, toward whom he evinced no rivalry whatsoever and, in settings in which they were both present, inevitably deferred. Jorge was also involved, in a minor capacity, in the laboratory project—he was supposed to supply samples of **guirakillo** and other medicinal plants for ongoing assays by the La Paz–based Bolivian Universidad Mayor de San Andrés researchers (and some French ethnobotanist colleagues). According to them, mostly he did not do this, but he wasn't confrontational about it. He just agreed to do it and then, as time went along, contributed less and less carefully sorted material, instead handing over sacks of apparently random leaves and sticks and, still later, stopped contributing anything at all.

When I first began visiting Don Jorge, it was usually in the company of Doña Beatriz's husband (his advisor) and the elected village capitán—who, like Jorge himself, was settled in Ibasiriri because he had married an Ibasiriri woman but was originally from another village in Isoso. These visits were excruciating. There was no menace or unfriendliness, just mild and patient silence. I'd try to prepare questions, at first in Spanish, and later carefully practiced ahead of time in Guaraní. Jorge would answer amiably, with at most a sentence. Neither of the other two men would contribute. We would sit for a bit, and I'd trot out another question. A visit that lasted thirty minutes was, in my view, a triumph of willpower achieved by ignoring every social instinct I possessed about not being intrusive and leaving people alone who wanted to be let alone. After several days or a week had gone by, I'd do it again.

This was fieldwork, at first. But then something changed, after I had made the rounds of many other households in Ibasiriri and particularly as I began to pay regular (sometimes even invited!) social visits to several women in Isoso. What changed was that Jorge's wife, Apolonia, began to play hostess during my visits. Their daughters and grandchildren and kin and other visitors would join the circle, and people would cross-talk, and sweetest of all, Don Jorge would begin to crack little jokes. Never for my benefit—these were obviously gambits aimed at getting Doña Apolonia to laugh. He played to her audience of one, though anyone else around was welcome to enjoy the performance. He was transformed by her presence, which from my perspective worked a kind of magic on everything: the household opened up. Sometime after this, Don Jorge invited me to observe several curing sessions, but these were uncomfortably intimate—they took place inside the house, while social visits happened outside. The method of treatment was familiar, in the sense that I had read about it—he sucked the illness-causing **mbaeruvi** out of his patients' bodies with his mouth.[4] But the whole time I was inside during these sessions, I wished I were outside again, with Apolonia and everyone else, laughing and talking. When Don Jorge talked about the hardships of being a shaman, I suspect that one of those hardships might have been that he often found himself wishing the same thing.

TWO KINDS OF SHAMANISM

Don Jorge was younger than Don Miguel, which could have explained Jorge's deference to Miguel, but a more important reason was probably the respective sources of their shamanic powers. Unlike Don Miguel, who had inherited his **paye** directly from another shaman,[5] via a long apprenticeship, Don Jorge's **paye** derived extrasocially. As a young man, around the time he was doing his military service, Don Jorge disappeared in the forest for several days. He returned in a weak and disoriented state. He had been taken by the **kaaiyareta** (owners of the forest). As he gradually recovered, it emerged that he now had new powers, and was possessed of a **paye**. He never told me the story himself, but in versions told to me by others this was a far-from-welcome gift. The experience was traumatic, and being a shy and retiring man, he was quite a reluctant shaman. Nevertheless, by the time I arrived in Isoso (many decades later), he had a well-established reputation within Isoso and had on several occasions collaborated with outsiders as well (a program run by the Swiss Red Cross during the 1980s, that attempted to combine conventional with traditional medicinal practice; the ethnobotanical research program described here; the willingness to speak with me). With respect to outsiders, he always positioned himself as the junior partner to Don Miguel and a third, very elderly shaman in the most upriver village, Kuarirenda (this man died while I was doing my fieldwork; I visited him for a single afternoon as part of a group and never spoke with him directly). In the one multivillage meeting I saw Jorge attend in Don Miguel's company, he deferred to Don Miguel when shamanic opinion was called for (regarding a complicated case of potential witchcraft: see Lowrey 2007) and did not speak publicly. In village meetings in Ibasiriri, he rarely spoke up. Occasionally he made quiet asides that caused the men sitting immediately around him to laugh but I never heard what he said, and my Guaraní, even at its best, was far from equal to slantwise repartee, so I probably would not have understood his comments if I had.

In his gentle, soft-spoken persona Don Jorge did not resemble the "canonical" Tupí-Guaraní **paye** assembled from the ethnohistorical evidence in H. Clastres's famous book ([1975] 1995). Nor did he in his domestic arrangements: his marriage was uxorilocal (the most common pattern in Isoso, followed by neolocal and virilocal—all forms, however, are present and none was ever supremely valorized in my hearing). He settled in Ibasiriri as a young man to live with Apolonia's family but had been born and raised in a downriver village, Tamachindi. Jorge and Apolonia's own daughters, in turn, raised their children in and nearby their parents' household.

I last saw Jorge in 2013. It had been four years since my last visit, at the time my longest stretch of time away from Isoso. Each time I go back (since I finished my doctoral fieldwork in 2000 I had returned to spend the New Year there in 2003/2004 and then gone again during boreal fall 2005; during the boreal summers of 2007, 2008, and 2009; and for shorter visits in the boreal springs of 2013, 2018, and 2019) I hear, of course, of people who have died since I was last there. On that visit in April 2013, I learned of Doña Apolonia's death the year before, in May 2012. Lourdes, an Isoseño friend, told me about Apolonia when I stopped for a night in the Chaco town of Charagua to visit her on my way to Isoso.

When I got to Ibasiriri I learned Jorge was still living in the home he had shared with Apolonia, which had been expanded and to which two outbuildings had been added over the years, with their daughters and grandchildren. Without Apolonia, our visit was in the "original" fashion. Once I had offered my condolences, we sat in painful near-silence. He told the story (which others had conveyed to me as well) of the horrible final days, of taking her to Santa Cruz for treatment where she had died and of having to arrange to bring her body back on a bus, for burial. We talked about how good and kind she was. As I got ready to leave, I said I hoped to return in two years. Jorge told me that he did not see a reason to go on without Apolonia, and didn't think he would live to see me again. Despite my sincere condolences on that April visit, I didn't pay this too much mind, as I knew well that Jorge was prone to moroseness when Apolonia wasn't around for him to perform for and play to. That October, I got word from a young Isoseño man with an email account that Don Jorge had passed away earlier in the week.

A POWERFUL MAN

Just as Don Jorge never showed the least rivalry toward Don Miguel, Don Miguel always spoke well and fondly of Don Jorge. On the two occasions I saw them together, they seemed to take a quiet comfort in one another's companionship. Although Don Miguel took the responsibility for public speaking at the one multivillage meeting at which I saw them both, in general their affect at village meetings and social gatherings was quite similar: no oratory, just soft, laughter-provoking asides to their immediate companions, always the senior men of their respective villages.

After Don Miguel's death in 2005, Miguel's widow, Neli, sought treatment from Don Jorge when she was ill, and she also sent her daughter to him after the daughter had lost a baby. Neli deeply mourned the death of Jorge's wife, Apolonia. The two women had not met often, but just as their husbands seemed to recognize in one another a sort of shared burden, the two women obviously felt for one another as wives of shamans. Apolonia was very sorry for Neli after Miguel's death and I suspect that when Neli went for treatment at Jorge's, it was as much to see Apolonia as to see Apolonia's husband. When they knew I was traveling between their two far-flung villages, each inevitably asked me to convey her greetings to the other and each asked after the other when I would return.

Apolonia's and Neli's marriages, though, were very different. Neli was four decades younger than Don Miguel and the last in a long series of wives. Don Miguel's many wives and many children were famous elements of his persona—less in what he said about himself than in the stories others told about him. He was supposed to have married more than a dozen women during his life and by his own account he had fathered more than thirty children, maintaining relationships with all of them. Neli, his final wife, was the niece of her predecessor, who died young. Neli's grandmother (who married more than once herself) was another past wife of Don Miguel; she lived at Aguarati-mi also, with her daughter, Victoria, by Don Miguel. Victoria's husband was the half-brother of another son (by another mother) of Don Miguel—this son and another son (by yet another mother) of Don Miguel were married to two of Neli's sisters. These two couples also settled for a while in Aguarati-mi. Isoso's villages are small, but the degree of inmarriage found at Aguarati-mi is unheard of elsewhere, and the intensely patrilocal pattern of marriage settlement is also unusual. Married sons and married daughters alike gravitated back to the orbit of their father.

This image was brought home to me very powerfully one evening, not too long after I'd finally come to live at Aguarati-mi, where I finally moved in February 1999 for a few months and to which I returned for several more months in 2000. Don Miguel, who in addition to being a shaman was an accomplished violinist, brought out his fiddle one evening after dinner. In the days before evangelical Christianity had made so many inroads, when there were more dancing parties in Isoso, he had played quite often; by the time I came to the field, it was rather rare for him to do so. It was a lovely evening. The months from February to May are the pleasantest in Isoso—June and July are often cold, the river "leaves," and in August the winds begin; September and October are windy and increasingly dry, with stinging sand blowing everywhere. November and December are suffocatingly hot, with occasional rain; heavier rain comes in earnest in December and January, the river "returns" (augmented by rain, but fed mostly by Andean snowmelt), and February through May are warm and green.

In the sort of good weather we were then enjoying, the solar panels attached to the laboratory supplied enough power to their attached batteries to hook up an outside light, suspended from a tree limb, at the shaman's house. Neli's (then) five children stayed up, even tiny toddler Dorotea, with the baby Fernando in Neli's arms. Two of the children by Neli's deceased aunt were also there—the oldest girl, in her late teens, had married recently but the younger teen sister and preteen brother were still living at the house. Victoria and her mother and husband and their four small children were also over, and Lourdes (at the time resident at Aguarati-mi as a patient of Don Miguel's) and I sat together on a bench. Don Miguel was in a *sillón*, which in Spanish means armchair but in Isoso means a metal lawn chair with comfortable, stretchy plastic webbing that is the chair of honor in any Isoseño home (ordinary seats are either wooden benches or wooden chairs with goat or cowhide seats), in the center of the circle of light provided by the electric bulb, playing *chacareras* (Chaco region country music) while the small children and grandchildren danced happy orbits round him, delighted by the impromptu party. He was like Aguarati-mi's sun.

POWER, SUSPICION, AND HUMBUG

In Paraguayan Guaraní **pai** means Catholic priest and in much older Tupí-Guaraní literature **pai** or **paye** appears paired with another term, **karai**, meaning something extraordinary and used to distinguish exceptional prophets from "ordinary" shamans: "The great shamans were those carrying the title of karai . . . All paje did not enjoy a similar prestige" (H. Clastres [1975] 1995: 27).

In Bolivian Guaraní usage, **karai** now means "white" in a very ordinary manner—descendants of white settlers living in Isoso are **karaireta** (plural, whites) and the city of Santa Cruz de la Sierra is **Karairëta** (home of whites). The word has been stripped of its supernatural connotations, though these connotations of strange power are undoubtedly why it became attached to whites in the first place. Clastres also emphasizes that karai were "outside of that which precisely constitutes a community, that is, the network of kinship" and, again, "exterior to kinship" ([1975] 1995: 32). This historical usage, almost certainly, is among the reasons the term **karai** came to be applied to strange, powerful, and utterly exterior whites.

The physical apartness of Don Miguel's home in Aguarati-mi from the village proper of Aguarati is reminiscent of H. Clastres' famous description of pre-Columbian Tupí-Guaraní shaman-prophets:

> It is known of course that the karai lived in seclusion, apart from villages . . . Self-chosen isolation . . . was a way of indicating that the karai had a different status, that in effect they did not really belong to a community, that they were from nowhere. ([1975] 1995: 30–31)

This observation aligns in interesting ways with Don Miguel's "exteriority" to normal kinship rules. As mentioned above, Isoseño households are most often uxorilocal or neolocal. In Aguarati-mi, by contrast, Don Miguel was the patrilocal sun around which a set of closely related kin-planets revolved. He was an ambivalent figure who comprised in his person the suspended tensions of being exaggeratedly beyond society, literally in his living far beyond the boundaries of his own village and at the far northeasterly limits of all Isoso, while also attracting a closely related minivillage to live around him.

Although **paye** used to contrast to **karai** in Tupí-Guaraní society and does no longer, there is a contrastive category to that of paye in contemporary Isoso: **mbaekuaa**, "witch." Mbaekuaa, means "thing-knower" or "knowledge-thing" and as with paye means both the person and designates the magical object they have inside them that is the source of their power (see Lowrey 2006c). In older accounts, **mbaekuaa** was not necessarily pejorative. It was used as often as paye to translate "shaman" (and *brujo*, Spanish for "witch," was often used for persons who contextually seem to have been viewed as shamans). Even in contemporary Isoso, people speak of feared and respected **mbaekuaareta** of long ago.[6] They were known to be able to kill and held in high regard for it, especially when they used their powers against collective enemies. In contemporary parlance, however, to call someone an mbaekuaa is to be making an accusation while to call someone a paye is to be paying a tribute of respect.

But the situation is only clear in that the first term is now almost exclusively pejorative. The latter role, paye, is ambivalent in two ways. First, there is the issue of simple fraud. People in Isoso had different opinions about which **payereta** were truly effective and which were **payejanga** (an unreal "reflection" or "image" of a paye). Don Miguel and Don Jorge were the most widely acknowledged, but there were several others in Isoso (some called also **payerai**, "little paye"). It was not uncommon for Isoseño people to seek treatment from several in sequence—Don Miguel was in some ways a paye of last resort, for hard cases. While I never heard Miguel or Jorge disparage one another, they both disparaged other payerai on occasion as payejanga, as did some other Isoseño people in my hearing.

It was impossible for me to collect unbiased data about Jorge and Miguel, as everyone in Isoso knew that I was studying shamanism, spoke to them often during my fieldwork (and in fact lived with Don Miguel's family for several months) and that I took them seriously. I don't know, then, whether they were sometimes disparaged as payejanga themselves. I suppose it unlikely that no one in Isoso ever doubted their powers, though the only people who directly expressed such doubts to me were karai Isoseño (who did so in Spanish, and didn't use the term **payejanga**). It was nevertheless impossible to remain unaware that Don Miguel, in particular, was both publicly respected as a paye and quietly feared by many people as an mbaekuaa. I never heard such talk about Don Jorge.

In fearing Don Miguel as a potential mbaekuaa, people were attributing to him a kind of occult superefficacy. People hope and expect that eventually witchcraft will "fall back on" the witch, killing him or her. There are cannibalistic rituals—more spoken of than performed, I suspect—that are supposed to bring this about, involving a shaman being called in by the family and eating a tiny part of a witchcraft victim's corpse. The witch, who has through sorcery "eaten up" the victim, finds him or herself then being magically "eaten up" instead (Lowrey 2006c). If shamans are supposed to be able to make this happen (even if, as I suppose, this ceremony is never really performed), they are potential intentional causers of magical death. So why was Jorge never—to my knowledge—suspected by anyone of being a malevolent witch? Here I think we must consider the sources and natures of their respective **ipayereta**.

GENTLENESS AND POWER, GENUINENESS AND HUMBUG

Jorge's paye was extrasocial in origin and visited upon him privately in an ordeal that took place in the wilderness. Miguel's was inherited from the previous generation in a public process that culminated with a public ceremony in his village. After I had lived at Aguarati-mi for several months, Don Miguel invited me to copy his "biography," contained in a small notebook. It is not, at readers will see, his biography so much as it is the biography of his paye. The original text (which I did not see) was in Guaraní. The voicing of the text is unclear. Miguel, who did not read or write, had asked Lourdes, who had finished high school, to translate it into Spanish; she did not tell me (perhaps she did not know) who had written the Guaraní original (see Lowrey 2003, appendix D, for the Spanish version). My English translation, with some place-names that would be confusing to non-Isoseño readers excised, is as follows:

The life of Miguel Cuellar, that is to say his story when he was titled as a paye in the year 1956, 26th of November. The paye that titled him was Piñoa Lopez. He who was most concerned that Miguel C. become a paye was Apiyare, he had great friendship with this paye Piñoa, at every opportunity he would say to the paye Piñoa that he give his title to him so that he could cure already, and it was in this way that this man always insisted with him, until the day arrived when he said, "very well, make corn beer, but well-made corn beer," thus he directed, and "that it be rich with oil, in this way the task will turn out well," he told them. And it passed Saturday 26 November of 1956 we assembled to await the paye Piñoa at midday. He issued his question. "And so it is that you all desire that I title Miguelito?" he asked in a loud voice. The people replied, "we want for you to title him well, in order that he cure us. We don't want him to be a **payejanga** [Guaraní: a reflection, or imitation, of a paye]." He answered in this way, "I am going to return him to you when he is well; he is going to walk with me until I see that he cures well." When he finished he said, "now there is one part, but it is lacking, after the rest period, that is to say within 15 days you are going to take him to me," he said to Apiyare, "to my house," but he directed them to take him at night, so that no one would see him, but "it is jealous," he said "for this reason," he said to them, "you must take him to me at night." And so it was that Apiyare took him. They arrived there by night and he spoke to them and came out and said, "I was already awaiting you." And so it was that Miguel stayed with him in his house, he was there with him for 10 months, his instruction was quite long that is to say orations. Every three days he would ask him if he already knew them. That was Miguel's task, after the 10 months he knew all those orations and also already went out with him to practice. Thus with him, wherever people took this paye to do curing he would go also, he would do it for him and when Miguel couldn't, he would show him how, and thus he went along training him, until one day there was a boy who was ill, there he made him work and he worked well and he said, "now I have fulfilled that which I told you all I would, that I had to return him well and I am going to give him advice: that he be good to his kin, that he take care of his people, that he not be proud, that he not be lazy about going where they seek him, that he be of good heart." This advice Piñoa gave to Miguel when he completed curing the boy, thus he delivered him, since that year Miguel was titled, from the year 1957 on.

I don't want to attempt to parse this text too closely, though I have many times puzzled over certain aspects: the "jealousy" and the "titling," in particular. What it makes clear is that Don Miguel's becoming a shaman was an eminently social process, though the forces harnessed in that process are clearly not entirely sociable. Don Jorge's process was markedly asocial. For reasons addressed at considerable length in chapter 6, I suspect it is not at all accidental that I only had stories of Jorge's receipt of his paye as a consequence of that shamanic seizure in the wilderness at second hand—never from Jorge himself. In marked contrast, Don Miguel participated in the creation and dissemination of a canonical version of his paye: in Guaraní, in Spanish, and now in English, too.

Turning, now, to the fact that it is wilderness (the **kaaiyareta**) in one case and society (a negotiated inheritance, and a public investiture) in the other that were the sources of Jorge's and Miguel's respective powers, two Amazonian sources seem relevant here. The first is Stephen Hugh-Jones, who distinguished "vertical" from "horizontal" shamanism in Amazonia. He says that for vertical shamanism, "the predominant component is esoteric knowledge transmitted within a small elite" while for horizontal shamanism "the emphasis is more democratic, depends less on 'saying' than on 'doing,' and involved the more classic shamanistic features of trance and possession." (1994: 33). Hugh-Jones says that in a few cases, including Arawakan societies, "HS occurs together with VS . . . VS appears to be associated with more complex, ranked societies . . . and with less emphasis on warfare and hunting" (33). Here of course, Don Miguel would be the "vertical" shaman and Don Jorge the "horizontal" one; the point about Arawakans, hierarchy, and relative lack of predatory features is also noteworthy.

The second Amazonian source is Terence Turner's work on the Kayapó of the Brazilian Amazon. Turner has argued for there being two supreme forms of value for the Kayapó: beauty and dominance (sometimes this latter is called "power"; Turner 1980, 2003). The first, beauty, is thought by Kayapó people to be ultimately external to society in origin. "Beautiful names," for example, which function as an important form of Kayapó wealth and which are bestowed on particular individuals via elaborate collective rituals, are supposed to have originally been gifted to Kayapó by natural, extrasocial beings. Although there is certainly a hierarchy involved in determining which Kayapó obtain beautiful names, "beauty" is a more accessible quality—even for "commoner" Kayapó—than is dominance, or power. Everyone can (and indeed, for them to come off successfully, must) participate in collective occasions of beauty: ritual and festive occasions of costuming, dancing, and singing at which "beauty" is simultaneously produced, expressed, and consumed by everyone present. Notably, these beautiful costumes and associated paraphernalia, dances, and songs all pertain to and imitate (or animate) extrasocial ways of being: anteaters, birds, and supernatural entities.

Dominance, by contrast, is reserved for a small subset of senior men, accomplished at ceremonial oratory, who embody the supreme expression of a fully successful Kayapó life. The means by which one becomes a dominant senior male are entirely social, and involve strategic accomplishments in the field of marriage, reproduction, and—most crucially—father-in-law-hood. A dominant senior man (and not all men achieve such dominance) controls his daughters and, through his daughters, his daughters' husbands and their children. Hypernucleating kinship is essential to power in Kayapó society.

So far, so resonant to the related-yet-contrastive cases of Don Jorge and Don Miguel. Even more interesting about this comparison is that as far as one can gather from Turner's ethnographic accounts, beauty is not a contested quality. That is, while there might be quite a bit of jockeying around the bestowal of beautiful names (which can be acquired by both men and women and are often bequeathed to small children), no one seems to claim, for example, that one or another name isn't "really" beautiful and while one supposes one ritual or festival can be judged as having come off rather better or worse than another, they are all equally occasions of collective beauty. There is not a lively discourse of sham or suspect beauty. On the other hand, judging by the evidence Turner has presented over many articles over many years, there is a tremendous amount of doubt, contestation, and pooh-poohing attached to one or another claim by Kayapó men to power or dominance (1984b, 1991, 1993, 1996, 2002).

In sum: Beauty is an important social value but its font is ultimately extrasocial, it is relatively generally accessible, and it is not hedged about with talk of humbug. Dominance is an important social value and its font is entirely socially internal, it is exclusionary of access, and it is constantly hedged about with talk of sinister humbug.

This summary seems to fit the case of Jorge and Miguel, the sources of their shamanic power, their relative potency, their relative menace, and their very different societal/kinship situations extraordinarily well. It also resonates with the way I had experienced as Isoso being two kinds of societies in one, a naive feeling that was, I found, amply confirmed by the ethnohistorical evidence (Combès 2005a; Combès and Lowrey 2006; Combès and Villar 2004; Lowrey 2003). Here again, points made by Turner about the Kayapó case resonate with the Isoseño data.

Kayapó kinship terminologies are "Omaha" in form, meaning they classify kin in a way that is puzzling to someone accustomed to, say, English kinship nomenclature (which is "Eskimo" in form, to use Lewis Henry Morgan's [1871] terminology). Kayapó kinship nomenclature displays "generational skewing" in the naming of certain cross-cousins, treating the mother's brother's children as "aunts and uncles" and the father's sister's children as "nephews and nieces" rather than as "siblings" (as parallel cousins are treated). Turner's explanation for this system has to do with the specific pattern of household formation in Kayapó life and how this reproduces Kayapó society as a whole. For my purposes, what is interesting about his argument is his assertion that

> societies with Omaha or Crow terminologies will generally be found to constitute
> hierarchical systems, with a lower level of segmentary units of identical structure, and
> an upper level comprising a communal framework of collective groups and ritual
> activities. (2013: 17)

In Isoso's case, this hierarchy would not take the topographical form it does among the Kayapó, with their tidy round village plans with clearly marked moieties, elaborate circular rituals, and a supreme focus on a central men's house. Social hierarchy is not spatially marked in Isoso, but it is much remarked there. There are ordinary Isoseño, and then there are the **tuicha vae reta**, literally, "those who are big [or great]." More than twenty years after I began my fieldwork in Isoso, I am constantly learning of new ways that the people and families whom I knew best there turn out to be kin to one another, in relationships that span far flung villages but which appear again and again in the ethnohistorical record (see Combès 2005a) down to present-day access to opportunities for schooling, leadership, and preferable forms of nonmanual employment—as with NGOs (Combès and Lowrey 2006; Combès and Villar 2004; Lowrey 2003, 2008a). Had the **kaaiyareta** (owners of the forest) not seized upon Don Jorge, I am not sure as an outsider that I ever would have come to know him and his family well, if at all. While I did of course meet many "ordinary" Isoseño families during the course of my fieldwork, they were not the families to whom I became closest.

ANARCHY, HIERARCHY, GRANDMOTHERS

The language that Isoseño people speak is Guaraní, and Tupí-Guaraní social structure is famously a-structural: take P. Clastres's argument in *Society against the State*

FIGURE 4.1. Village center, Ibasiriri (photo by author, 2008)

FIGURE 4.2. Homes tucked beneath trees (photo by author, 2000)

([1974] 1977) about Guaraní "anarchy." And indeed, the layout of Isoseño villages is meandering. Higgledy-piggledy paths connect homes, clusters of homes, or pairs of homes. Village centers are less geographically central than customarily so. Unlike Amazonian groomed circles, or Andean paired moieties, indigenous Chacoan settlements are invisibly tucked away into the forest. They have, unlike the stonework of the Andes and earthworks of the Amazon, left few traces for archaeologists to study, at least by methods presently available.

As Eduardo Viveiros de Castro has said in one of the few discussions of these social architectonics, "Compared to the crystalline properties of Ge societies, the Tupí-Guaraní evoke images of amorphous bodies—clouds or smoke—in their weak and casual social organization" (1992: 5).

However, the Guaraní were not the original inhabitants of Isoso. The Andean foothills of Bolivia were first settled by Arawakan Chané, who were in turn conquered in the pre- and peri-Columbian period by Guaraní invaders from the east (Métraux 1946b). Isoso's population descends from Arawakan Chané driven off more fertile agricultural land in the Andean valleys to the north and west; they pushed into the Chaco (and against its hunter-gatherer populace, speakers of Zamucoan languages; Combès 2004, 2008, 2009) and along the Parapetí. Chané was still spoken in part of Isoso in the first years of the twentieth century (Nordenskiöld [1912] 2002: 147).

In the ethnographic literature, Arawakan societies are much remarked for two features: hierarchy and complex systems of irrigation (Hill and Santos-Granero 2002). The latter is certainly present in Isoso—in fact, cultivating the periphery of the Chaco proper would be impossible without it. The arid interior of the Chaco cannot support agriculture, and the feat of using a river that is only seasonally present to channel the pell-mell rush of snowmelt to grow maize and even rice at the Chaco's northern fringe is no small accomplishment.

What about social hierarchy? This would seem anti-Guaraní, with its famous ethos of anarchic egalitarianism. The hybrid population of Guaraní speakers produced by Guaraní invasion of Arawakan territories was once known by the now-disdained ethnonym "Chiriguano." Relatively more Guaraní Chiriguano called the relatively more Arawakan Chané of Isoso **tapii**, "slaves." This ethnonym is now vigorously rejected in Isoso, and Ava Guaraní also avoid using it when they are being "politically correct" in contemporary lowland Bolivian indigenous politics. Interestingly, however, a leading family in Isoso—prominent in the nineteenth and twentieth centuries—is surnamed **Iyambae**, which means "without owner" in this community of people sometimes called **tapii**, slaves. There is considerable irony in putatively egalitarian "Guaraníness" being held as the supreme expression of what looks in many respects like an Arawakan dominance hierarchy, with lineages, differentials of material wealth, and a propensity to truck readily with high-status outsiders (Guaraní invaders, followed by Spaniards and then republican karai, followed by NGOs).

In fact in Isoso one very often has the feeling of being in two parallel societies—there are some families that are relatively more dominant, the **tuicha vae reta**, the "big ones," the most prominent of whom are variously related to the Iyambae lineage. But not everyone in Isoso participates in producing the dominance of the tuicha vae reta consistently. In this zone that seems to have been settled by refugees, much of the time Isoseño people tolerate the airs of the tuicha vae reta but "vote with their feet" when they find them intolerable. Dissent in village meetings called by the tuicha vae reta, for example, usually takes the form of simply not turning up rather than confrontation (see Lowrey 2007). Recall that when the less powerful shaman Jorge became disillusioned with the laboratory project he did not protest it; he simply stopped contributing to it.

To the extent that it is possible to reconstruct the historical events by which Guaraní people arrived to Arawakan territories in the Andean foothills and valleys, these incursions seem to have been at least as much pragmatic as prophetic. Catherine Julien (2007) has persuasively argued that a major attraction was Andean metallurgy and control of trade networks in the intervening territory between the Andes and Guaraní territories in the eastern part of South America (originally extending as far as the Atlantic).

What seems clear, however, is that trade and martial expeditions by Guaraní from the east were predominantly male. These Guaraní men married into Arawakan families, and the result is a society that is Guaraní speaking with an explicit ideology of male dominance and warrior ethos. These latter characteristics, as has been shown in previous chapters, are ever more readily elicited in the contemporary context: the defiant Chiriguano **kereimba**, which is now embraced also by lowland white elites interested in "autonomy" from indigenous Andean Bolivia (Lowrey 2006b).

The Arawakanness of complex irrigation, social stratification, and networks of female kin are less available as a conscious political resource. There are two reasons for this, which seem separate but may in fact be related. The first is that Guaraníness is explicitly valorized by Bolivian Guaraní people, to such an extent that at least one sympathetic scholar has made attempts to show that the Arawakan ancestry of present-day Bolivian people is a colonial invention (Bret Gustafson, personal communication). But the second may be that Arawakan "values," so to speak, are not in modern fashion: their collectivity, their relationality, and their admission of dynamics of dependence are currently embarrassing. The possibility that there is a gendered dynamic to this is well worth exploring.

The people who ended up farming the marginally cultivatable region of Isoso were by all accounts the Chané underlings who fled Guaraní invasions of the fertile valleys; this process accelerated in the colonial period, when the Spanish began "ransoming" Chané slaves from Guaraní captors. This was actually a convenient fiction that allowed the Spanish to avoid papal edicts prohibiting the enslavement of Indians: if they were "ransomed" from other Indians (particularly Indians, such as the Chiriguano, known to sometimes practice cannibalism), they didn't count as having been bought. This slave capture by proxy meant that long-standing relationships of dominance and subordination were channeled into raids and kidnapping.

Chané ended up in Isoso as runaways, headed ever more downriver, away from better agricultural lands in the foothills, settling finally along the very last stretches of the Parapetí that allowed for agriculture, a thin stream of seasonal water flowing into the arid Chaco.[7]

It just so happens that the very last, downriver-most bit of the Parapetí, where it peters out into a swamp, is called **Ñande Yari**: "our grandmothers." The current, ecologically inflected explanation of this name is that it refers to the nurturing role of the swamp as a fish nursery (the twice-annual running of fish into Isoso, when the river "comes" and then when it "goes," is a much anticipated feast for Isoseño people). Ethnohistorically rather than ecologically, however, the name suggests that Isoso itself was known to be progressively "more Chané" along these nether reaches of the Parapetí (which has its headwaters in the Andes, winds through Chiriguano country in the valleys, and ends along the northwestern border of the Chaco, where Isoso lies) and that the very downrivermost portion of the river is explicitly labeled as feminine.

Returning to Turner's point about Crow and Omaha kinship terminologies, the hierarchy he describes among the Kayapó is definitively masculine at its apex. This is much-remarked in the literature on Omaha kinship—they are supposed to be associated with "patrilineal" societies (Trautmann and Whiteley 2012 offers an excellent overview of this literature). For the argument I lay out here, it would be very nice if it turned out that Chané kinship terminologies showed the same generational skewing, but in the "opposite" direction—as it is in "Crow" systems, which are associated with "matrilineal" societies. Thus Chané kinship would be "feminized" as Kayapó kinship is "masculinized," with both, however, sharing hierarchy. Unfortunately, no data exist on Chané kin terms and despite considerable searching, I have not been able to find direct data on the nearest proxies, the Mojos (an Arawak group of the Bolivian Amazon supposed to be related to the Chané). Intriguingly, however, France-Marie Renard-Casevitz writes of the matri-uxorilocal settlement pattern among the Mojos and the scandalized remarks of at least one early traveler about the way that Mojo "women do not recognize subjugation to their husbands" (Orellana [1687], cited in Renard-Casevitz 2002: 137–138).

It is well documented that in those Bolivian Guaraní-speaking communities designated "Chané" rather than "Chiriguano," the status of women could be high indeed—as long as the women in question were elite women. About his time in one such community in 1908, Nordenskiöld wrote,

> The true chief in the Itiyuro River region [a Bolivian Chané area] is a woman. I have visited the old lady Vuayruvi who received me with great dignity reclining in her hammock . . . I asked Vocapoy [his Chané guide] why Vuayruvi, being a woman, was

the chief. 'Her father [chief before her] taught her to speak' answered Vocapoy . . .
The individual village chiefs belong also to the lineage of [Vuayruvi's father]. ([1912]
2002: 212)

In Isoso, a well-established tradition holds that a woman, **Kaa Poti**, was once
mburuvicha in Isoso (Combès 1999: 16). She is in fact the first named leader of
Isoso and brought her people to the present-day territory of Isoso, to which they are
described as having arrived after fleeing a series of (mostly supernatural) difficulties
elsewhere. Her name appears, as it were, at the transition from myth to history: the
legendary Kaa Poti, like the historical Vuayruvi, is said to have been the daughter of
a previous (male) leader, but Kaa Poti's father's name is unknown and he died eaten
by a monster. It is interesting that the origin story of Chané Isoso, founded in the
last cultivable stretch of land between the Chiriguano foothills and the arid Chaco,
that ends in the swamps of "our grandmothers," involves female leadership.

At present, one village in Alto Isoso long had a woman as its *capitana*, including
into the time of my own fieldwork. In more recent years, principally at the insistence of outside funding agencies, Isoseño villages have implemented a system of
dual captainship: a *capitán*, alongside a women's *capitana*, each elected annually.
This is the position held in Ibasiriri by Marta, the woman who helped me carry out
my first survey there. My own impression is that this has in fact had some of the
gender-equalitarian impacts intended, but it is also the case that it has effectively
abolished extant internal pathways to women holding "real" leadership positions in
the way they occasionally were able to do previously in Isoso.

To return to the kinship question, it seems that Iroquois kinship systems are the
most common type in Arawak-speaking groups (Alexandra Aikhenvald, personal
communication, 2015), though a Crow terminology is documented among the
faraway (from the Bolivian Chané) Arawak Wayú of Colombia (Mancuso 2008).
Arawak kinship systems have been described as "matrilineal" in general (Murdock
1957; Rouse 1948), including in one older essay that makes systematic recourse
to ethnohistorical documentation (albeit for analytical purposes we would now
find very antiquated): "As far as I have gone into the matter, both Guaraní and
Carib Indians seem to be patrilineal, whereas the Arawaks are matrilineal" (Lafone
Quevedo 1919: 424).

Recently a pair of authors declared a "common pattern of patrilineal descent"
among the Arawak, though they offer no direct evidentiary basis for the statement (Walker and Ribeiro 2011). One of the secondary sources they cite speaks
only of Arawakan groups of the northwest Amazon, albeit with caveats (Hornborg
2005: 597); the author in this case added the additional caveat when I contacted
him about it that "their 'patrilineality' could of course be a consequence of their

intermarriages with Tukanoan sibs in the region" (Alf Hornborg, personal communication, 2015), while the other text they cite is simply an edited volume about
Arawakan ethnohistory that in fact speaks in one place of matrilineality among
the Arawakan Taino (Santos-Granero 2002: 38–39) and the Arawakan Lokono
(46), and in the case of Renard-Casevitz (2002) about the matri-uxorilocal Mojos.
When contacted directly, Walker said, "You are right, I probably should have been
much more careful with this comment" (Robert Walker, personal communication,
2015). He offered three examples of Arawak groups reported as being "patrilineal"
in the anthropological literature; in each case, the source of the information was the
same *Encyclopedia of World Cultures: South America* edited by Johannes Wilbert
(1991) rather than an original ethnographic or ethnohistorical monograph. Let me
explain why I belabor this point.

HISTORY, KINSHIP, AND THE LIFE CYCLE

The notion of "lineage" generally, whether uterine or agnatic, is not a particularly
useful one in lowland South America, as kinship reckoning there is rarely predicated primarily on descent. This ethnographic fact has been one of the spurs to a
considerable comparative literature treating Melanesia, which is similarly indiffer-
ent to descent, and also explains why many lowland South Americanists find work
that tries to generate evidence for descent-oriented obsessions of the Western culture (as, e.g., male "reproductive fitness") from Amazonian materials so profoundly
silly.[8] It is easy to make mistakes about "patrilineality" and "matrilineality" when,
in fact, most of the practices in question are neither. At issue instead is what is
emphasized about the ways in which the proliferative relations of alliance that are
so important to lowland South American social dynamics preferentially get made.
In some societies, making these alliances seems clearly to be "masculinized"—that is,
thought of in terms of hunting, warfare, capture, predation. In other societies, the
making of these alliances seems clearly "feminized"—that is, thought of in terms of
feeding, taming, adopting, protecting. It is striking that even the sociocultural (as
opposed to the evolutionary-ecological) South Americanist literature has polarized
around these two versions of kin making as if they were mutually exclusive. One
would have to be naive indeed to be surprised that the version that has been the
higher status and more widely influential of the two is the "masculine" one, made
most famous by Eduardo Viveiros de Castro (1992) but seen in its purest form in
the work of Carlos Fausto (Fausto 2000, 2007, 2012). Joanna Overing (1975, 1988
and 2000 [with Alan Passes], 2003) and Peter Gow (1991) have written the most
influential accounts emphasizing what might be called the distaff variation. But,
of course, kinship—the empirical rather than the theoretical kind—encompasses

both. Considered from the perspective of lived experience, the figuring of the essence of Guaraníness as prime-age masculine dominance might have a counterpart in the figuring of Chanéness as nurturing grandmotherliness. There is some evidence for this in life as I have seen it lived in Isoso, which relates also to the shamanic complex there.

Lourdes was a long-term patient of Don Miguel's who lived in Aguarati-mi for much of the time I did during my doctoral fieldwork in Isoso between 1998 and 2000. She is originally from Alto Isoso and had been under the care of Don Jorge before the seriousness of her case meant she moved on to Don Miguel. She knew both men well and was very fond of both of them. When I was in Bolivia in 2013, I spent a night in the small town of Charagua, which lies about three hours upstream from Isoseño territory.[9] Lourdes had moved there with her husband because of the better schooling opportunities for her daughter. We are the exact same age and both had our children quite late by the standards of our respective societies—Lourdes in her early thirties, I in my late thirties. In both cases we had daughters, another parallelism that has reinforced our sense of affinity. It was she who first told me about Doña Apolonia's death. Lourdes commented to me that quite aside from his grief, his wife's death made it difficult for Don Jorge to carry on his shamanic practice because Doña Apolonia had known so well "how to take care of people."

Lourdes's comment about the importance of Apolonia's care work to Jorge's shamanic practice brought to my attention that what Apolonia had done for me was a familiar kind of work for her, not a one-off effort for a lonely foreigner. When patients seek out shamanic ministrations, they sometimes come from other villages and so are relative strangers. It is also customary to plead one's case in several visits before the shaman agrees to undertake care. The pleas are made very indirectly: relatives accompany the patient, the shaman's advisors accompany the shaman, and relatives and advisors speak to one another in the silent presence of the shaman and would-be patient. I used to suppose that visiting patients and the families who happened to be visiting Don Jorge when I came by often looked so uncomfortable because my presence made them so. It has only occurred to me with time that just as I was posing a large and awkward dependency request—to be accepted as an anthropologist-supplicant—that necessitated slow familial deliberation, so were they—to become patient-supplicants, and probably felt similarly ill at ease during the preliminary stages. When I returned to Ibasiriri in 2013, it was eleven months since Apolonia had died, and people in the village were organizing a commemoration for her the month following, something to console Don Jorge but also as a recognition of the loss to the community in Apolonia's own right.

The route I took to Miguel during my fieldwork—preceded by time spent with Jorge in Ibasiriri—and the much warmer reception there I received once I had done so—was also the "correct" pathway in Isoseño terms. Miguel was not to be appealed to directly. Lourdes has told me about the long process by which she resigned herself to needing to resort to him after visiting both Bolivian doctors and other shamans in Isoso and the delegations of kin that interceded on her behalf, going to visit Don Miguel and asking him to take on her difficult case. In retrospect, my dread and avoidance of Aguarati-mi at the start of my fieldwork seem to me to attest not so much to the ethnographer's magic as to the magic of ethnography, the way local norms force you willy-nilly into correct ways of behaving.

Both Lourdes and I love and marvel at Neli, Miguel's widow. Lourdes had been there when the baby Fernando had been born and said that she had taken over many household duties while Neli rested after the birth, "but," she said, "I could not do it all so well as she could." When I was living at Aguarati-mi, it was Lourdes who told me that Neli knew how to read and write. Before Lourdes arrived as a patient, Neli had dealt with any paperwork that came Don Miguel's way. Neli very effectively feigned ignorance of Spanish in the presence of foreign visitors when it suited her, I had figured out by then, but I hadn't guessed she was also literate.

It was only in 2013 that I began to consider Neli "anthropologically." When I was doing fieldwork, the person who fascinated me, of course, was her husband. As my terror of him faded, I was ever more charmed by him. He was very witty and most seductively sweet-natured (though by reputation he could have a dark temper, about which I heard stories but rarely witnessed). His youngest daughter adored him, and would sing out, **Papa ou! Papa ou! Papa ou!** ("Daddy's coming! Daddy's coming! Daddy's coming!") whenever he returned from any sort of outing at all, even a short walk to the corral. He indulged his smallest children totally and was beloved by his grown daughters. His relationships with his grown sons were more fraught. After he died, Neli told me, the last little boy born during his life asked after him and cried for months—"when is Daddy coming?" His final child, also a baby boy, was born posthumously.

Neli was born into a family already structured across two generations by Don Miguel's kinship rule-breaking, and from my perspective during my first fieldwork it seemed to be coiling itself ever more tightly around her during her life. She was surrounded by multiple layers of intermarriage, in-laws, stepchildren, an aunt, and even a grandmother who all orbited around Miguel. She had, too, many children by him—the first died very young, when she too was quite young, followed by seven more children who lived, including of course the one born shortly after Miguel's death. In the first years that I knew her, I often thought of her as someone inescapably trapped by circumstance. She seemed never to be at rest: everyone came to Don Miguel's house for visits, for meals, for gossip, for treatment; patients came and stayed for weeks—most Isoseño, but a few from elsewhere in indigenous

FIGURE 4.3.
Miguel's violin hung on the wall in the lab after his death (photo by author, 2013).

Bolivia—an Ava Guaraní man for a while, some Simba Guaraní visitors for a bit, some Guarayos, even a *kolla* (Andean) indigenous man (who, horribly, died and had to be buried at Aguarati-mi); foreigners came, including a young American anthropologist who hung around for months.

Years later Neli laughed as she told me her reaction when Miguel had announced to her I'd be coming to live with them in 1999 for "six whole weeks"—which in the end became six months—and that Neli would have to prepare lots of "traditional foods" for me because that was the sort of thing in which I was interested. "I thought, so long! Too long!," she recalled. But she never protested aloud. On days when her own mother and sisters visited, she'd get a bit of a hand with food preparation but still was the one to pop up and down to keep the water for the *porro* (mate-drinking gourd) heated, chairs provided, children's squabbles soothed over.

Once she took me with her to help dig manioc from their fields. This was extremely hard work, as manioc roots very firmly, and despite having a good six inches and forty pounds on Neli I was nearly useless at it. She hacked up root after root with cheery, slightly brutal rapidity. She was similarly quick and efficient when it came time to pick a chicken to have its neck snapped for dinner, or to butcher meat brought in from hunting, or carving up a cow or a goat carcass using a massive cleaver wielded with lithe agility. But she also minded the ins and outs of which children were feverish, which sulky and why, which marriages tense and which adult feelings hurt, and even which household dogs were soon to whelp and which pigs were likely to attempt eating the puppies if given half a chance and, in incidental asides, the progress of a long-running interspecies love quadrangle between an imperious rooster, ruler of the household patio, a patiently cuckolded drake, an indignant old duck, and a lovely, much harassed young duck. She possesses, in other words, a lively sympathetic heart.

After Don Miguel's death in 2006, though still only in her early thirties Neli already began to be called Doña and Tía (Madame and Aunt) by men and women very close to her age. Once wiry, she now has hints of softness now that bespeak a bit more time sitting and being served rather than standing and serving. Her daughters have begun to have children of their own, and both they and her older sons have spent periods of time working in the city and bringing back gifts to make her house a finely equipped one. I was surprised on one visit to be served coffee from ceramic mugs—a gift from one of her daughters after a working sojourn in Santa Cruz—rather than the enameled tinware that is the standard dishware in Isoso. Neli is ably managing the herd of cattle and the several horses left to her by Miguel. She is a beloved grandmother and both helps her daughters with their small new dependents and minds that they carry out their own dependency responsibilities well—**nde membi oyaeo**, "your child is crying," is a regular admonishment—while her own younger children bask contentedly in her experienced mothering.

The most poignant aspect of visiting now is the way the smaller children treat me as a kind of talisman-like connection to the father they had barely known or had not known at all. With the laboratory project abandoned, my foreignness and my return to his orbit are evidence of the power he'd once exercised and the way the world they live in had once been his world. Neli, though, is now its center: as society matron, mother, and grandmother.

OUR GRANDMOTHERS

I noted in chapter 2 that a certain hypermasculine version of "Chiriguano" cultural history as "Guaraní" cultural history has been in the ascendance in recent Bolivian Guaraní politics and that the reason this should be so has both shallow and deep historical roots. The erasure of the Chané "grandmothers" who formed families with those peripatetic Guaraní who arrived to the eastern flanks of the Andes and the Chaco in several waves, even in zones like Isoso where their historical presence had once been most remarked, poses an underanalyzed cultural-historical problem. The Guaraní migrants were overwhelmingly (perhaps exclusively) male. Their subjugation of the Chané involved quite a bit of family formation with Chané women, and it is not a stretch to suppose that polygyny involving women from different generations was one of the forms it might have taken.

Nevertheless, these kinds of families would have been in the minority, simply because Guaraní men were in the minority in the Chané territories to which they arrived. They would have been powerful, yes, but also viewed with quite a bit of reserve and suspicion and gossip. To make a historical leap, Don Miguel's marriages were of a "traditional" but unusual type, Don Jorge's of a "traditional" and common type. In the long run, a family of Don Miguel's type did not break society apart but was folded back into it. The youngest Chané women in it emerged after the deaths of their powerful husbands as grandmotherly pillars of the hybrid, hierarchical, social establishment. We don't have to choose between these dynamics to determine which one was "really" the socially determinative one. Both types were present historically, just as both were present when I was in the field in the late twentieth century. They exist as simultaneous possibilities within the social field.

Gow (2014) offers a thought-provoking treatment of cases of different modes of kinship making existing sustainedly in a single lowland South American community. Thinking specifically about shamanism, P. and H. Clastres' account of Tupí-Guaraní shamanism as a kind of mechanism for preventing the emergence of the state is predicated on the existence of multiple possible configurations of a given social order, so the dominance of one form over time is the result of schismatic rather than automatic processes.

Suggestively, Soviet anthropological analysis of Siberian shamanism (with which Amerindian shamanism shares many commonalities) supposed shamanism itself to be an indicator of sharpening class antagonism. Unlike the Clastreses, who proposed that shamanic visions and subsequent prophet-led migrations perpetually foiled incipient state-formation in lowland South American societies, Soviet ethnographers suggested shamans in Siberia were the equivalent of kulaks in peasant agricultural societies, that is, an emergent class of parasites historically marking a transition from nomadism to more settled pastoralism (Hutton 2001: 99, Znamenski 2007: 117). In these Soviet accounts, the powers shamans pretended to possess and use for healing were the alienated capacities of their supplicants, and their rituals were therefore a primitive opiate of the people (323). Without wishing to adopt the deterministic dialectics of these Soviet accounts, what is interesting is their noticing of and attempt to explain the evident relationship of shamanism to power and inequality. In his fascinating exegesis of this body of work, Andrei

Znamenski relates an amusing anecdote about a native Siberian trained as an ethnographer who stubbornly recorded that in his experience, not all shamans were in fact kulaks in terms of their standing in and relationship to their communities. His Soviet-era professors appended a skeptical note to this native account (340). My own field experience makes me wonder if everyone involved might not be a little bit right: shamans do have a special relationship to inequality, and some shamans are markedly powerful in ways that rouse local resentment and suspicion, while others are not. It is even the case that Don Miguel was materially far better off than Don Jorge. He owned cattle, horses, and an expensive mule; Don Jorge's husbandry was limited to the ordinary herd of goats. The Soviet anthropologists who thought they were bringing something new, clever, and world historical to the scene by spotting humbug in the shamanic field were thus carting Marxist coals to a native Newcastle.

When outsiders hone in on hyper-Guaraní, hypermasculine figures such as Don Miguel as the most "authentic" bearers of Guaraní culture, they are embracing a version of Chiriguano history that emphatically rejects any Arawakan element. They are taking a culturally specific polarization as a culturally specific essence. When these ultra-Guaraní turn out to be viewed with suspicion in their home communities in Isoso (as they inevitably are), outsiders worry that they did not find the really real, ne plus ultra Guaraní with whom to work; they only found the phonies.

I suspect, instead, that the bearers and proclaimers of masculine superpotency in Chiriguano society have always been viewed with suspicion. This in fact is their burden and role. The arc I experienced with Miguel, from menace to charm, is a stereotyped one. Most of the society mostly works along unshowy (and in fact, hierarchical and stratified, not "proudly egalitarian and constantly declaring defiant independence," as the "official" version of the Chiriguano character goes) lines, which are Arawakan and in many ways female. Jorge's marriage was one in which the distaff element was determinative, as was in many ways his variety of shamanism. People did not think he was Isoso's most powerful shaman, but they did treat him as an entirely trustworthy one. Jorge's kinship relations were quite unremarkable: one wife, with whom he spent his life, and whom he did not long outlive. Unlike Don Miguel, apart in his own little minicosmos, Jorge lived the way most ordinary Isoseño men do, spending his adult life in his wife's village of Ibasiriri, in amongst the cozy paths linking everybody to everybody else.

Like other outsiders, I didn't (at first) go to Isoso to see Jorge, let alone Apolonia or Neli. I went to meet Don Miguel, the shaman who was so powerful, renowned, and charismatic that foreigners paid to build a laboratory next to his house. Anne-Christine Taylor writes of the attention paid by "Jivarologists" to the *arutam* complex (which will be examined at length in chapter 6):

[We] have tended to consider the *arutam* complex, because it is intellectually
spectacular, and also because of its esoteric aspects, as the heart of Jivaroan culture . . .
by positing that the *arutam* complex lies at the heart, rather than the boundaries, of
Achuar culture, we have misrepresented not only the *arutam* complex but Jivaroan
culture in general . . . I suspect that a great many of our ethnographic accounts are in
fact based on a similar conflation between "culture" and "extreme states." (1996: 210)

She's quite right. But it is also the case that anthropological accounts tend to privi-
lege masculine perspectives, and when mistakes get made about, say, kinship they
somehow err on the side of airily asserting too much patriliny and not on spotting extra matriliny (as in Walker and Ribeiro 2011). The arutam complex is associated with superpotent hypermasculinity in Jivaroland, just as a certain kind of
shamanism and the ethos of "Guaraní independent egalitarian defiance" are in the
Chiriguanía. As I began to think through my materials not from the perspective
of Miguel or even Jorge, but instead from that of Apolonia and Neli, I was struck
by the relevance of Kathleen Gough's (1971) perceptive restudy of Edward Evans-
Pritchard's landmark research on kinship and marriage among the Nuer.

Giving due credit to the excellence of Evans-Pritchard's empirical work, which
allowed her to critically reassess his interpretations using his own materials, Gough
shows how Evans-Pritchard took the handling of aristocratic Nuer men (his principal informants) of "the agnatic principle" (not their term for it, of course) to indicate a real organizational principle, rather than an ideological ideal. As Gough puts
it, "For the aristocrats, and for those few lineages of stranger Nuer origin which
have somehow managed to become dominant over a section of tribal territory and
have acquired a certain depth, the agnatic principle is indeed strong" (1971: 113).
However, she continues, since "non-aristocrats form the great majority of the population in any Nuer tribe, we must conclude that the agnatic principle is far from
supreme in it operation among the Nuer although the ideal undoubtedly persists"
(114). Nuer society shares with Chiriguano society a colonial-era history actively
shaped by interethnic conquest and invasion, pitting Nuer against closely related
(and in many ways despised) Dinka, a dynamic intensified "in the nineteenth century . . . by Arab slave-raids and slave-trading." One of the factors driving Chané-
Chiriguano relations in the seventeenth and eighteenth centuries, resulting in the
flight of many Chané to agriculturally inhospitable Isoso, was precisely the slave
trade or, more precisely, the "ransoming" of captive Chané from Chiriguano by
the Spanish, on the pretext that that cannibalistic Chiriguano would otherwise eat
them. The dynamics of aggressively martial, masculine, polygamous dominance as
a supreme ideological principle absorbed into, and made use of, by a social field
of stably reproduced hierarchical relations among networks of female kin—and

including many unremarkable and unremarked "ordinary" marriages—might be something that is often present in the history of humanity, though undernotedly so in the anthropological literature because, as Gough puts it:

> It is sometimes argued by male anthropologists that relations with and between women are of only minor relevance to an analysis of the political aspects of kinship. This argument scarcely, however, holds good, at all events for a society where men are prohibited from cooking and so much attach themselves to some kinswoman's hearth, where some women may own cattle and live, legally autonomous, where they choose, where women may provide men with their local and political affiliations. (ibid: 115)

All of these points hold true in Bolivian Guaraníland, including Isoso. Men are not prohibited from cooking, and those few men who are such skilled hunters that they go on hunts lasting several days cook for themselves in the bush. But I have never seen a man tending an Isoseño hearth at home. The possibility is not expressly forbidden; it is never even considered. In any event, the role of women in "male-dominated" structures or "masculinist" ideologies can never be one of simple absence. Returning to the problem of Amerindian shamanism generally and lowland South American shamanism in particular, it is striking that for such an intensively studied anthropological problem, the legacy of kinship studies and the potential relevance of women and family to this famously manly practice are so understudied.

The next chapter unpacks a hypervirile popular discourse around shamanistic practice that has had tremendous policy-making influence on the late twentieth-century lives of South American indigenous peoples even while being a pastiche of preposterous nonsense. But to borrow—rather awkwardly—the old-fashioned divisions of Africanist anthropologists, even in accounts that anthropologists can take seriously, shamanism has been more often treated in terms of the jural than the domestic sphere. In these accounts, shamanism does grand things, having to do with history and power and colonialism or nature and culture and supernature. It's a big manly deal, not a small homely womanish one. Taussig's *Shamanism, Colonialism, and the Wild Man* (1987) is one such, casting shamanism as a cure for historical ailments and featuring only men. Eduardo Viveiros de Castro's *From the Enemy's Point of View* (1992) has shamans as ontological operators, literal axis mundi. Carlos Fausto (2012) and Fernando Santos-Granero (2016) align shamanism with hunting, warfare, and predation generally in a way that oddly leaves little light between their visions of lowland South American life and that of Napoleon Chagnon's, making the generations-long showdown between their respective theoretical traditions look in many ways like drum solo variations beat out upon a single brawny chest.

As I slowly wrote up my own fieldwork, new work by scholars younger than me such as that of Harry Walker (2012) and most especially that of Oiara Bonilla (2005, 2013) have given me confidence that I am not the only person to notice what has gone underremarked in lowland South American social worlds; the work of Joanna Overing and Peter Gow and Suzanne Oakdale, previously cited, gave me considerable inspiration before I even began. Chapter 6 considers the work of another senior Amazonianist—Anne-Christine Taylor—who has gotten the importance of ambivalence all along.

It's not that I don't get the lure and fascination of the macho version of shamanism. Even as over the years Don Jorge came to seem the more unambiguously admirable man, I was infinitely more charmed by Don Miguel, as had been so many people, perhaps especially women, before me. Znamenski records the admission on the part of a Hungarian anthropologist working in the Soviet tradition about his first reaction to hearing shamanic chants, in the late 1950s: "I have to confess rather embarrassedly, I was immediately impressed by it" (Vilmos Diószegi, cited in Znamenski 2007: 327). As a Marxist ethnographer, he evidently felt silly falling for what he knew he was supposed to dismiss as a primitive opiate of the people. When it comes to misplaced cynicism, I get where he's coming from.

5

Shamans and Spies

It is not an anthropologically novel observation that belief in witches operates as a kind of conspiracy theory, a logic of connection that emerges from social settings of intense interconnectedness. When, with time, the shamans I knew in Isoso and especially their wives began to share with me their dark suppositions about what the laboratory project and investigators coming to study traditional medicine were really about, at the time I thought, Eeyore-like—how like them, believers in sorcery that they are. They had suppositions about embezzlement (these, I knew from conversations with NGO workers, were not unfounded) but they also imagined that outside researchers collecting plant samples might be selling them on the streets of distant Andean La Paz for a tidy profit. I knew this was not true and pitied their paranoia.

Sometimes my interest in shamanism provoked suppositions about my own potential occult powers. Once at Aguarati-mi, when I asked about the whereabouts of a young relative shortly before he turned up for an unexpected visit, this was much remarked because the ability to predict visitors is a shamanic gift. On another occasion in an Isoseño village that I visited from time to time a shopkeeper who had always seemed very ill at ease in my presence suddenly asked if I could see everyone's sins just by looking at them. I assured him I could not. It emerged that the question arose from the fact that anthropologists study **teko**, way of being, which is now often used to translate "culture" but which in Guaraní also means guilt or fault, as in **mbaeti sereko** (not my fault) or **jae jekopegua** (his fault). More generally, though, I think I escaped most kinds of local suspicion about whiteness and power

DOI: 10.5876/9781646420360.c005

precisely because my overall air in the field did not seem confident or successful. Once Don Miguel and one of his sons were telling me about certain places (eerie spots in the high sand dunes by the riverbank and in the caves in one of the lone hills in the otherwise flat Chaco landscape) that give access to *Salamanca*, a magical font of shamanic power (for more on this place, see Lowrey 2006c). Would I like to go there?, they asked, teasingly—and seeing the look on my face, then laughing delightedly: "No, look at you, you are scared! You are going to fail because you are scared!" This joke was, I think, reassuring to everyone (including to some extent me) about the possibility of my having a sinister impact in Isoso. Its perceptiveness about my career, especially with respect to a place of knowledge that takes its name from a Spanish university of great renown at the time of European contact, even at that early stage seemed depressingly on the money.

In any event, that the conspiracist mindset of people who, after all, believed in witches would extend to their encounters with assorted outsiders fit comfortably within my anthropological assumptions. The "natives," with their status society ways, would of course assume everything was personal and related. Less comfortably, as I researched this book, and particularly as I puzzled more and more seriously over why exactly anyone had ever supposed it would be a good idea to build a laboratory next to the home of a shaman, I found myself delving into a vast labyrinth of semischolarly literature and tooling around weirder and weirder crannies of the internet, gradually becoming a convinced conspiracy theorist myself. I am now persuaded that what lay behind the shaman's laboratory was that old black magic after all.

TRY TRY TRY TO UNDERSTAND . . .

The last time I saw Don Miguel was in 2005. He died the following year. At the time, he was not yet ill, but he was very sad. While I was visiting he wanted to talk to me about his plans to build a new house for his entire family: his (at the time) six children with Neli, and the five young children of his daughter Victoria, who had died suddenly and unexpectedly the previous year. Her death had followed the death of her mother, the children's beloved grandmother, in 2002. The children were living in Aguarati with their father and their father's sister but the situation was a heartbreaking one—the youngest child, a little girl, was hardly more than a baby. Don Miguel wanted, desperately, for all of them to be together again, as his children and Victoria's children had grown up in neighboring homes and were very close. Her sons and daughters came often to visit from Aguarati while I was at Aguarati-mi in 2005. On one slow afternoon two of Victoria's sons, whom I had known since they were tiny toddlers, spent a couple of hours singing *chacareras* (Chaco folk music) in Spanish, a language I hardly otherwise heard them use, into my tape recorder and listening to them played back, over and over. The older of the two boys—then about nine years old—was surprisingly good. Their quiet somber sadness as they sang the haunting adult lyrics of love and loss and their intentness as they listened to the playback, again and again, were hard to witness.

Don Miguel had bought bricks for the planned house and erected its posts. He was now saving up for the roofing. The site was just behind his current home, and one day he walked me through his plans, just the two of us. Suddenly he stopped in mid-sentence, and put a hand out for support, resting it on a stack of bricks. He was weeping. He worried, he told me, he worried all the time, about what was going to happen to everyone when he died. So many of his plans had come to naught—the whole horrible collaboration with the laboratory project, which had ended so badly, all of the burdens of treating patients, and then to have lost the daughter to whom he was so close and to see his grandchildren so bereft. Long before I knew Victoria, she had begun to train to be his shamanic heir—but then she got married, and the responsibilities of wifehood and motherhood meant she couldn't really fulfill the duties of a shamanic vocation. This, I was told, was common, and was why one almost never came across women shamans. There was no reason in principle a woman could not become one.

Being the center of his own little antisociety wore heavily on Don Miguel at the end of his life. The community had put him forward, again and again, to engage in external relations. Even the story of his "titling" as a shaman (previous chapter) makes clear that his fate was not quite self-chosen. Many people (himself included) told me stories of his behavior in childhood that marked him out as destined to be a shaman. He had strange food cravings, would fast if they could not be satisfied, would faint, would predict visitors, seemed gifted with healing powers when an epidemic of measles came through his community while he was still a child. I was told he had spent some years as a young adult outside Isoso, living and working in Santa Cruz. During the 1980s he had once traveled to Mexico as part of a shamanic congress under the auspices of the Swiss Red Cross. At some point he had acquired a Willys military jeep, though it had ceased to run long before my time in Isoso and was for years a favorite playing spot of the household children. In 2018 Mennonite settlers bought it for scrap and took it away on a horse-drawn cart.

He kept a replica of Copenhagen's Little Mermaid on a bookshelf in the laboratory, a gift from one of a trio of IWGIA-employed Danes who had filmed him for a documentary and agitated on his behalf about putative biopiracy. For that documentary, and sometimes in other posed photos, he donned a black gaucho hat, Argentinian style. He also had a rather striking print of a mounted Apache, drawing his bow in mid-gallop, on a pink-sunset–lit plain. I don't know where it came from. He'd been awarded a diploma of traditional medicine by CIDOB, the lowland Bolivian indigenous peoples' umbrella political organization. He had visited the university laboratory of Alberto Giménez in Bolivia's Andean capital, La Paz, and had been struck by the many cages of experimental white mice. He'd answered the questions of visiting French and Bolivian ethnobotanists. He'd hosted patients from other indigenous communities in Bolivia. He'd put gas workers up in the laboratory. He'd had an American anthropologist live with his family for months. But now he felt he had nothing to show for it but disappointment and loss and even—in the case of the laboratory project particularly—betrayal.

Why was the laboratory project such a disaster? The immediate reasons are simple and straightforward. The plan to have the laboratory become a production site for a commercially marketable antifungal medication was ill considered. Bolivia may be a poor country, but it has regulations governing the production of over-the-counter medications, and the conditions in the laboratory could not meet those standards. The site could not be regularly inspected due to its remoteness, and transport from Isoso to urban centers was always a logistical challenge. However, in the end this was a rather distal problem. The fallback plan was to distribute locally medications made in the laboratory. For a while after I first arrived in 1999, an occasional **karai** customer would turn up on horseback to purchase some ointment. Don Miguel and his assistant, Don Nelson, drew up lists of potential medicines and price lists, and for months stacks of plants were collected and arranged for drying in the lab. I occasionally had a very good herbal tea made from one of them, that was supposed to be good for coughs and that, once sugar was added, tasted rather deliciously of Trix cereal (a sort of sweet-tart fruit flavor). The problem here was that the additional components—plastic packaging, petroleum jelly to make a base for ointments, and the like—would have to be supplied continually to the laboratory by external funding. With only a potential local customer base of fellow poor people, the lab was not going to make any money. Finally, external funding (principally provided by the French government) to the laboratory project was handled under the auspices of the Capitanía del Alto y Bajo Isoso, which at the time was also managing a much larger amount of external funding from the United States Agency for International Development in order to run a national park project (again, for details, see Lowrey 2003, 2008a). All of this funding was subjected, at least in theory, to very tight controls, though in the end much of it went unaccounted for (Estrada 2010).

One way or another, after the laboratory was built, much of the funding intended for its completion disappeared. The most plausible version I heard about what happened to it was that it had been used to reimburse funds CABI leaders siphoned

FIGURE 5.1. Water supply with laboratory and family home partially visible in background (photo by author, 2005).

off the park project, which were subject to tighter controls than was the laboratory funding. Be that as it may, much of that park funding disappeared without explanation as well. In any event, though the laboratory did have electric lights, supplied by solar panels, it was never supplied with running water. Its built-in sink and taps were thus unusable. The supply even of well water to Aguarati-mi was a perpetual problem and one into which Don Miguel and his family sank many of their own resources and to which they applied considerable ingenuity. In the early 2000s, Don Miguel allowed visiting Bolivian gas workers to spend about a month living at the laboratory. In return, they promised to use their test well equipment to drill a new drinking water well and reservoir for him. They did so, but its pump never worked properly. This is a subject on which I could spend pages and did in my field-notes and letters to family and friends. For a memorable few months, the system for pumping water involved a hand crank on a bicycle wheel, which was breathless making. Once, after I'd gotten a bucket filled for a bath in the dry season, a thirsty cow eagerly knocked the whole thing over. Not only is water scarce in Isoso, but the brambly spikey prickly flora of the Chaco means an easily graspable stick is rarely at hand when you'd most like to have one.

The misappropriation of funds that passed through CABI during the late 1990s and early 2000s eventually produced a major leadership crisis in Isoso, the fall-out from which continues to the present day. But all of these explanations for the project's failure suggest it could have succeeded and thus miss the most fundamental reason it did not. The project was poorly executed in practice, yes; but more important, it was conceptually totally misbegotten. The fault for this does not lie at the feet of Don Miguel, nor of CABI, nor of Alberto Giménez, who hoped for a Bolivian science that could help Bolivian citizens, nor of the well-meaning French ethnobotanists who helped secure international funding for the project, nor of the vacuous Danish NGO do-gooders who felt sure the project was an example of "biopiracy" and "theft of indigenous knowledge" and fostered considerable ill will and suspicion in a situation already charged with bad faith (Lowrey 2003, 2008a). The usual thing in contemporary anthropology at such a juncture is to gesture in the direction of some sort of more general, overarching structural-historical context in order to explain a sad local muddle like this one. In what follows, I instead use the formula of witchcraft accusation and make the case for an individual culprit and a few guilty associates.

IN THE JUNGLE WITH THE LEAF PRESS: INTRODUCING THE SUSPECT, RICHARD EVANS SCHULTES

As is the case for many if not most lowland South American shamans, plant medicine and plant lore formed almost no part of Don Miguel's nor Don Jorge's practices, nor that of any other **paye** or **payerai** in Isoso. The plant pharmacopeia in use in Isoso is, as I found in my household survey, limited and widely known. It is not a field of esoteric knowledge in which shamans specialize. Shamans' diagnostic and treatment techniques are magical rather than parascientific. The Isoseño are farmers and have been since pre-Columbian times. Were they hunter-gatherers, the range of plant medicines in use would likely be somewhat larger, but the truly spectacularly efficacious elements of indigenous plant knowledge throughout the Americas (curare, quinine, hallucinogens, arrow poisons, fish poisons) are few in number, are widely known across lowland South America, and have been researched and published upon since the arrival of Europeans—that is to say, for hundreds of years.

Nevertheless, in the second half of the twentieth century (and now well into the twenty-first) it has been an article of popular faith, and one that has had a tremendous impact on policy making and international funding as it pertains to South American indigenous peoples, that their pharmacopeia is vast, mysterious, woefully understudied, and principally in the hands of shamans. The person most often credited with "discovering" this set of facts is Richard Evans Schultes (1915–2001), hailed as the "father of modern ethnobotany." Despite hagiographic biographying and no small amount of self-mythologizing, the facts of his story are a little hard to nail down. The story of his story, though, is a doozy.

Schultes's first foray into ethnobotany was in the company of anthropologist Weston LaBarre—whom, recall, we met in chapter 3, with his mature thesis on the Ghost Dance religion as an expression of native neuroticism, published in 1970. Years before that writing, in the early 1930s, Schultes and LaBarre traveled together to Kiowa country, in Oklahoma, to study the use of peyote. LaBarre based his 1937 doctoral thesis on that research. Schultes, for his part, wrote an MA thesis in 1938 on the basis of the peyote work and then a PhD dissertation in 1941 on the identity of botanical hallucinogens referred to in colonial-era chronicles of Mexico. After finishing the doctorate, he went to the Colombian Amazon to research the indigenous arrow poison, curare.

In a late-life interview, Schultes said he traveled with a grant from the "National Academy of Sciences" and the timing was due to the fact that tubocurarine had in the late 1930s been isolated as the active compound responsible for curare's effectiveness as a muscle relaxant and as a result was beginning to be used in surgical anaesthesia such that it needed to be more effectively sourced (Gorman 1995). His student and biographer, Wade Davis, tells the story slightly differently: identifying the funding agency as the National Research Council and mentioning, as a bit of color, the immediately previous work of someone Davis calls Schultes's "distant comrade, a man with a colourful past," Richard Gill, who in 1938 had brought twenty-five pounds of properly sourced and identified curare to the United States, where they were "introduced into medical practice for a host of muscular and neurological ailments" (W. Davis 1997: 215). However, "all of this remained unknown to Schultes, who began his own search for arrow poisons on the Putumayo in January 1942" (215).

It is unlikely that this is true. In 1941 Schultes's old friend Weston LaBarre published a review of Gill's swashbuckling 1940 account of his expedition, entitled *White Water, Black Magic*, in the important journal *American Anthropologist*. Given their friendship and shared interests, one imagines LaBarre would have discussed the book with Schultes prior to publishing a review of it. The review is short and worth quoting in full:

> A frankly popular book (and excellent reading on this score), the present work will be of interest to the ethnobotanist, the ethnologist, and the anthropologist concerned with advances in modern psychiatry. It contains a complete account of the preparation of curare by the tribes of tropical Ecuador, as well as incidental ethnographical notes. Standardized curare has largely been made possible through Mr. Gill's

"functional exploring" of the region. The same substance on the Jivaros' deadly arrow-point is recently being widely used in conjunction with metrazol shock-therapy of schizophrenia and the affective disorders. Preliminary reports (e.g. those of Dr. A. E. Bennett and Dr William Menninger) indicate that the relaxing action of curare reduces the danger of fracture and dislocation in the tonic phase of the metrazol convulsion, formerly a drawback in this therapeutic procedure. The book contains maps and an index, and is profusely illustrated with the author's own photographs. (LaBarre 1941: 103–104)

These uses of curare—as an adjunct to shock therapy and in psychiatric treatment—are quite different from those mentioned years later by Schultes and his biographer Davis. They did, however, precede curare's use as a surgical anaesthetic. In the early 1940s, LaBarre was working at the psychiatric clinic of the Dr. William Menninger mentioned in the book review, located in Topeka, Kansas. At the time, Dr. Menninger was serving as the chief of the Army Medical Corps' Psychiatric Services Division, where by the end of the Second World War he attained the rank of brigadier general. At the Menninger Clinic, one of the treatments in which Dr. (General) Menninger specialized was convulsive therapy for schizophrenia and depressive disorders. The medical application of curare in the late 1930s and early 1940s was not yet to surgery but instead to psychiatry, where it made the application of various kinds of convulsive or "shock" therapy to psychiatric patients less physically dangerous because it rendered them unable to flail about during its administration. They otherwise sometimes injured themselves badly.

The National Research Council (founded during the First World War) mentioned by Davis as having funded Schultes's research was at the time much more closely allied to military and defense purposes than the National Academy of Sciences (to which Schultes referred when interviewed), which is a much older entity into which the NRC was absorbed after the Second World War. According to Margaret Krieg (whose apposite book is not cited by Davis), in 1935 there had been "some discussion about using curare as a military weapon" (1964: 225). At the start of World War II, William Menninger's brother and colleague Karl was one of the founding members of the "Committee for National Morale." which brought together psychologists and anthropologists to study propaganda and psychological operations in support of the Allied war effort (Chase 2002: 253). The launch of Schultes's postdoctoral career, then, was to study a psychoactively useful drug during wartime.

Once in Colombia, across January and February 1942 Schultes collected several other psychoactive plants (the stimulant *yoco*, the intoxicant *chiricaspi*, some "roots cooked to relieve hysteria"), and he also tried the hallucinogen *yagé* and recorded local information about plant admixtures said to vary its mental effects. In March, he had the fortuitous good luck to "run into Colonel Gomez-Pereira, the Columbian army officer responsible for security in the borderlands" (W. Davis 1997: 219). Somehow Schultes persuaded this Colombian military man to mount a frontier patrol, and "escorted by the Colombian army, Schultes headed upriver into Kofán territory" (219). Davis's accounts suggests a kind of jolly serendipity to all of this, but it is astonishingly implausible that this kind of military cooperation would have been forthcoming on the basis of Schultes's personal charm alone. According to Davis's account, as soon as they arrived to a Kofán village, the local shaman emerged in full headdress to greet them whereupon they were immediately offered a hallucinogenic brew: they were now among "a people who evidently took the drug as casually as Englishmen take tea" (222). Although during his time with the Kofán Schultes did not in fact collect any arrow poison species new to science, he did collect "dozens of folk remedies, stimulants, hallucinogens, fish poisons, and wild fruits" (225). After a bit more riverine exploration on a military launch, "quite unexpectedly" (227) the services of a military plane were made available to Schultes in May 1942, to courier his collections to Bogotá. He traveled with the cargo, then returned to another Colombian naval base on another Amazonian river, on another military plane. In July 1942, again using military transport, he returned to Bogotá. This record of fortuitous military compliance with pure scholarly research is, for anyone who has done purely academic fieldwork, rather amazing—in fact simply unbelievable. But Davis is only getting started.

In Bogotá, Schultes was told to abandon the curare research in favor of collecting rubber for the war effort to replace Southeast Asian sources that had fallen into Japanese hands. As it turned out, synthetic rubber production obviated the need for natural rubber. Although Schultes did collect many potentially blight-resistant varieties of rubber and establish test plantations in Costa Rica (since, unfortunately, destroyed according to Davis 1997: 369), in fact very little Latin American rubber was put to use during the war (334). For some reason, though, Schultes was exempted from conscription—according to Davis, due to the vital wartime importance of the rubber work (334). Schultes stayed on in Colombia after the war ended, ostensibly to continue his important research on rubber. Although a prolific scholar, for whatever reason Schultes never did publish his planned opus on South American rubber plant species. On into the late 1940s and early 1950s, in Davis's account, Schultes continued to manage to avail himself of military transport in the Colombian Amazon on a regular basis. Despite this inexplicably obliging relationship with the Colombian military, Schultes, according to Davis, was more or less totally unaware of the outbreak of "La Violencia" in Colombia in 1948 (408). Not all observers of the period affirm this obliviousness: Gerard Colby and Charlotte

Dennett say, "His [Schultes'] reports [to US officials] included descriptions of the politics of various individual Colombians during the civil war" (1995: 505).

In Davis's version of events, however, Schultes spent almost all of his time with "the Indians" (this very general descriptor appears frequently in the hagiographic work on Schultes by Davis and others). Davis claims that Schultes spoke "two indigenous languages . . . fluently" (1997: 476), though it is difficult to see on the basis of the evidence in Davis's own book how this could be true. It is a feat almost unmatched in the history of South Americanist anthropology, rare even among missionaries who spend their entire adult lives working in indigenous communities. Schultes's time in the field amounts to some weeks among the Kofán,[1] a stay as the guest of a Catholic mission priest among the Huitoto (W. Davis 1997: 232), and eighteen months (interrupted with returns to both Bogotá and Boston) at one of two Colombian trading posts for the commercial exploitation of rubber in the establishment of which Schultes was involved in ways that Davis does not make an effort to elucidate (1997: 465–466; 478).[2] This rubber trade recruited Indian labor of diverse linguistic origin. During expeditions from the posts, Davis admits, "[Schultes] would not spend a great deal of time in any one village" (1997: 479). In a collection of Schultes's photographs from the Amazon, posthumously edited by Davis, he says, "It is perhaps no accident that so many of Schultes's finest photographs were taken at only four localities, all relatively brief interludes during his many long years in the forest" (2004: x). Yes, perhaps not.

Even the most minimally critical reading of Davis's account of Schultes's life produces misgiving. But it has been, for all that, flamboyantly successful. Why? A striking feature of Davis's account of Schultes's time in the Amazon is that—despite all the US federal funding behind it, the Colombian military boat and plane trips facilitating it, the series of local men Friday accompanying it—Davis's overwhelming emphasis is on Schultes's autonomy and self-sufficiency during it. For Davis, Schultes is always setting off with a minimum of gear, assistance, and guidance; spending long periods of time alone in the forest; paddling up and down hundreds of kilometers of rapids practically unassisted and eating almost nothing along the way; turning up his nose at most of the human company on offer (though Davis assures us Schultes had a kind of magical rapport with "the Indians"—astonishingly rarely specified by individual names, however). This figure—the strong, self-contained man, who just needs to be let alone to accomplish great things—fits with Schultes's politics.[3] It also has a powerful hold on modern sensibilities.

To recapitulate points made in the introductory chapter, modern society in some respects is, and in many respects imagines itself to be, a society cobbled together from the choices of free individuals. The figuring of Schultes as a uniquely gifted chooser—someone who knew his preferences and went wherever they led him—is very powerful in such a society. There is a doubling of this in the fact that Schultes figured Amerindian shamans as, themselves, uniquely gifted clever male choosers as well. That in fact shamanism is a feature of status societies in which people both are and imagine themselves as so thoroughly enmeshed in networks of sociability connecting people, animals, and spirit powers that they are constantly vulnerable to relational disturbances that can only be treated by relationally attuned specialists is erased by the essentially false Schultean account.

The Schultes version of shamanism is for all intents and purposes the contemporary Western apprehension of shamanism. A popular audience of modern Westerners has found the Schultes version so persuasive that they have failed entirely to notice how farcically implausible it is, even when much of the evidence of its falsity is contained within one of the key metatexts constructing it, W. Davis's *One River*. None of this would be worth tracking down were it not for the fact that the story of Schultes is intimately connected to the story of ethnobotany and that this humbug narrative of the humble lone (who was in fact backed by a vast imperial apparatus) scientist (who was in fact a pater fabulist to many junior fabulators) didn't eventually come smashing destructively into the life of someone in fact rather powerless—Don Miguel—on the pretense that he, and lowland South American shamans like him, were possessed of powers beyond fathom. It also wouldn't matter (except to people who knew and cared for him) if it were just Don Miguel the narrative affected—but the narrative has had a tremendous impact on lowland South American indigenous experience in the latter part of the twentieth century. It provided a rationale for the sowing of seed funding on shamanic and local community backs on the promise that these would sprout into towering edifices of indigenous entrepreneurial self-sufficiency. It intersected with hardnosed, pitiless late modern ideologies of what is usually called neoliberalism with magical efficacy, producing a putatively technocratic boomlet in fanciful projects. As we have seen in chapters 2 and 3 and as is usual with these sorts of double-dealing operations, only indigenous people have ended up getting hurt by these processes. In a crowning injustice (but one that should not, by now, surprise us) the charge of humbug is sometimes doubled back upon indigenous peoples themselves, that they are pretending to a body of medicotechnocratic knowledge they do not in fact possess in order to bamboozle dewily innocent national and international aid agencies into funding them (Widdowson 2008). Again, the modernist temptation is at this point to invoke abstractions about the global circulation of discourses about indigenous knowledge, shamanism, and entrepreneurship. I want instead to think the way Isoseño people urged me to do right from the start—conspiratorially, "witchily"—and to explore the connective web of relations between the identifiable people that created and sustained these phony fantasies of powerful loners and autonomous autochthonous knowledges.

"THERE IS SOMETHING"

As Davis describes it, after his long (but in point of fact, multiply interrupted) Amazonian sojourn, in fall 1953 "Schultes returned to his beloved Harvard and accepted a job as curator of the Orchid Herbarium of Oakes Ames at the Botanical Museum" (1997: 369). Schultes remained at Harvard until his retirement, increasingly lionized and occupying ever-more-prestigious berths at the institution and producing a fascinating crop of acolytes, of whom more anon. The timing of this hire is at the coming together of several interesting astrological houses. Davis says that in September 1952, two amateur investigators into Mexican magic mushrooms "received a letter from Robert Graves, who somehow had stumbled upon Schultes' 1939 paper identifying *teonanacatl*" (1997: 118). This is less serendipitous than Davis makes it sound. Although Davis does not mention it, Schultes had traveled "numerous times to the south of Mexico" in the late 1930s in the company of engineer Robert Weitlaner and Weitlaner's anthropologist son-in-law Jean Basset Johnson (Hagenbach and Werthmüller 2011: 92). Johnson was a student of linguist Morris Swadesh. Swadesh would go on to work for the Office of Strategic Services (precursor to the CIA) during the Second World War. The mushroom researchers (staunch anticommunist Gordon Wasson—friend of CIA head Allen Dulles—and Wasson's Russian wife, Valentina) who "somehow stumbled" across Schultes's work in the early 1950s were on at least one later trip to Oaxaca, in the mid-1950s, accompanied by the CIA-funded researcher James Moore (Riedlinger 1990: 203).[4]

John D. Marks, in his well-known account of the founding of the United States Central Intelligence Agency's MKULTRA program devoted to researching methods of human behavioral modification and so-called mind control via specialized methods and materials, mentions something relevant to this story. He says that the director of the ARTICHOKE project (the immediate precursor to MKULTRA) arranged in late 1952

> for a young CIA scientist to take a Mexican field trip and gather samples of piule [teonanacatl] as well as other plants of high narcotic and toxic value of interest to ARTICHOKE . . . [the scientist] assumed cover as a researcher interested in finding native plants which were anesthetics. Fluent in Spanish and familiar with Mexico, he had no trouble moving around the country, meeting with leading experts on botanicals. (Marks 1979: 114–115)

Marks does not identify the young researcher, though these attributes (note the interest in anesthetics) align well with Schultes's.

In April 1953, the United States Central Intelligence Agency established MKULTRA. Psychoactive drugs were of course of tremendous interest and had been since at least 1949, when the CIA became convinced that the Soviets and the Chinese were already in possession of "truth drugs" and America was falling behind in the mind control race (Chase 2002: 270). According to John Marks, "[CIA Director Allen] Dulles ordered the Agency's bookkeepers to pay the costs blindly on the signatures of Sid Gottlieb and Willis Gibbons, *a former U.S. Rubber executive* who headed TSS [the Technical Services Staff]" (61; emphasis mine). Gibbons was, in fact, "research director" for U.S. Rubber (Albarelli 2005: 65), while Gottlieb, for his part, had previously worked for the National Research Council (the entity that funded Schultes's first foray to Colombia), where he was "exposed to some interesting work concerning ergot alkaloids as vasoconstrictors and hallucinogens" (Albarelli 2005: 103). The TSS was a part of the agency "full of PhDs with operational experience" (Marks 1979: 32) and which was according to Marks closely involved in behavioral work after 1953. As this research expanded, "money started pouring through CIA-linked conduits or 'cutouts' such as the Geschickter Fund for Medical Research, the Society for the Study of Human Ecology, and the Josiah Macy, Jr. Foundation" (Lee and Shlain 1985: 19–20).

According to Davis, Schultes had no involvement whatsoever in MKULTRA; Davis says that Schultes "was once asked if he had been associated with the agency. He famously replied something along the lines of no, but I would have been delighted to help out if I could" (Davis, personal communication, 2015). Schultes made no secret of his reactionary politics, though admirers such as Wade Davis, Mark Plotkin, and Andrew Weil tend to treat this set of attitudes as having been a harmless foible. For whatever reason, though, the concerns of MKULTRA were all around Schultes. He coauthored a book, *Plants of the Gods*, with LSD chemist Albert Hoffman; his Harvard colleague Timothy Leary was at the center of the popularizing of LSD use; and William H. Burroughs once traveled to the Colombian Amazon to try ayahuasca in Schultes's company. Schultes's student Andrew Weil—who went on to become an alternative medicine guru—took his first class with Schultes in 1960 and in 1962 wrote a "sensationalized" article in for the *Harvard Crimson* about faculty opposition to Leary's radical approach to LSD research that contributed to Leary's firing (Lee and Shlain 1985: 87). In 1963, Schultes—always careful to distance himself from Leary—became Weil's thesis advisor. According to at least one researcher, the "CIA was less than pleased about the activities of Professors Timothy Leary and Richard Alpert at Harvard" (Albarelli 2005: 361). The psychedelic researcher Alexander Shulgin, in a tribute to Schultes, recalled, "I remember a couple of trips to London with him, to small, intimate conferences at the Macy Foundation House" (Shulgin 2001: n.p.). This is the same Josiah Macy, Jr. Foundation that was a "sometime Agency conduit" for funding into psychoactive research (Marks 1979: 127). According to chroniclers such as Davis, however, Schultes was merely elegantly bemused by all the drug culture nonsense of the 1960s and felt very removed from it all.

Be that as it may, his students consistently focused on psychoactive plants. His most beloved protégé, Timothy Plowman, who died young, carried out work on coca. In 1968, Plowman and another of Schultes's students made riverine collecting trips in Peru under the auspices of the Amazon Natural Drug Company. According to Davis, this collaboration was a naive mistake, and Plowman and his companion ended the collaboration once they twigged that ANDCO was not a legitimate entity and that its "research director . . . displayed less interest in plants than in the whereabouts of Che Guevara" (1997: 25). Amusingly but allusively put. ANDCO's founder J. C. King was "involved in chemical and biological warfare after he retired as chief of Clandestine Services in Latin America" (Colby and Dennett 1995: 497) and had been the "CIA's former Western Hemisphere chief" in the 1950s and 1960s (Albarelli 2005: 173). That would cover the latter part of the period Schultes spent meandering around Colombia, hardly aware of "La Violencia" in Davis's telling but turning in reports to the US government about individual Colombians' political inclinations according to others. Marks, for his part, says Plowman was "unwitting of the CIA involvement" (1979: 218). Perhaps he was. But just as it is difficult to imagine, if you think about it flatly rather than through the golden haze of mythologizing, how Schultes simply beguiled the Colombian military into providing him with transport on a regular basis, it's hard to understand how two of Schultes's students accidentally ended up working for a CIA front company in the Peruvian Amazon.[5]

In his book, Davis describes Schultes as having been legendary at Harvard for getting students off marijuana possession charges by making a botanical argument about there being several species of hemp, and the consequent impossibility of prosecutors' proving that students weren't caught with the innocent fibrous sort rather than the naughty resinous one (1997: 24). Davis does not mention that Schultes's early 1970s interest in cannabis extended to actual fieldwork—not in Latin America, but in Afghanistan—which was at the time a source of legendary hashish and a profitable drug trade (see the photo in Schultes et al. 1992: 98). Strange coincidences proliferate: the period of Schultes's Afghan fieldwork would have been around the time of the coup that brought down King Mohammad Zahir Shah. The usurper was his cousin, Daoud Khan; Khan, of course, was in his turn overthrown in 1978 in a Communist coup that featured accusations of his having been a CIA client.

In a manner reminiscent of the first humbug we met in this book, Hernando Sanabria Fernández, who came in later life to elaborate upon stories he himself had invented in his "biography" of Apiaguaiki Tüpa, Schultes loved Davis's 1997 account of his life, with all its glorifications and elisions, so much that he began to use it as a reference for improving his own memory about himself:

In Schultes's last years, Davis has reported, the book took on a sort of "magical reality" for Schultes. He would open the book at random, and use passages to index forgotten episodes and conversations. In Davis's words, "the book had become his life." (Davis 2004, xi; Davis, qtd. in Sheldrake n.d.: 4n15)

From Davis's account, Schultes delighted in self-invention, happily allowing himself to be described as a "Boston Brahmin" after he had become enough of a Harvard fixture to pass for one, though in fact he was of humble, East Boston immigrant origins (Davis 1997, 63–65). The famous photos from the field of Schultes costumed for native festivals go in hand with his general commitment to costume and dress-up.

Margaret Krieg—the author of a 1964 book that goes notably uncited by Davis in his 1997 one—describes how at her first meeting with Schultes he was kitted out in a suit and top hat, with his commencement day regalia in view (71). This outfit was, she supposed, happenstantial; Schultes had not realized at the time they made the appointment that the day for her interview coincided with Harvard's graduation, when he'd be draped in his ceremonial garb. Maybe. During the 1960s Schultes took to wearing a white lab coat during lectures, the instrumental utility of which is dubious but the message in the context of the decade's sartorial politics quite clear. By all accounts, exotica were always on full display in his environs; no one who visited his office failed to mention the impressively long blowpipe prominently on show in it. These details about Schultes, and what they reveal about his attention to others' impressions, go a long way to explaining his charm. They even work a kind of wry magic on a skeptical-to-hostile observer such as myself (as did, of course, some of Sanabria Fernández's flourishes). There's often something rather flattering about humbug. It pays a lot of attention to impressions made, and ipso facto to impressees. Andrew Weil's memorial remembrance of Schultes, from his foreword to Davis 2004, is worth quoting at length:

> I first saw Dick Schultes in September 1960 in the Nash Lecture Hall of the Harvard Botanical Museum. He wore a long white lab coat, and he looked and acted every bit the Harvard professor. Though only forty-five at the time, he appeared rather stiff and stuffy, and his style of lecturing was very formal. Yet he had a twinkle about him that suggested something far livelier. He felt very familiar to me from the moment I first saw him, as if I had known him before. I sensed a connection with him that held my interest. His face fascinated me. His elegant patrician air, the resonant voice: both seemed so familiar and comfortable. I knew that I wanted to spend time with him. He had this effect on people. For those who fell under his spell, he was the ultimate mentor. (in Davis 2004: xiii).

PLANTS, PATRIARCHS, AND PROJECTION

Dr. Schultes produced several loyal academic sons. Preeminent among these is the Boswell to Schultes's Johnson, Wade Davis, Schultes's student and biographer. In a manner isomorphic to the shambling, accident-prone gait with which in Davis's telling of it Schultes and his students moved through the world, Davis's doctoral thesis was on the ethnopharmacology of Haitian zombies. Davis argued that zombies were not mere creatures of fantasy but that through a combination of drug dosing, psychological trauma, and cultural belief it would in fact be possible to create these eminently biddable persons. The specifics of his argument, having to do with the presence of neurotoxins derived from puffer fish, entombment and disinterring, and subsequent psychic capture by a witch doctor (supplemented by use of the poisonous plant known as the "zombie cucumber"), have been subjected to withering critique on scientific grounds (Booth 1988; Kao and Yasumoto 1990; Yasumoto and Kao 1986) and his fieldwork challenged on its ethical merits—during the course of it, he paid informants to dig up the body of a dead child for use in preparation of one of the zombie powders he sought (both his 1986 dissertation and 1987 book include photos of the disinterred small girl). Since the production of a very lurid Hollywood horror movie on the basis of a popular book by Davis on the subject, this study has been treated (not least by Davis himself) as something that began as an earnest inquiry, that was made silly by others, and that he has now distanced himself from as befits a serious academic. After a long and peripatetic career, Davis since 2011 holds an endowed chair in the Department of Anthropology at the University of British Columbia and has intimated he sees a future for himself in Canadian politics (Macdonald 2014).

The trajectory is continuous from curare in the 1940s to the "zombie cucumber" in the 1980s: the focus by Schultes and, later, his students on plant-derived psychoactive substances. According to Albarelli, the CIA's ARTICHOKE program hoped to find means of producing "chemical lobotomy" (2005: 294)—zombification, in essence. In the course of researching his book on MKULTRA, Jonathan Marks learned "a good deal of the human testing on new psychoactive drugs was done in Haiti" (cited in Albarelli 2005: 369). Davis's research journey into Haiti began when Schultes put him in touch with psychiatrists Nathan Kline and Heinz Lehman. These two men, in turn, recommended the young Davis to one of their former students, Lamarque Douyon. Dr. Douyon was working at the time as the head of a psychiatric center in Port-au-Prince.

Dr. Douyon had done his psychiatric residency at McGill University during the Ewen Cameron years and at Dr. Cameron's urging had done some preliminary work on the so-called zombie cucumber (Davis 1987: 58). Dr. Cameron headed a

CIA-funded program of human experimentation at McGill involving heavy LSD dosing and intensive electroshock "therapy" that has since become notorious (E. Dyck 2007); he also made extensive use of curare to immobilize test subjects on whom he was performing his unsuccessful "psychic driving" experiments (Gillmore 1987: 88, 128).[6] Davis mentions Cameron's association with McGill, but only to insist that Cameron's "dark" practices ended with his retirement in 1964 (1987: 59).

They had not. Everyone supporting Davis's Haitian foray had extensive ties to the same sort of research done by Cameron. Dr. Nathan Kline also carried out CIA-supported LSD research at his Rockland Institute (Albarelli 2005: 370); Lehman, at McGill, pioneered the use of Thorazine among psychiatric patients at very high dosage levels (Swazey 1974). The person who eventually analyzed Davis's "zombie powder" samples (and was the only researcher to document their zombifying effect on animals, in unpublished personal communication to Davis [1987: 147]—these effects were never independently reproduced by other investigators) was Dr. Leon Roizin. Some of Roizin's best-known work was on the brain-damaging effects of electroconvulsive therapies (Ferraro and Roizin 1949). With this we come full circle: Davis has Kline offering the same justification for sending him after zombie drugs as Schultes and Davis do for Schultes's curare research in the 1940s—that these were to be used in surgical anaesthesia (Davis 1987: 23). In both cases, however, this is misdirection; the motivating interest was psychiatric.

The themes of projection and misdirection that arose first in chapter 3 around Wounded Knee become quite acute in the bad-faith works of Davis and Schultes. Davis actually makes a joke about CIA funding in his 1987 popular account of his zombie research: he has a technician working on one of his puffer fish samples ask, "'Schultes have you working for the CIA, or what?' He laughed out loud." (134). This technician-character then launches into a story involving the greatest of all fictional cloak-and-dagger men, James Bond. The way Davis raises this possibility, joins it to laughter and fantasy, and dismisses it is rather good. Less adroitly, in his original doctoral thesis he makes a series of statements about the role of voodoo in Haitian society that purport to explain the rise and hold on power of Papa Doc Duvalier in terms of voodoo and secret societies, saying these latter "explain the rise and fall of the Tonton Macoutes" (1986: 16) and as he elaborates in his conclusion:

> In the end, one might almost ask whether or not Francois Duvalier himself did not become the symbolic or effective head of the secret societies . . . One thing is certain. The members of the secret societies will continue to function as an underground government with their emperors, kings, queens, presidents and cabinet ministers, army officers, soldiers and diplomats and their leaders will continue to engage in local and national politics. (1986, 427–430)

Davis ends resoundingly:

> In outlining the sociological role of zombification within the peasant society, this research reveals the political and legal dimensions of an understudied belief system. The network of power relations that this investigation has revealed relates to all levels of Haitian political life, and as such sheds light on many recent aspects of Haitian political history which have yet to be explained adequately: in particular, the meteoric rise under Francois Duvalier of the Tonton Macoute. (1986: 433)

Other commentators have suggested that the rise to power of Papa Doc Duvalier and his employment of a brutal personal disciplinary force in Haiti are not actually that mysterious and certainly not endogenous to Haiti. Early on in his rule, in 1958, a coup attempt was made against Duvalier, which he faced down with US military support; in the years after that, US Marine military advisors came and trained the forces that would become his Tonton Macoutes (Sprague 2012). In fact, the "secret society," the role of which goes most consistently underexplored in understanding Haitian dynamics, cannot be traced back to West African religion but instead to North American imperialism.

FROM COLD WARRIOR TO ECOWARRIOR

How is it that these immensely well-connected men so consistently have been able to throw the switches on where power lies and which inscrutable mysteries actually remain unplumbed? How is it that their obfuscatory accounts inspire such boundless, credulous trust in modern Western (particularly North American) audiences? Schultes's name is synonymous in many quarters with virtuous eco- and indigene-friendly inquiry, and Wade Davis has been fondly hailed as "Canada's Indiana Jones" (Hampson 2014). It is difficult to separate out, across the 1990s, who is the student and who the master in the business of recasting a couple of pretty weird and shady shared trajectories into those of two scientific eminences interested in nothing so much as the hidden potentials of indigenous knowledge, the precarious position of indigenous peoples, and—encompassing both—the protection of the environment.

In 1990, Schultes published his crowning opus, *The Healing Forest* (with Raffauf). For a work of science, it is surprisingly derivative: a list of plants from the Northwest Amazon purported to be medicinally useful, each paired with an overview of other sources referring to them, and a note as to when plants were tested for the presence of alkaloids (which could potentially correlate to applied usages but only at the level of a preliminary screen). It repeats, in many places, data already presented in a previous book copublished with the Swiss discoverer of LSD Albert Hofmann and entitled, *The Botany and Chemistry of Hallucinogens*. This earlier book was first put out by a commercial publisher in 1973 and in a second edition in 1980, though the 1980 edition does not bring readers up to speed about the fact that the series editor, the spectacularly monikered Isaac Newton Kugelmass, whose introduction appears in both versions, had had his license to practice medicine revoked by the state of New York in 1978 for being "guilty of practicing the profession fraudulently, with gross incompetence, and with gross negligence, and of unprofessional conduct" and had died in 1979.

The manuscript of *The Healing Forest* was completed during a residency at the Rockefeller Foundation's Study Centre at Bellagio, Lake Como, Italy (Schultes and Raffauf 1990: 38), and it does rather better than Isaac Newton Kugelmass for prefatory matter. It features a foreword from HRH Prince Philip, then president of the World Wide Fund for Nature (WWF). The Prince mentions the award by the WWF in 1984 of its Gold Medal for Conservation to Schultes (since Prince Philip's retirement in 1996, this has been renamed the Duke of Edinburgh Medal for Conservation in his honor). The WWF is notorious for its elite, corporate-friendly approach to conservation (Barker 2008; Huismann 2012).

With this reference, we can begin to return to Isoso. Thomas Lovejoy, former director of the WWF-US, was among the architects of the international conservation policies behind the national park project in Isoso, which left behind at least as much bitterness and recrimination in the community as the traditional medicine project did at Aguarati-mi (see Lowrey 2003, Lowrey 2008a). The direct agents of the national park project were Conservation International—a 1993 CI "Rapid Assessment Program" working paper provided much of the scientific justification for establishing the Parque Nacional Kaa-Iyaa del Gran Chaco; Thomas Lovejoy sits on CI's Conservation Council (Barker 2009)—and the Wildlife Conservation Society (WCS), which has long been associated with the Rockefeller family. Laurance Rockefeller was a major funder and former executive committee member of its predecessor organization, the New York Zoological Society.

As it happens, the Rockefeller family has contributed considerable funding to the cause of "alternative and integrative medicine," endowing a Laurance S. Rockefeller Chair in the same at Memorial Sloan Kettering Cancer Centre in New York. The WWF's Prince Philip's eldest son, Charles, is similarly boosterish about alternative medicine in the United Kingdom (Barker 2013). Canada is home to the world's largest prize for complementary and alternative medicine, the $250,000 Dr. Rogers Prize annually awarded for "excellence" in it. It is endowed by the Lotte and John Hecht Memorial Foundation, otherwise notable for aggressively funding educational reform of the "school choice" variety. The original source of the Hecht fortune is arms dealing (Gutstein 2005). As Michael James Barker notes, "Providing placebo therapies for patients is much cheaper than providing real medical treatment.

Thus alternative medicines offer a cheap alternative to those members of the ruling class intent on gutting existing health services" (2013: n.p.).

Little by little, the congruence of the traditional medicine project and the national park project in Isoso has come to me to seem less and less accidental and more and more like a kind of heartless human experimentation on a vulnerable population, the Isoseño. Thomas Lovejoy is known as a proponent of free-market approaches to biological conservation and first proposed "debt for nature" swaps, by which heavily externally indebted nations such as Bolivia might be forgiven some of their external debt in return for establishing protected areas. When I began my fieldwork, American WCS employees repeatedly emphasized to me that the *parque* was absolutely not established on a "debt for nature" swap basis, though given the extensive USAID funding flowing into it, it was also not established absent American intervention. Bolivians with whom I spoke did not contradict this; what they consistently insisted upon was the relevance of the Chaco's extensive subsoil hydrocarbon resources to the park's establishment. Thomas Lovejoy sits with Wade Davis on the advisory board of Hunt Global Partnerships, which, according to its website, since its establishment in 2006 "advises Hunt Oil Company on the best approaches for mitigating the social and environmental impacts of Hunt operations in Peru."[7] What was "friend to the Indian" Schultes doing on military transport after military transport in Colombia in the 1940s and early 1950s? What are noted conservationists Thomas Lovejoy and Wade Davis doing advising one of the world's largest oil companies? Maybe I spent too long in Isoso talking to Isoseño people about witchcraft. Nevertheless, like Don Jorge diagnosing witchcraft, there are times when I feel right down in my **pia** that "there is something."[8]

SHAMANS AND PLANTS

In 1975, Schultes's friend and colleague, the Colombian anthropologist Gerardo Reichel-Dolmatoff, published a study entitled *The Shaman and the Jaguar*. It makes an analysis of a by now familiar type—that the work of the shaman is to embody and manage native neurosis and that these neuroses are internal crises projected on to the external world. To reiterate, then: "natives" are neurotic and prone to projection; you can tell by looking closely at shamanism.

Schultes writes in his invited foreword to his friend Dolmatoff's book: "Man in primitive societies lives in a much closer and more personal association with his ambient vegetation that man in our modern technological cultures. Shamanism depends in great part on the supernatural powers resident in certain plants" (p. xiii). The first sentence is indubitably true; the second, just as certainly, untrue. It is true that shamanism in a few places (and, perhaps even more delimitedly, only in a few time periods; see Gow 1996) depends on plant hallucinogens. In the overwhelming preponderance of instances about which anthropologists know, and collect in one way or another under the header of "shamanism," it does not. Why, then, would Schultes say something so easily disproven and wildly at odds with the empirical facts and why would this false statement become so widely circulated, repeated, and believed?

There are two reasons, one ideological and one material. The ideological reason returns us again to white projection onto Indians. Schultes, who went into Indian territory in search of plant sources of psychoactive mind control in the service of dealing with a collective white society neurosis (worries about the specter of communism and various liberatory social agendas—anticolonial, antiracist, feminist—after the Second World War), ends up asserting that his own particular agenda is a key feature of Indian existence. He repeats the idea in *The Healing Forest*, saying, "the shamans or medicine men who are repositories of tribal lore and almost always men with impressive knowledge of the properties and uses of vegetation" (1990: 17). Again, while the first part of the statement is generally true, the second is generally false.

Some of what Schultes ends up saying is toweringly ludicrous. He calls ayahuasca "the most important medicine of the Amazonian Indians" (Schultes et al. 1992: 12), which it certainly is not. Most Amazonian Indians do not use ayahuasca at all. He says, "hallucinogens . . . become the firm basis for 'medical' practices of most, if not all, aboriginal societies" (14), which is not remotely borne out by the ethnographic and ethnohistorical literature. He projects these ideas onto the history of Europe, describing how among medieval witches "one concoction containing belladonna, henbane, mandrake, and the fat of a stillborn child was rubbed on the skin or inserted into the vagina for absorption" (89). Here an obviously misogynistic psychosexual poison fantasy from the era is subjected to a double twist: earnestly noted as fact and then processed through a separate (but equally perverse and elaborate) set of fantasies about the ur-nature of "primitive man," giving premodern Europe a history invented in Cold War America by way of a fabulated version of "Red Injun" lore.

All of this reaches its apogee when processed through the ethnohistorical speculations of Schultes's erstwhile travelling companion, Weston LaBarre. Their research relationship of long standing began of course with that joint trip in 1936 to study the so-called peyote cult among the Kiowa in Oklahoma. The use of peyote in the United States is associated with the emergence and expansion of the Native American Church, which combines features of Protestant Christianity with Amerindian practices of diverse origin (usage of peyote, ceremonial tipi, drumming, and gourd rattles). The history of the Native American Church is intertwined with the spread of settler colonialism in the American West in the late nineteenth and early twentieth centuries.[9] It is precisely not a window into a prehistoric

Amerindian past, still less a primeval human past. The same may well be true of aya-huasca shamanism, which plays such a key role in Schultes's accounts of Amazonia (Gow 1996).[10]

The rather fantastic conclusions at which Schultes and LaBarre arrive are worth quoting at length. These are taken from an edited volume published in 1972 enti-tled *Flesh of the Gods: The Ritual Use of Hallucinogens* to which both Schultes and LaBarre contributed essays. Schultes's opening essay introduces an idea that LaBarre's closing essay will repeat and elaborate: that the New World shows more usage of hallucinogens than the Old because the societies of the Americas were primitive hunter-gathering societies; shamanism is the religion of primitive hunter-gathering societies; thus as hallucinogens are central to shamanic (and, thus, primi-tive religious) practice, they will be found more in places that still maintain such primitive ways of life. The first two premises being entirely wrong, the conclusion is of course wrong as well. The wrongness of the first premise is becoming more clear with every passing year (a well-written and accessible summary of recent findings can be found in Mann 2005); the wrongness of the second premise has to do with the fact that shamanism in all the places where it has been studied seriously has turned out to have an intimate rather than innocent relationship to history. In no place where shamanism is practiced does it give evidence of being "primeval" but rather the reverse. For the moment, though, let us consider LaBarre's florid asser-tions on the basis of this totally wrong constellation of ideas.

LaBarre's mode of analysis was reviewed at length in chapter 3, of course, but it is worth rehearsing when considering why Schultes's ersatz vision has proved to be so popular with modern audiences. La Barre says, "Like the paranoid schizophrenic, the vatic personality pretends to be talking about the grandiose outside cosmic world but he is really talking grandiosely in symbolic ways only about his narcis-sistic self and his inner world" (1972: 265) and "A neurosis or psychosis is the patho-logical operator of the defense mechanisms of a confused and troubled individual under stress. A religion is in origin the defense mechanism of a society in confused and crisis-torn times" (265) and, most deliciously, "The unreal omnipotence of the shaman is the reciprocal of the unreal helplessness of the cultist" (207).

This last statement does not resemble the actual practice of shamanism in Isoso (or, as I will show in the next chapter, other places either) in the least. As we have seen, the more powerful the shaman, the more suspect he is, and in fact no one seeks or expects perfect curative efficacy from a shaman there (or anywhere else from which we have actual ethnographic accounts of shamanism, as opposed to erratically sourced inventions about it). What LaBarre's statement does resemble rather per-fectly, however, is the entire faux edifice of pseudoshamanism puffed up by Schultes and his devotees. They postulate the existence of a primeval body of knowledge and associated practitioners who can heal all ills, bodily and ecological, and they do so from a position of "unreal helplessness"—that is, a position that in actual fact is, without hyperbole, allied with the CIA, the Rockefeller Foundation, Hunt Oil, the gilded World Wildlife Federation, and the stuffiest male members (in a stiff competition)[11] of the British Royal family. The charges of craziness and paranoia that fly off the pages of LaBarre, directed at superstitious Indians, are manifestations of white chicanery that support quite seriously the cartooniest of conspiracy theories. By now when I read a LaBarre saying something like "shamanism is, so to speak, culturally programmed for an interest in hallucinogens and other psychotropic drugs" (272), well, I reach for my blow gun.

Trudging, as I have in the course of researching this book, up and down the mountains of bad faith with which its landscape is lousy, the faux-folksy earnestness of certain Schultes devotees begins to wear very thin. One last exorcism, and then I'll stop. Mark Plotkin is the author of the popular 1993 book *Tales of a Shaman's Apprentice: An Ethnobotanist Searches for New Medicines in the Amazon Rain Forest.* Plotkin was not a favored son of Schultes in the way that Plowman or Davis were. Slightly younger, he grafted himself onto Harvard and the Schultes legacy but he obtained his PhD at the much-less-prestigious Tufts.

Plotkin cites some of the precursor popularizing accounts of ethnobotany much less obliquely than does the more successful Wade Davis, who is probably more alert to what this somewhat embarrassing older literature means for its present prospects and so more cautious about invoking them. Two important such texts are Nicole Maxwell's 1961 *Witch Doctor's Apprentice: Hunting for Medicinal Plants in the Amazon* (to which Plotkin's title pays very direct homage) and Krieg's *Green Medicine: The Search for Plants that Heal* (1964). Davis cites the first book as being about "medicinal plants, especially of the Iquitos area" (1997: 513) and gives as its publication date that of its third edition (1990). This is a telling bit of misdirection. The Krieg he does not cite at all, which is strange considering how many Schultes-related anecdotes that appear in Davis's 1997 *One River* first appeared in her 1964 text.[12]

Both Maxwell's and Krieg's books, properly considered, are rather depressing indicators for the contemporary ethnopharmaceutical enterprise because their rhetoric, projections, and commitments are so identical to everything said 30, 40, 50 years later—with no new results in the interim (Estes 1994). A further embarrassment in Krieg's book is that Schultes is one in a series of "plant hunters" interviewed with great seriousness and admiration by Krieg (as is his *Healing Forest* coauthor, Robert Raffauf). Another is Bruce Halstead, convicted in California in 1986 of administering fraudulent "natural" therapies for cancer.[13] Small wonder that Davis let this text and the associations it suggests pass quietly unremarked. Maxwell's book, for its part, in 1961 writes of the amazing properties of *sangre de grado* (sometimes also written "sangre de drago," "dragon's blood") and *uña de gato* (cat's claw), which continue to be trotted out right up to the present as worthy of "further" investigation, as if anything new could be discovered about either after fifty more years. Worst of all, both of these early 1960s authors were women—saying and doing the same things years earlier but to almost no acclaim that Schultes's acolytes reprised decades later as swashbuckling male adventure (to much greater popular success).

Maxwell amusingly reports, as later works fail to do, on the enthusiasm of her informants for remedies derived from animal sources. This absence is especially telling of the vastly more intense scrutiny the entire ethnobotanical enterprise ought to receive than it has. The arguments for ethnobotanical investigation would apply equally well to traditional remedies derived from animal sources—the jaguar and red **teyu** (lizard) fat mentioned by my informants in Isoso, or, say, the bear bile and rhino horn advocated in some quarters of Chinese medicine. Mutatis mutandis, the same people pressed for plant wisdom should have their suggestions about lizard fat taken seriously on the same grounds; they have known their environment for years, have experimented over many generations with the possibilities afforded by its flora and fauna, such that both their plant- and animal-derived ideas ought to merit solicitation, documentation, and screening. Nevertheless, I have yet to read the memoirs of a celebrated collector of bear bile lore and harvester of lizard grease, nor met an undergraduate who aspires to become one (all anthropology professors have met dozens of undergraduates interested in "traditional plant medicine").

Returning to Plotkin, his book about himself is reminiscent of Davis's book about Schultes in that it is full of telling elisions, but they are more notable for appearing in a first-person account. There are things Davis couldn't know about Schultes's past, but surely Plotkin remembers his own life. Nevertheless, Plotkin does not explain how he arranged his first extended fieldwork in Suriname, though he mentions political upheaval upon his arrival in December 1982: "The politics of the situation were obscure . . . no one really knew the details" (Plotkin 1993: 81). This is a peculiar way to describe the notorious "December murders" under the military dictatorship of Dési Bouterse, the details of which certainly were well known by the time Plotkin was writing his book. According to Plotkin, he "hung around" an airplane hangar until he met a pilot planning to go to an Indian village the next day (82). Upon arrival, finding that it was inhabited by people of several origins—Trio, Waiwai, and Apalai—he was delighted to have "stumbled on to an ethnobotanical gold mine" (85). Anyone who has done fieldwork in an indigenous community in South America knows that this story is at best undertold and at worst egregiously obfuscatory.[14] Plotkin spent two months in the community, Kwamala. Writing of when he went back for a month in 1983, he refers to a man whom he nicknames the "Jaguar Shaman" as his "mentor" (1993: 135); in 1985, on another month-long trip, he meets a shaman from a different village whom he says "obviously considered me a student or apprentice" (212). In 1986, under auspices again not specified, he visits a Yanomami community in Venezuela for perhaps two weeks. In 1988, he returns to Kamala in Suriname, allegedly finding it drastically transformed in the lapse of three short years by "civilization," which somehow had not reached it between the beginning of time and 1985.

When I contacted Plotkin while researching this book, he told me I would not be able to obtain a copy of his doctoral thesis because he had made special confidentiality arrangements in order to protect the valuable indigenous knowledge contained within its pages from prying Western eyes. I was, in fact, able to obtain it via the usual university interlibrary loan arrangements. What I wanted to know was if the thesis was any more forthcoming about the logistical details of his research than was the book. It was not. He did at one point in the thesis mention, with disgust and relief, that he'd managed to do all of his fieldwork without once sampling manioc chicha, a staple of Amazonian diet. This comment alone raises questions about the seriousness of his time in the field. It's akin to asserting that one did fieldwork among the Nuer whilst avoiding all beef and dairy products or lived for years in the suburbs of Canada whilst managing never to discuss ice hockey.

How did such a silly and dishonest set of ideas come to be so influential? Why did Susan Sarandon narrate a documentary about Plotkin's book, and why do so many undergraduates, thirty years on, parrot its assertions uncritically? Plotkin simplifies and amplifies Schultes's claims when he says: "Shamans are not only the crucial link between the tropical rain forest and our neighborhood pharmacy: I believe they are our greatest hope for finding cures to currently incurable diseases (cancer, AIDS, the common cold)" (1993: 14). Time has not borne this hope out even remotely (Dalton 2004).

Reading the literature in ethnobotany, many of its most exalted claims refer back to the authority of Schultes himself. The trappings of power and authority serve as their guarantee in his case. That he was a Harvard man, that he was lionized, that his magnum opus featured a foreword from British royalty seem to have dazzled everyone about the less credible portions of his own story, the fishier dimensions of the careers of his mentees, the way his most fundamental assertions about the value of ethnobotanical knowledge have never been validated, and, most fundamentally, that his assertions about the intimate connection between shamanism and esoteric plant knowledge in South America are simply fraudulent. In place of doing or citing serious ethnographic research, Schultes conjured up just-so stories:

> Beset by hunger, early man experimented with all plant materials he could chew.
> He could not have avoided discovering the intoxicating properties of *Cannabis*, for

in his quest for the nutritious seeds and oil, he certainly ate the sticky tops of the plant, the most narcotic part. The euphoric, ecstatic, and hallucinatory aspects of the intoxication may have introduced him to an otherworldly plane from which emerged religious beliefs, perhaps even the concept of deity. The plant became accepted as a special gift of the gods, a sacred medium for communication with the spiritual world. And such it has remained in some cultures to the present. (1973: 62)

Schultes was a flagrant humbug and sower of a flamboyant series of humbug seed-lings and yet is immortally surrounded by an odor of sanctity. Thinking about why this should be so returns us to the problem at the heart of the book, which is what set of positionings is met with suspicion and scrutiny in different cultural contexts: power and autonomy in some, weakness and dependence in others. It also brings us to a final reason this narrative gained such ferocious purchase in the final decades of the twentieth century (in the hands of men and governments) despite rehashing buoyantly optimistic claims put forth (by obscure, and sometimes actively obscured, women) as early as the early 1960s and never borne out.

CAN'T INDIANS AND THE ENVIRONMENT SAVE THEMSELVES AND PAY FOR IT TOO WHILE THEY ARE AT IT?

As I have analyzed at length in a previously published article (Lowrey 2008a), both the traditional medicine project and national park project that were active in Isoso during my first forays partook of global exhortations to self-sufficiency emerging with considerable ferocity in the 1980s and into the 1990s. In the field of health care provision, the World Health Organization's 1977 Declaration of Alma-Ata proclaimed an agenda of "Health for All by 2000," which directly guided ethno-botanical research in Isoso (Gallo Toro 1996: 1). Part of its plan was to incorporate "traditional medicine" into systems of health care provision in parts of the world where this was the only kind of medicine to which people had access. Devoid of cynicism though this call may have been at the outset, it fit a global aid and develop-ment agenda emergent across the 1980s and 1990s that was cynical in the extreme in the context of aid from donor nations dropping between the 1960s and 2010 from 0.5 percent to 0.3 percent of Gross National Income (OECD 2012). The appeal of a narrative in which diversity (cultural and biological), properly investigated and appreciated, could be turned to the twin ends of capitalist profit (obviating the need for external aid) and "cure," thereby ending "dependency" (financial, social, physical, moral, and spiritual), was gargantuan. Mindful of the ableism embedded in the term, I still will deploy it this once to point out that the notion that the people with some of the worst health indicators in the world ought to get busy sav-ing all of us with their secret stores of medical knowledge was totally crazy.

The profoundly confused notion that shamans are "like doctors" or "like scientists" had some very powerful policy consequences during the 1980s and 1990s. Articulating a condescending tribute made by modern Western rational-technical utility to a diverse cultural array of essentially magic-minded phenomena, it intersected during those decades with the tremendous expansion of funding to international nongovernmental organizations all clamoring for support in the name of promoting somebody else's self-sufficiency (usually very, very vulnerable somebodies). I speak here to the outcomes in Isoso, but what took place there was also happening in local versions in many places around the world in the 1980s and 1990s and into the early 2000s.

In Isoso, the Swiss Red Cross funded a medical care initiative during the 1980s that sought to incorporate Western and non-Western approaches and perspectives. Shamans such as Don Miguel and Don Jorge were enrolled as paid consultants in an ambitious project that brought medical supplies, visiting doctors, training programs for local midwives and local "health promoters" to Isoso. There were some of the usual problems with misdirection of funds but for the most part this program was a success, at least in Isoseño eyes. For many years afterward people spoke of it wistfully, as a kind of health care golden age. The Swiss Red Cross was less pleased with it, because of the failure of repeated schemes to make it self-sustaining. One such attempt was the creation of "community farms" in each village. People were supposed to volunteer time to their cultivation, and the sale of the harvested products was to underwrite health care costs. This plan did not work. Another scheme assessed a direct (and low) fee to each family as a kind of collectively funded health insurance coverage. Fee collection had dismal yields. By the late 1990s the Swiss Red Cross left Isoso, and the programs it had paid for came to an end.

While the traditional medicine laboratory at Aguarati-mi absorbed a lot of my attention, it was relatively small potatoes in Isoso during the 1990s and early 2000s. This era was the high-water mark of NGO attentiveness, including that multimillion dollar project that recruited the Isoseño leadership to act as coadministrators of that enormous national park in the Bolivian Chaco established in 1995 (again, see Lowrey 2003 and 2008a for a detailed treatment). Every Isoseño village longed for a small subproject of its own, and though the laboratory was affiliated specifically with Don Miguel, the village closest to his home welcomed its proposal and establishment. All of these projects eventually suffered similar fates, with outside funders becoming exasperated by the inability of Isoseño people to find ways to make the undertakings financially independent and eventually withdrawing support. Financial mismanagement by Isoseño leadership tasked to direct these projects from offices in Santa Cruz was also a continual problem. Since 2009, the once-powerful Capitanía del Alto y Bajo Isoso has been effectively supplanted by two separate entities: one Capitanía for Alto and one Capitanía for Bajo. These entities continue to pursue project funding of various stripes, but now work much more closely with the departmental and national governments than with international NGOs.

Leaders in the two new organizations blame past mismanagement by CABI for the apparent unwillingness of NGOs to continue investing in projects in Isoso. The remnant of CABI, which still exists, albeit in hollowed-out form, meanwhile, blames the existence of the two new organizations for undermining CABI's former position as the sole, genuine, and unitary representative of Isoso for purposes of external collaboration. Amidst this strife, Isoseño people from the village level to that of urbane leaders who have been city dwellers for years all speak in one voice of their desire for new "projects" (the Spanish term, *proyectos*, is used). It doesn't matter, really, what the projects are about (environment, cattle raising, women's empowerment, education, health, and agriculture are the usual suspects): the point is to have more projects. Whenever I go back to Isoso, I am asked by many people to establish a project of some sort, or at least to seek out contacts with entities that might fund projects in Isoso.

There is nothing easier than being cynical about this, and, of course, everyone is. External funders and NGO employees lament the insincerity of Isoseño commitment to project aims; Isoseño people lament the insincerity of external funder and NGO employee commitment to Isoso. Each side charges the other with bad faith and phoniness. In many instances the charges can stick all too easily all round; examples of farcical development projects the only real purpose of which is to pay salaries for a while to all involved are all too common in Isoso (as elsewhere). The most recently recounted to me, in 2013 (and by an Isoseño person) was of a "women's apiculture" project that harvested a total of two liters of honey in a year, at the end of which it failed, and into which $14,000 dollars disappeared: two $7,000 liters of honey, a price even the global rich would hesitate to pay. I haven't seen its funding proposal but am confident it proposed a promising-sounding formula for involving women in a relatively low-labor enterprise that would (given the proverbial industriousness of bees) provide a reliable source of cash income over and above the costs of maintenance and production. I don't know why it failed, though I imagine it did so for the same reason many similar projects fail. I do think I know why people (including Isoseño people) like to tell this one story out of all the possible similar stories about failed projects one could choose (sexism). The general point, though, holds: self-sufficiency is not as easily achieved as it is prescribed.

In all of these projects, very poor people have to promise a fealty to future states of nondependence in order to have immediate dependency needs addressed. Nongovernmental organization workers (and external funders) are not required to design farcical plans for their own eventual emancipation from salary earning or grant pursuing, though it must be said that the entire expanding universe of NGOs is premised upon its own abolishment on that happy future day when all of the projects everywhere throw aside their external funding crutches and walk. A kind of performance is the price of entry to the world of projects, in which one must disavow the motives for playing along. You must make believe that you have no dependency needs in order to get those very needs met.

While doing my doctoral fieldwork and for a few years afterward, I spent tremendous amounts of time trying to track down funding numbers relating to projects, to figure out where the money was going. It was for that reason gloriously satisfying to read the report of an external consultant eventually brought in to do exactly that for the national park project and learn how unable he was to locate relevant documentation (Estrada 2010). When the money was rolling, lots of people—outsiders and Isoseño—were zipping around in four-wheel drive vehicles, holding informational meetings in the villages, and traveling to "capacity-building" (*capacitación*) workshops in the city. Without wishing to flog the point too heavy-handedly, I do ask the reader to note, again, the focus on "capability" as the supreme virtue to be cultivated in these efforts.

HUMAN EXPERIMENTATION

During the time I was doing fieldwork, a gas pipeline was built across one corner of the Kaa-Iya National Park. The Wildlife Conversation Society cooperated with Shell Oil and Enron in order to facilitate the building of the pipeline with some degree of environmental oversight and attention to the needs of affected indigenous communities—mostly Chiquitano and Ayoreo, as the pipeline was far from Isoso proper (Hindery 2013)—but with some indemnification for Isoseño people included in the plans. Many people built new homes under the auspices of this part of the deal, including Don Jorge. For a while, Bolivian pipeline roughnecks were traveling through Isoso regularly, churning up dust with their SUVs and heavy equipment, causing all kinds of gossip and speculation (e.g., that they were going to build a bridge across the Parapetí in Isoso and pave its roads, at least with gravel: neither came to pass). Some oil employees stayed, for a while, at Don Miguel's laboratory, in return for which they dug that new well and poured a cement tank for watering his cattle. This was around the time I was moving from Don Miguel's home to the third and final village in which I lived during fieldwork, Güirapembirenda (more commonly known as Rancho Viejo). The village *capitán* there, with whose family I came to live, told me that the gas companies had to negotiate with the **iyaareta** (masters of the forest) about extracting oil and gas: a certain number of lives would have to be given in exchange. The reason the company employees had come and left again episodically over the years was because of the haggling: the gas companies would agree to a few lives without a second thought; if they went away again this time (which in the end they did), it would be because the iyaareta had asked for "too many lives."

It is interesting that I heard this version of "impact assessment" in Rancho Viejo, the village in Isoso most affected by the War of the Chaco (1932–1935) in ways I will explore further in the final chapter of the book. Rockefeller-owned Standard Oil (on the Bolivian side) and Royal Dutch Shell (on the Paraguayan side) played either a directing or contributing role in that conflict, depending on the account. For many years, a conceit I attempted to deploy to frame my fieldwork was that of the shaman and his laboratory being a sort of surrealist, Marcel Duchampian ready-made, as "beautiful as" in Lautréamont's words "the chance encounter of a sewing machine and an umbrella on a dissecting table." The strange juxtaposition of a sha-man and a laboratory in the arid eerie "netherlands" of the Chaco! No doubt this gnomic, poetic phrase insistently suggested itself to my plodding social-scientific mind thanks to the actual abandoned sewing machine that was a permanent feature of the waste space behind the laboratory. But the lab, in general, charms me in its incongruity much less than it once did, not least because the graves of two people whom I knew and loved now rest beside it: that of Don Miguel and his adult daugh-ter Victoria.

It didn't end badly just for Don Miguel, the shaman in Isoso who most closely approximated a set of misguided external ideas about what being a paye was all about. The traditional medicine "laboratory" is abandoned. The Parque Nacional Kaa-Iyaa del Gran Chaco still exists, but in many respects the involvement of Isoseño people with it has been destructive for their community. Before and during my fieldwork, the **Mburuvicha Guasu** ("Grand Chief") of all Isoso was Bonifacio Barrientos Cuellar, "Boni Chico," son of Bonifacio Barrientos Iyambae, **Kuaraya Guasu,** "Great Shade." As his star rose with the parque project, Boni Chico became closely involved with regional "Camba" politicians, white agrobusiness and hydro-carbon elites who have adopted a Chiriguano identity in order to fend off accu-sations of anti-indigene racism while still ferociously opposing government policy radiating from the Andes (see Lowrey 2006c). Their rallying cry is regional "auton-omy," which sits very well with modernist discourses of independence and invul-nerability. The aspects of Chiriguano identity they most promote are exactly those championed by Sanabria Fernández in his humbug account of Bolivian Guaraní his-tory: that of the masculine warrior, the **kereimba.** Don Boni was elected to politi-cal office on one of their party platforms but later pursued on corruption charges for selling Isoseño lands to private, non-Indian buyers (including Mennonites) and was denounced in 2006 by representatives from the new Isoso, now divided into rival Alto y Bajo Capitanías that dispute the remains of CABI's united and once rather formidable powers. The language in which they expressed this denunciation is telling: they say Boni betrayed the memory of the "**Kereimbas** and **Iyambaes**": the warriors and those "without owner," a funny old set of avatars for a Chané slave society to concern itself with defending (Bolpress 2009).

I last saw Don Boni in 2013, when I dropped by the formerly bustling but then rather lonesome offices of CABI in a posh-approximate neighborhood in the city of Santa Cruz de la Sierra. Bonifacio Barrientos Cuellar was found dead in an empty lot in a suburb of Santa Cruz in 2014. His body lay unclaimed for five days in a city morgue before his family located him. He had last been seen in the company of karai associates. His death, and that of Don Miguel, seem to me outcomes of impossible traps set by phony notions of power and masculinity that never catch the white men who set them, only the Indians who fall in. I know that this makes whites seem all-powerful and indigenes defenseless in a way that is badly out of favor according to current sensibilities, not least anthropological ones. But to tell it otherwise would seem to me to be faithless to Don Miguel's and Don Boni's memories and to the way the Isoseño people and families that I know actually see the world. Don Boni's family found his death extremely suspicious, though the Santa Cruz coroner's office counted it as heart failure (Don Boni had suffered heart problems stemming from Chagas disease for many years). Similarly, Don Miguel's family is quite convinced he was done in by an accursed conspiracy stretching far outside Bolivia, into rich Western donor nations, and involving shady white characters. I no longer think they are wrong. Not one bit.

6

Wizards and Ghosts

Like many Amerindian shamans, Don Miguel sang inaudible songs when curing people. Don Jorge, to my knowledge, did not. This may be related to the latter's acquisition of his **paye** extrasocially and not through an apprenticeship that involved acquiring a repertoire of songs. In both of their cases, others aspects of their practical repertoires were also consistent with what is reported about shamanism in many other parts of lowland South America: determining, while in a very mildly altered state (in Isoso, induced by smoking cigarettes and chewing coca; hallucinogens are unknown), the location of malevolent objects and removing them by sucking them out by mouth. These objects are called in Guaraní **mbaeruvi**, a term translated in Spanish as *bicho*, or bug (possible etymologies of the term can be found in Lowrey 2003: 183n11). The witch who causes illness manages to get a **mbaeruvi isi**, or "mbaeruvi-mother," into the body of the victim, which then proliferates. A variety of quite inconsistent means whereby the witch accomplishes this were described to me during my fieldwork in response to my prompting, but it is not a problem of much interest to Isoseño people. The point is that witches (who may be men or women) manage to do it, and if shamanic treatment proceeds as it ought, the **isi** will eventually be found. Along the way, offspring mbaeruvi are removed across many sessions while the mother is sought and the patient is prepared for the final excision. This may take months or even years. The patient may die or choose to end treatment or seek alternate treatment before this last step is reached. It is only when the mother is found and removed that the paye clearly "sees"

DOI: 10.5876/9781646420360.c006

the responsible witch, though he may have an idea of his or her identity sooner. While other kinds of supernatural illness are possible—caused, for example, by offending spirit masters of the forest or the river (the handling of these illnesses was something with which Don Jorge was particularly adept)—Don Miguel specialized in illness caused by human witches. If either thought a case was best referred to a medical doctor or different shamanic specialist, they would indicate this to the supplicant. They could sometimes be disparaging of younger **payerai** within Isoso and were quite disparaging about urban practitioners known as *espiritistas* but not of the fact that people sought help from a wide array of sources to deal with their problems. All of the illness histories I recorded during my fieldwork included a long recitation of treatments sought from the most varied of sources (shamans, medical doctors, espiritistas and *naturistas*—spiritualists and naturopaths—in the city, faith healers of various denominations: see Lowrey 2007). These sorts of open-ended attentiveness to the condition of debility and vulnerability and continuous experimentation as to modes of amelioration go on, for most of their supplicants, for years.

People in Isoso, of course, have many maladies that are attributable to poverty, and health indices in Isoso would be much improved by access to affordable medical care. I don't want to overattribute to cosmology what is in large part due to inequity. That shamans are something like doctors used by people who don't have access to Western medicine for reasons of culture, poverty, and history isn't an entirely wrong idea. In fact it is something that Isoseño people often say themselves: they would consult medical doctors more often if they could, but it is far too expensive to do so. However, "shamans as doctors" is an idea that overattributes Western models of cure as a restoration to "normal health" to worldviews and associated practices that have no such model of normalcy in mind.

Shamans might be better understood as ideal "allies." I am borrowing the sense of this word from feminist, antiracist, and disability activist accounts of how relatively privileged people (men, whites, the relatively abled) might best act in solidarity with less privileged ones (women, people of color, disabled people). Shamans listen to patients without judgment, they believe their narratives, they agree that what they have been through is unjust, and they take their patients' sides against the injustice they face. Shamans don't challenge patients' accounts ("are you sure you are bewitched, really, or are you just overreacting?"), offer suggestions about how patients could handle things better ("maybe you did something to provoke the witch, and you should knock it off or apologize"), or try to be objective ("okay, it might seem that way to you, but I'm just trying to also keep the witch's point of view in mind here"). Shamans accept that the patients that come to them have had their vulnerabilities trod upon and they know this is commonplace, agonizing, and very unfair. They don't send patients out "cured" but instead are reliable and attentive in times of hardship and disease. They do not promise vengeance, but they don't dismiss its importance and they certainly never scold anyone for wishing for it.

In the modern West, there is almost no aspect of feminist and antiracist and disability activist prescription more subject to condemnation, scorn, and—above all—suspicion, than that having to do with the work of alliance. The critique is as follows: When someone positionally vulnerable claims harm, why should we believe them? How will we be able to sort out the fakers, of whom there are no doubt a lot? Shouldn't our first concern be to withhold sympathy and solidarity from the vulnerable until we've screened them very thoroughly for humbug? Because, after all, everyone knows they are rife with it: the weak, the vulnerable, the less able, the dependent. They're a suspect lot.

A subheader of this reaction involves, unsurprisingly, disavowing vulnerability itself. The assertions are as follows: women and people of color and people with disabilities can be just as able, autonomous, agentive as whites and as men! It's insulting to not hold them responsible for their own sad fates when they get themselves into risky situations! Sure, maybe they do have some bad outcomes, but what they ought to do is stop making themselves vulnerable to bad things happening to them.

What is interesting here is how vulnerability to others itself is treated either with suspicion or as a temporary, aberrant state of affairs—one that will be abolished in a more truly emancipated future with absolute vigorous autonomy and self-sufficiency for all. I know in this extended comparison I have provided delicious fodder to reactionaries: so rape accusation and "playing the race card" and talk about ableism really are just like witch hunts after all! Such claims to harm are as fantastically unreal as belief in sorcery! A feminist anthropologist has admitted as much in published work!

That's not my aim, of course. What I want to draw out is the contrast between, on the one hand, a worldview in which constant positional vulnerability to others is taken so seriously as a basic feature of existence that intimations of witchcraft attack are continuous, a body of specialists exists to manage them, and they sometimes end in violence and, on the other hand, a worldview in which the possibility of positional vulnerability to others is treated as so inconceivable that when the topic is broached it is heaped with suspicion, scorn, and rhetorical (and sometimes actual) violence. The point is not that Western society is purely the second type and Isoseño society is purely the first and that one or the other is superior and right about everything. The point is that each type of society picks its emphases and, having done so, is prone to carrying them to terrible excess.

The first white interlocutors of Amerindian shamans—Europeans who were themselves then living in a status and not a contract society—took shamans seriously on their own magical terms. They considered them native agents of Satan. A slightly later, less pejorative characterization had them as native priests. Witchcraft was, for these Westerners, first taken seriously as indistinguishable from Satanism and, later, dismissed as a primitive version of religion.

Across the twentieth century and into the twenty-first, however, instrumentalist accounts of shamanism have proliferated. Shamans are supposedly native medical doctors or native environmental scientists, or (in a more humanistic mode) native psychiatrists or (sometimes) native standard-bearers of colonial resistance. As long as they can be described as doing something practical, they can be redeemed. In all of these recent guises shamans are held in anything from fairly to ludicrously high regard. However, the supernatural assault—and particularly the witchcraft attacks—to which most Amerindian shamanism is meant to respond is nowadays held in dim regard by Westerners. It is treated as so dubious and embarrassing it often goes unmentioned or is recast in terms of some sort of New Agey concern with ecological or social or cosmic-harmonic imbalance.

Although I hesitate to posit perfect inversions, here there is something that comes very near to one. In Isoso—and from my reading of ethnographies about other lowland South American societies (I haven't read widely enough to extend this claim to elsewhere in the Americas, though from what little I do know, I suspect it holds)—it is shamanism that is viewed with considerable skepticism, and supernatural attack that is treated with utter seriousness. I have had many conversations with Isoseño people about the credibility of one or another shaman's claims to special powers or benignity and about the relative superiority and inferiority of Western and shamanic treatments for maladies of different kinds. I have never had a conversation in which anyone expressed serious skepticism about supernatural attack (as by the **kaaiyareta** and particularly witch attack). People disagree about whom they suppose to be witches. No one doubts that witches exist. Early in my fieldwork, people often ventriloquized the skepticism they supposed I, as an outsider, felt about witchcraft ("you may not believe me, but . . .") before telling me witchcraft attack stories. People now sometimes preface witchcraft attack stories by noting that they know that I know about these things, having spent a lot of time in Isoso. My sense is that they are articulating a kind of disjuncture and are acknowledging that I belong to a "normally skeptical" class of persons but can now be relied upon to listen informedly if somewhat perplexedly. My own contention (that I only offer when asked) that there are no witches in my country even though they seem to exist in Isoso is dismissed out of hand as the most laughable of naiveté on my part and on the part of my similarly blinkered compatriots.

Witchcraft stories are stories of debility, vulnerability, relations, and dependence. All adults can tell a story of witch attack—if not involving themselves, then involving someone to whom they are close. Accusations, however, rarely coalesce around a single person. During my original doctoral fieldwork, when I was actively collecting instances, I heard of eleven such cases. Only two "coalescing accusations" as opposed to idiosyncratic (in the sense of being held by a single individual or family group) speculations took place while I was in the field. The others were notorious instances—still spoken of—from the previous two decades (Lowrey 2003: appendix F). In a few of these instances, some form of collective hearing and/or punishment (usually banishment from Isoso) was the result. There were no clear patterns that I could discern as to what sort of person might be accused as a witch (marginal or privileged, old or young, female or male, relatively poor or relatively wealthy in local context). From my evidence, in Isoso talk about witchcraft does not seem to be the vehicle for social enforcement or sanction that stigmatizes certain behaviors or categories of people that so many anthropologists have posited, including about Isoseño witchcraft (Hirsch and Zarzycki 1993). People hold private opinions regarding who they think might be bewitching them or their loved ones but also suppose there to be many other witches active bewitching others whom they don't even begin to suspect as such. This view might help to explain the relative rarity of public, collective witchcraft accusation. The gains from any such undertaking are hard won, topical, and temporary while the problem of witchery is intractable, pervasive, and permanent.

For the outsider, one of the initial puzzles of Isoseño existence is the way this continual state of paranoia coexists with a way of life that is full of cooperative collective activities. Agriculture would be impossible in this part of the Chaco, where the river only runs for half the year, without the excavating and maintenance of an extensive network of irrigation canals for the fields in every village. These canals are major and continuous collaborative undertakings of hundreds of years' standing. Isoseño crews keep the dirt road connecting their villages, and their villages to the world beyond, in a good state of repair. Indeed, the dirt road between Aguarati and Aguarati-mi was maintained by the collective contributed work of Aguarati residents. Weekly village meetings are generally well attended, evangelical church services led by Isoseño pastors and featuring extensive hymn-singing happen almost every other night (with rival denominations, it is true, but with many people—especially women, young people, and children—attending whichever service is on any given evening). Children troop about in great jolly gaggles outside of school hours, and during the two annual fishing seasons men and older boys spend companionable evenings and early mornings gathered at good spots for casting small and large nets. I have written elsewhere of the crisscrossing, higgledy-piggledy, rabbit-warren–like network of paths connecting homes and fields in Isoseño villages (Lowrey 2011), which are rapidly and confidently traversed by villagers even on

FIGURE 6.1. Dogs at a hearth (photo by author, 2000)

moonless nights but which always had me getting lost or turning up, embarrassed, at households I hadn't set out to visit. What could feel to me like snares were to residents merely cozy. Every household has a Goldilocks-ready array of handmade wood and cowhide chairs (along with a couple of metal and plastic lawn chairs) in sizes from adult to toddler so that every member has a comfy seat at mealtimes, and in cold weather it is not unusual for someone to build a second household fire around which the family dogs and cats can warm up unperturbed by competition from humans. How can these kindnesses, large and small, be reconciled with so much mutual suspicion?

This is a research problem to which the ethnographic method and its principal instrument—the anthropologist herself—do not lend themselves. It is impossible for anthropologists to apprehend village life fully—a whole life, spent with the same others, who bring you all of your life's joys and sadnesses. Isoseño people don't compensate for private failures with professional successes, or the reverse. Even if they pull up stakes and leave Isoso for life in the city, they almost inevitably move into a poor neighborhood in Santa Cruz full of other migrant Isoseño families. The overwhelming power of relationships with a circumscribed set of others to truly make or break you is something that no amount of empathetic imagination or extended fieldwork can conjure for the anthropologist, whose very ethnographic method is predicated on personal mobility and compartmentalization of experience.

So Isoseño people are not wrong when they now suppose I am not, really, a skeptic about witches. I listen to witchcraft stories knowing they are part of the lived texture of a way of life I have experienced but shallowly. To be a skeptic about such stories would be to object to the form in which part of the experience of that life is expressed, without ever having grasped its content (one of the points, by the way, of tips about "how to be a good ally").

One observation, however, strikes me with great force with respect to witchcraft. In my world, all the principal relations and institutional settings for relation formation—education, jobs, marriages and family, a rented or purchased home—are contractual relations from which one can release oneself (or be jettisoned) from one day to the next. To fail at any of them—to fail to form these, to choose badly, to be involuntarily severed from them and be consequently debilitated, vulnerable, relationally incomplete—is a tremendous source of personal shame. Access to education is preferentially directed toward the highly educated and their offspring, and becomes more competitively exclusionary at each stage. To show a real need for education would be an embarrassing misstep in applying for it. No one wants to hire or date the "desperate," let alone give them a home loan. To show these vulnerabilities is to risk being trapped in them. It is also the case that one must continually reject consciousness of and conscientiousness about others' vulnerabilities in large and small ways every living day. In my native culture, lying and posturing about vulnerability and dependence are matters of basic socialization.

By contrast, no one in Isoso is ashamed of relational vulnerability. Witchcraft stories, which are perhaps the limit case of vulnerability to others' intentions, are inevitably told with a sort of proud defiance. The witch, perhaps jealous, perhaps simply malevolent, has chosen me (or my loved one) as target. Wait and see: sooner or later, they'll get theirs (witches are universally supposed to come to eventual bad ends, no matter how powerful they may once have been; see Lowrey 2006a). People are not frightened of witches but angry and indignant about them (as Evans-Pritchard noted long ago among the Azande). Claims about vulnerability and dependence are regularly and explicitly made. People in Isoso often call themselves poor and importune others (bosses, anthropologists, NGO workers, the government) on those grounds (see Bonilla 2005, 2013 and Walker 2012 for similar cases elsewhere in lowland South America). More than one evaluator of articles I have submitted for publication about Isoso has objected to my describing Isoseño people as "poor." Reviewers protest that this is insulting, pejorative. This is a contract society reaction, in which a relational status is apprehended as an individual attribute. There is a disingenuousness involved in wanting to protect Isoseño from the misunderstood implications of something they say about themselves that fails to grasp that it is something they are simultaneously saying about richer others. This variety of bad faith is refreshingly absent from the Isoseño worldview, witches and all.

Not that I prefer their world of witches to my own. I don't. I saw a friend heart-broken by the persecution of her sister as a witch, an old couple frightened and isolated by similar calumny. I met on one memorable occasion a man in late middle age, hounded out of Isoso by a particularly notorious campaign of witchcraft accusation, on a brief return visit. He looked so tired and so wanted to stay in the village of his youth but had in the end to return to the city. Another friend told me how her father had been murdered because of witchcraft accusation. Contract-organized societies have one set of heartrending bugaboos, status-organized societies another. Each have their distinct proclivities to vicious, damaging denial about important aspects of human experience and human social life. Each also have their funny peculiar fantasies about the same. This chapter explores these facts and their sequelae.

IN THE REALMS OF FANCY, PLAYFUL AND VICIOUS

Lyman Frank Baum, fabulist of that most famous of American wizards—the Wizard of Oz—was born in 1856, very nearly contemporary to the Chaco prophet Apiaguaiki Tüpa and the Plains prophet Wovoka. To the extent we can rely upon Sanabria, Apiaguaiki was most probably born around 1864. Wovoka was born between 1858 and 1863 (Hittman 1997). The massacres at Kuruyuki and Wounded Knee as we know were also very nearly contemporary, and just around that time Baum was self-employed as the financially strapped publisher of a weekly newspaper in Aberdeen, South Dakota: *The Aberdeen Saturday Pioneer*. Upon the murder of Sitting Bull, one of the events presaging Wounded Knee, Baum published a eulogy for him that contained a condemnation of all other Indians still living:

> Sitting Bull, the most renowned Sioux of modern history, is dead. He was not a Chief, but without Kingly lineage he arose from a lowly position to become the greatest Medicine Man of his time, by virtue of his shrewdness and daring.
>
> He was an Indian with a white man's spirit of hatred and revenge for those who had wronged him and his. In his day he saw his son and his tribe gradually driven from their possessions: forced to give up their old hunting grounds and espouse the hard working and uncongenial avocations of the whites. And these, his conquerors, were marked in their dealings with his people by selfishness, falsehood and treachery. What wonder that his wild nature, untamed by years of subjection, should still revolt? What wonder that a fiery rage still burned within his breast and that he should seek every opportunity of obtaining vengeance upon his natural enemies?

The proud spirit of the original owners of these vast prairies, inherited through centuries of fierce and bloody wars for their possession, lingered last in the bosom of Sitting Bull. With his fall the nobility of the Redskin is extinguished, and what few are left are a pack of whining curs who lick the hand that smites them. The Whites, by law of conquest, by justice of civilization, are masters of the American continent, and the best safety of the frontier settlers will be secured by the total annihilation of the few remaining Indians. Why not annihilation? Their glory has fled, their spirit broken, their manhood effaced; better that they should die than live the miserable wretches that they are. History would forget these latter despicable beings and speak, in latter ages of the glory of these grand Kings of the forest and plain that Cooper loved to heroise.

We cannot honestly regret their extermination, but we at least do justice to the manly characteristics possessed, according to their lights and education, by the early Redskins of America. (December 20, 1890; cited in Koupal 2000: 93)

One of Baum's more apologetic biographers calls this editorial "thoughtless," "unthinking," "incoherent," and "irrational" (Loncraine 2009: 127), but it takes such a stereotyped format it can hardly be credited as an outburst of spontaneous passion. It presents one of the most familiar set pieces of nineteenth- and even twentieth-century American Indian policy and popular discourse, with its "sentimental pessimism" (Sahlins 1996) that made of genocide the white man's regrettable burden. Baum repeats it to perfection. Anthropologists have dissected at length the bad faith that animates these creepy discourses of celebratory lament, in which "Indian identity crystallizes at the point of surrender" (Guthrie 2007: 528). We also note the rote attribution of hatred, revenge, and vengeance to the man killed rather that to the men who killed him and the potted mythologized biography—elements with which the subject matter of chapters 2 and 3 have made us so familiar.

After Wounded Knee, Baum published another editorial:

The peculiar policy of the government in employing so weak and vacillating a person as General Miles to look after the uneasy Indians, has resulted in a terrible loss of blood to our soldiers, and a battle which, at its best, is a disgrace to the war department. There has been plenty of time for prompt and decisive measures, the employment of which would have prevented this disaster.

The Pioneer has before declared that our only safety depends upon the total extirmination [sic] of the Indians. Having wronged them for centuries we had better, in order to protect our civilization, follow it up by one more wrong and wipe these untamed and untamable creatures from the face of the earth. In this lies future safety for our settlers and the soldiers who are under incompetent commands. Otherwise, we may expect future years to be as full of trouble with the redskins as those have been in the past.

An eastern contemporary, with a grain of wisdom in its wit, says that "when the whites win a fight, it is a victory, and when the Indians win it, it is a massacre." (*Aberdeen Saturday Pioneer*, January 3, 1891; Koupal 2000: 96)

The middle paragraph has become notorious. Two Baum descendants offered an apology to the Sioux Nation for these editorials in 2006. On the internet especially, Baum is excoriated as an advocate of genocide when the damning middle paragraph is quoted without the two bracketing paragraphs (Lone Hill 2013). With those two framing passages, the editorial becomes potentially more salvageable (Hastings 1990; Venables 1990): a maladroit attempt at a Midwestern Modest Proposal.

Parties to the fierce debate around this possibility come together on one point: that these editorials are shocking departures for Baum. The shock is either in the form of exposé (the vicious face of the beloved children's author revealed) or exceptionality (a rare moment when the genial good humor of Baum turns bitterly sardonic). But in fact these editorials are very much of a piece with the rest of Baum's creative oeuvre, which is replete with a consistent awkwardness that simultaneously proffers and denies nasty impulses. Indeed, the way this tension animates almost everything written by Baum probably goes a long way to explaining the enduring popularity of his fantasy universe for modern readers.

Oz has been called the "Utopia Americana" (Wagenknecht 1929) for its putative "jes' folks" ethos of egalitarian agrarianism. Someone who only read American praise for Oz might be as surprised by Oz itself as someone who only read American praise for America might be by America itself. Very little of the text of the Oz books is devoted to perorations on egalitarian agrarianism. The books are full of detailed accounts of strange bodily frailties and transformations, of mechanical semimarvels, and sporadic magic that has no discernible internal logic. Dreadful, nasty things happen all the time and are related without much remark; the humor of the books is by turns bleak and ham-fisted, and periodic declamations of fealty to the values of equality are wildly at odds with the events unfolding in the narratives. Nevertheless, the enormous and sustained popularity of the Oz books is beyond question (Rahn 2003). The question is, why?

In a perceptive pair of essays entitled "On re-reading the Oz books," Gore Vidal calls Oz an "essentially feudal society" (1977, n.p.). The observation gets us further than the notion that Oz is some kind of idealized version of democratic America or a self-conscious critique of the same. Oz is not a parable of plain folks practicality, though pragmatic analyses are perennially urged on to it. The most enduring of these is the decoding of Oz as an allegory about the monetary gold standard, which has become an American classic in its own right so regularly is it brought up in connection to Oz (Dighe 2002; Maurer 2006; Rockoff 1990). In fact the original author of that analysis intended it as a means to teach high school students about agrarian populism and not as a decipherment of Baum's real authorial intent (Littlefield 1964).

The impulse to find what it is that Oz is really about, and for that latent content to be something prosaic and ordinary, is of a piece with the perennial puzzle of Oz's literary popularity. By the mid-twentieth century the Oz books were several times targeted for removal from public library collections in the United States as a professionalizing corps of children's librarians objected to their manifest content as odd, silly, and excessively fantastical (Gardner 1962; Vidal 1977). The librarians were on to something that the code breakers missed, I think. The original Oz books are children's literature and are fantasy literature.[1] These are genres the unreality of which is important to the society that produces them.

LITERARY REALISM

Lennard Davis (2002) has offered a persuasive and illuminating account of disability-related aspects of the way that the emergence of the modern novel during the nineteenth century was marked by the championing of realism. Special cases and special circumstances became the province of lower forms of writing. While the impact of statistical thinking on both nineteenth-century regimes of governmental-ity and the accompanying rise of the social sciences has been much noted, Davis has explored the literary processes by which normalcy and the average emerged as synonyms for the real in the late eighteenth and across the nineteenth centuries: "Bourgeois society spent much of its culturally productive time trying to find out exactly what average meant" (2002: 93). He argues that "the novel emerges as an ideological form of symbolic production whose central binary is normal-abnormal" (95). Davis documents the modern valorization of realism in narrative fiction, the devalorization of romances and epics, and the way a central judgment of novelistic quality became whether the characters and themes were plausibly average, normal, and everyday. The middle-class able-bodied heterosexual is the antiheroic everyman protagonist of these accounts. What is expelled is the "abnormal," relegated to the zone of the freakish, fantastic, and invisible (or at least unacknowledged). Davis argues that what resulted was a socioculturally pervasive conflation of the normal and the real.

He writes of the way that disability appears in serious modern fiction only as a foil. I would add to his observations that major themes of modern fiction are com-ing of age (the end of childhood), and disenchantment itself. Disability, children, and fantasy are relegated to representational ghettos and stigmatized in overlapping ways having to do with abnormality, unseriousness, and unreality. So, concurrently, were indigenous people: genre literature about imaginary (and always, always on the point of extinction) "Red Injuns" proliferated alongside the literary canon of serious realist fiction (see Tompkins 1985 for a perceptive and very influential treatment of perhaps the best-known work of this sort, *The Last of the Mohicans*). As normal (in the sense of demographically predominant or average) came to be conflated with real, especially in the important imaginary space of literature, disability (and indigeneity) became somewhat magical—abnormal, unreal, invisible—or at least disappearing. Dying cripples and vanishing Indians became occasional foils within serious, realist modernist fiction, but were also central in critically derided but proliferating and extremely popular paraliteratures.

Turning from the sphere of literature to that of social policy, we can find that it is now well understood that disability's modern disappearing act was helped along by concrete practices of eugenics and institutionalization; even milder therapeutic approaches to disability became oriented toward a future in which it would just go away. The same of course must be said of indigeneity—"Indian policy" throughout the Americas was essentially genocidal in the late nineteenth and into the twentieth centuries. Notice, here, the overlap with childhood—which "goes away" in one sense (at the individual level, though never at the societal) and with nonwhiteness when it is figured as "primitive" indigeneity that ought to "go away" when true modernity saturates the globe. Note, also, given the themes of this book the way modernity, ability, adulthood, white civilization, and cure all travel together. This is a zone that is relentlessly and mutually overdetermined. But people didn't stop being interested in writing or reading about everything other than white male heterosexual able-bodied professional technocratic adulthood, because everything that isn't that occupies the larger part of human experience. Thus genre fiction proliferated, even if carefully remarked upon as such, from which good literature could be distinguished.

The secret to Oz's success is that it traffics openly in the dubious goods of childhood, abnormality, disability, gender fungibility, hyperracial difference, and fantasy while also indulging every fear/desire for cruel punishment of the same and every hope/want for solidarity and acceptance. Of course the books insist thematically on "humbug" as a sort of philosophical master key; how could they not? The empathy and cruelty, the gaudy emerald-encrusted folksiness, the contraption-embracing agrarianism, the gender bending, the draconian color segregation of the population simultaneous to its happy coexistence and so much else that parades on Oz's pages lets readers have a rather nasty sort of delicious cake and eat it too, courtesy of extended perorations on the perils and pleasures of bad faith—much like those *Aberdeen Saturday Pioneer* editorials and for much the same reason.

DISABILITY AND HUMBUG IN OZ

In her excellent biography of Baum, Katherine Rogers notes that although Oz has become a "socialist utopia" by the last book in the series, in Baum's personal life, "His best friends were prosperous businessmen, and he loved card parties, golf, and convivial meetings. He was ever ready to throw his energies into a scheme that he hoped would make him rich" (2002: 182). As a young man Baum aspired to an acting career but ended up a salesman. He was so talented a creator of trompe-l'oeil window treatments that he eventually edited a trade magazine, *The Show Window*, for several years (Rogers 2002: 55–59). Baum lamented, during his years operating an unsuccessful bazaar in Aberdeen, South Dakota, that "Barnum was right when he declared that the American people like to be deceived" (cited in Loncraine 2009: 102). These elements of Baum's biography have often been used to make of him a kind of populist critic of capitalism, which he clearly was, albeit of the American variety whose dearest hope was always, to his dying day, to make a quick fortune of some kind. As Vidal puts it, "inevitably, he settled in the village of Hollywood in 1909" (1977, n.p.) and he went on to lose great sums investing in moving pictures. His furious productivity in the field of children's literature was driven by recurrent financial exigency. The fourteen Oz books are the best known of his enormous oeuvre, and the only ones still regularly read, but he also wrote boys' and girls' adventure stories, other fantasy books for small children, short stories, plays, poems, and musical theater.

The fact of the matter is that Baum was an eager but never particularly committed or clearheaded critic of many aspects of American society, capitalism among them. During his years as editor of that small Dakota newspaper he editorialized in favor of women's suffrage (Koupal 2000: 62), but he also mocked the women's movement in a broad and clumsy satire in one of the Oz books (Baum 1904).[2] He was a theosophist and admirer of Madame Blavatsky and other luminaries on the subject of spiritualism but began appending defensive anticipatory rejoinders to his newspaper editorials on the subject of religion when attacked and was careful to note his church attendance and warm friendships with ministers as well (Koupal 2000: 91). He made relentless fun, in Oz, of grandiose pretensions and masquerade while being a lifelong enthusiast of amateur theatricals and, eventually, professional vaudeville and movie making. As an adult, he managed a baseball team and founded and joined no end of hearty businessmen's associations but had grown up as a delicate, dreamy child prone to heart trouble, had fled military school in early adolescence, and wrote several stories in which gender ambiguity feature strikingly. In *The Marvelous Land of Oz* (1904), the eventual heroine begins the story as a humble lad in the Munchkin countryside, but learns during the story's course that she was turned into a boy as a baby by a malevolent witch and is in fact a princess, the restoration of which status she accepts with little fuss. In *John Dough and the Cherub* (1906), one of Baum's less-successful non-Oz fantasies for children, the titular John Dough (a sort of gingerbread man) is at constant gruesome risk of being eaten while the ambiguous gender of "Chick the Cherub, the Incubator Baby" is repeatedly remarked upon (note also that the child is a turn of the twentieth-century technological marvel). The name and description of the child's downy head of fuzzy flaxen hair are no doubt a sly reference, for Baum, to the near-impossibility of sexing chicks. Baum was a chicken fancier from childhood and wrote a guide to raising Hamburgs before he became famous.

It is in his handling of bodies that we see the degree to which Baum is not in full intentional control of his own creations. Unlike English fantasy fiction (Lewis, Tolkien, Rowling) in which the conscious message relentlessly saturates and drives the narrative, in this American case the latent content of the narrative is out of pace with the manifest message and roiled by weirdness in spite of the simple folksiness of its overt propositions: forthrightness, love of home. Freud would not have been at all surprised that Baum was a compulsive enthusiast of punning. Baum's works are dream work, in the Freudian sense. They are unintentionally revelatory. They simultaneously proffer and deny their own disturbing content. They are committedly uncertain of the reliability or absoluteness of bodily properties.

The relationship between moral and physical integrity is subject to every possible treatment in Oz. Several characters are under constant threat of, and repeatedly experience, dismemberment and disablement—always temporary, for longer and shorter periods of time—but as a possibility that is constantly present even if usually in abeyance. There is the Scarecrow, afraid of fire, liable to lose his stuffing and collapse, with a face whose paint fades over time if not regularly touched up. There is the Tin Woodman, first met when rusted into stasis, who like the Scarecrow is a protective and chivalrous sort simultaneously in permanent need of friendly assistance—in his case to stay oiled and polished rather than rusty and immobilized. The Tin Man began life as a "meat creature" but is now the product of a remarkably gory series of accidental loppings-off of fleshly parts and sequential replacements by metal substitutes. There is Jack Pumpkinhead, whose head must be regularly replaced because it inevitably rots and goes soft. Scraps, the Patchwork Girl, is an animated doll who was brought to life to be a servant; her head is stuffed with an array of brains from different sources such that she is clever but rather mad. Tik-Tok, the "Patent Double-Action, Extra-Responsive, Thought-Creating, Perfect-Talking Mechanical Man—Fitted with our Special Clock-Work Attachment—Thinks, Speaks, Acts, and Does Everything but Live" is regularly involuntarily immobilized when his winding mechanism runs down so that he is continually dependent on the assistance of others to "live." When in a position to do so, these characters makes advance arrangements for his own upkeep: plenty of straw and paint, a handy oil can, a well-maintained pumpkin patch. But accidents and unforeseen circumstances often leave them in need of a helping hand. Because they are so sympathetic, their vulnerabilities are used for purposes of narrative excitement. The reader empathizes when they run risks, celebrates when they escape unscathed (or recover, as the case may be).

All of this works, of course, as a device for capturing the imaginations of children, themselves physically vulnerable and continually subject to bodily interventions not of their choosing (baths, hair brushing, insistence upon mittens and shoes, and the like). But the Oz books also feature wildly unsympathetic characters whose bodies are similarly fragile and unreliable. There is the Wicked Witch of the East, known only by her protruding feet, upon whose body Dorothy's house falls opportunely when first she is transported to Oz via cyclone. There is the Wicked Witch of the West, dissolved into oblivion by nothing more than a bucket of water. There is Bungle the Glass Cat, a beautiful transparent feline who is correspondingly vain, shallow, and at much-remarked lurid risk of death by shattering.

An argument often put forward in Oz itself is that appearances can be deceiving and that what matters is not the fragile casing of these creatures—pretty or ugly as the case may be—but the durable characters dwelling within. Take the Hungry Tiger, ferocious in appearance, who just as one might imagine longs to eat fat babies. But his soft heart won't allow him to carry out the terrible act. Just thinking about it (which he does constantly) so pricks his conscience that it brings him to tears, and so he carries a large damp hankie everywhere.[3] Here again, though, too much should not be made of Oz's vaunted fealty to the principles of essence over appearance. As Osmond Beckwith points out "The Emerald City ought by right to be a vast fake, since its people are compelled to wear green glasses, but actually it is a *fake-fake* and the emeralds are real" (1961: 240; italics mine).

Within the confines of the city's gorgeous ramparts, each of Dorothy's companions is made truly content with an object that is "manifestly a substitute" (Culver 1988: 99). Their symbolic personal quests—for courage, brains, and a heart—are satisfied by a mystery drink from a green glass bottle for the Cowardly Lion, a mass of pins and needles to stuff in the straw head of the brainless Scarecrow, and a silk valentine pillow stuffed with sawdust for the empty breast of the Tin Woodman. In each case, the course of the book has shown the Cowardly Lion already to be brave, the Scarecrow already to be wise, the Woodman already to be kind, and Dorothy already to be in her real home, long before the final transaction with the humbug hidden in the palace. For though Dorothy's own aim—to return "home" to the farm—is fulfilled to the letter (though not by the Wizard), in the long run this resolution is revealed as one more surrogate satisfaction. In a later book she will definitively decamp from Kansas and return with her old Uncle Henry and Auntie

Em in tow to take up permanent residence as a royal princess in the vastly preferable Emerald City.

But of course, the fakiest fake of all is the Wizard himself. Devoid of supernatural powers, he still manages to help everyone; when, at the end, Dorothy accuses him of being a "bad man" for having deceived her and her friends he famously replies, "Oh, no, my dear. I'm really a very good man; but I'm a very bad Wizard, I must admit" (Baum 1900: 189).

The reverse is true. He is a horrible man, who has knowingly sent an innocent girl and her friends into the clutches of a witch, from which they very narrowly escape unscathed. Nevertheless, he turns out to be a pretty good Wizard, satisfying them all with top-notch humbug in the end. This felicitous truck in manifest phoniness becomes the basis, in later books, for enduring friendships all round.

Both Beckwith (1961) and Stuart Culver (1988) have noted the way that many of the denizens of Oz are subjected to repeated physical assaults from which they rebound with no particular sense of injury or trauma. Beckwith analyzes these assaults in psychoanalytic terms, Culver in a cultural studies framework keyed to commodity fetishism. Along with the notice both take of dismemberment and fragmentation in the Oz books, the two essays share sustained attention to notions of falseness, phoniness, and humbug that also pervade the Oz stories.

These essays make for satisfying, suggestive reads. But both, I think, are a little too explanatory. They reconcile the violence, oddity, and charm of Oz much too tidily. My own interpretation—helped along in tremendous measure by disability theory—is that Oz is so popular precisely because it gives narrative and character to problems about which modern readers have irreconcilable kinds of knowledge and experience. It does not resolve or sublimate these contradictions but instead parades them shamelessly about while also making soothing clucking noises about phoniness. In his essay on the Oz books, Stuart Culver limns Horkheimer and Adorno on advertising: "Why do the people want what they know they can't have?" (1988: 103). As Culver notes, this is very like the famous complaint of the Wizard of Oz himself: "How can I help being a humbug, when all these people make me do things that everybody knows can't be done?" (Baum 1900: 199)

When one reads a psychoanalytic treatment of Baum's Oz that tells us, archly, that it is a world in which "half-crippled makeshifts stumble through a series of flights and escapes" (Beckwith 1961: 22) and in which anxieties about masculinity are all too clearly revealed by the obsessive reiteration of the theme of decapitation in the books that should be read as serial castration (28), to find it conclusively revelatory (as its author intends) one would have to agree that disability and nonmasculinity are conditions of being that merit supercilious takedowns. Instead, the self-satisfaction of such an analysis turns a lens as much on the analyst as on the analysand. When Beckwith tells us, sneeringly, that analysis of Oz reveals roiling undercurrents of debility and effeminacy, how worried should we be for the patient? One might better wonder at the demonstration of being shocked, shocked to discover weakness and femininity are going on here.

The fairyland is full of gender-fungible, physically parsable, technology-integrable denizens. Pages could be spent on the proliferation of flesh-machine hybrids found there and their folksy hominess. A land in which trees grow that sprout lunch pails is cyborg hog heaven. All of the vulnerability, dependence, fragility, and ramshackle rattle-trap weirdness that is abolished from sleek modern normalcy is flaunted in Oz. It's exactly the lopping and slicing and losing of one's stuffing forbidden elsewhere that is permitted there, and it is the illicit joining and merging and connecting, too.

STATUS, CONTRACT, AND REPRESENTATION

Gore Vidal called Oz a feudal society; what it is, in fact, is a status society. The denizens of Oz live lives according to their kind, some of which are very odd but all of which are accommodated. Oz proper is divided into four colored quadrants: the blue land of the Munchkins, the purple land of the Gillkins, the yellow land of the Winkies, and the red land of the Quadlings; the Emerald City is at its center. Beyond those civilized domains lie mildly more fearsome territories. Problems with evil characters, like the Nome King, are resolved by these characters being "put in their place," geographically and socially. This ought, really, to horrify modern readers. Why do generations of us instead find it so comforting? Why do we like Oz?

One answer, and it isn't a wrong one, is because most of Baum's readership has been white, and a world in which everyone knows his place and stays there appeals to people who benefit from white supremacist racism (see Ritter 1997). Certainly the rest of Baum's oeuvre trots out the schlockiest of racist stereotypes, and his notorious newspaper editorials put the most ruthless version of American racism on full display. While the invention for which he is most famous—the Land of Oz—is frequently celebrated as a copacetic multiontological domain, Baum's one extended peroration on the pluriethnic United States (*The Woggle-Bug Book* 1905) takes the form of the adventures of a giant bug who delights in flashy attire and falls in love with a garish dress which he single-mindedly pursues as it is worn by a series of stock racist types: a hefty and swinishly uncouth Irish housemaid, a hyperfertile Swedish widow trailed by an unprepossessing line-up of offspring, a slow-moving slack-jawed "Negress," a cantankerous laundry-owning "Chinaman," an avaricious Arab—the speech of each of whom is meticulously rendered in wince-making dialect. The inference to racism ought not to be fended off or mitigated, but additional explanations might simultaneously operate.

Lennard Davis writes of the way that "representation" is a serious problem for contract societies in a way it is not for status societies:

> [This was] not a problem for feudal or monarchical governments, since no representation of citizens had to take place. You had to postulate not individuals but rather groups, classes, realms of control. But in order to represent a citizen—as a painter or novelist would, for example—you must visualize, create, postulate a simulacrum of that citizen.
>
> Here is where we see the development of the average citizen in the literary form, of the average character in the novel, a genre that is devoted to the depiction of daily life, the quotidian ... Thus the novel is a form centrally concerned with the norm. (2002: 103)

Davis readily concedes that the championing of the average and the normal was not simply punitive. It was in important respects also liberatory as compared to the imperialist, aristocratic order that went before it. But it remains double edged, as disability activism demonstrates. To treat people with disabilities "just like everyone else" and to exhort them to think of themselves as such, to try and be such, is of course a somewhat liberatory practice. It is also an anxious insistence on the quashing of difference that can become annihilating.

Say what you will about feudalism, it didn't have the problems modern contract society does with difference. We are used to thinking of this not in terms of difference but in terms of inequality; feudal societies were bad because they were ineluctably structured by essential inequalities (differences) among persons. They were status societies. When we think of the move from status to contract as a way of organizing society, we usually lament only the slowness of our progress—the way things such as race, gender, and sexuality still affect outcomes when everyone ought to be recognized as equal under the law.

Disability bedevils this progressive arc (children present another kind of stubborn difference, as do indigenous peoples). Status societies may have treated these people badly, but it had a place for them; contract societies must behave as if they did not, or at least should not, exist. People who have difficulty forming social contracts—for education, for family formation, for employment, and for fundamental modes of self-determination—because of physical or mental disability, or developmental immaturity, or cultural incompatibility—pose challenges to contract society's claim of moral superiority in at least two ways. First, the manifest resulting hardship for people with disabilities, for children, and for indigenous peoples belies contract society utopianism. Second, contract society's vaunted championing of meritocracy as the fairest social order known to history looks less virtuous and certainly less logically defensible in light of the experiences of people with disabilities under its regime (Wikler 1979); the cruelties of sorting children and the way that traditional peoples are left out or opt out of that great game is also disquieting.

Here, the poor fit to contract society of children—who eventually grow up—becomes the model type. Indigenous primitives can eventually "civilize up," and there is broad social enthusiasm for charitable donations to "cures" for disabilities (so that they can "cure up") and correspondingly inadequate attentiveness to, funding for, or even tolerance of accommodations that treat disablement as permanently possible. Irritated laments about excessive numbers of disabled parking spaces are the classic example here. One consistent reaction of contract society is to assert that if even when the rest of society "bends over backward" (Davis 2002) for people with disabilities, they still seem unable to join in or keep up, perhaps the real explanation is that they are a mix of malingering fakers and hopeless cases. Many disability theorists have written about how bedeviled a relationship people with disabilities have with contract law. In the first decade after the passage of the Americans with Disabilities Act in 1990, 93 percent of cases brought before it were decided against claimants (Colker 1999). Lennard Davis, writing on one such case, says the "court implies that workers with disabilities are approaching asymptotically that classic stereotype of the worker who fakes a disability to shirk work" (2002: 109).

At the same time, to recognize disability as having a real claim on contract society, legal structures effectively require what Tobin Siebers has called "masquerade." Siebers quotes Goffman on stigma: the social interlocutors of people with disabilities "expect the cripple to be crippled; to be disabled and helpless; to be inferior to themselves, and they will become suspicious and insecure if the cripple falls short of these expectations" (Goffman 1963: 110, qtd. in Siebers 2004: 11). Even then,

> exaggerated self-presentation may not be sufficient to render disability visible since the public is adept at ignoring people with disabilities. Authority figures will attack people for "faking" their disability, and if in fact they are exaggerating it, what stance can they take? (Siebers 2004: 10)

Disabled people who perform disability are, to borrow a phrase, "fake fakes."

Henry Sumner Maine noticed much of this long ago. He specified the exceptions to the shift from status to contract, which

> illustrate the rule. The child before years of discretion, the orphan under guardianship, the adjudged lunatic, have all their capacities and incapacities regulated by the Law of Persons. But why? . . . the classes of persons just mentioned are subject to extrinsic control on the single ground that they do not possess the faculty of forming

a judgement on their own interests; in other words, that they are wanting in the first essential of an engagement by Contract. (1861: 100)

The child, the orphan under guardianship (the effective legal relationship of many indigenous peoples to modern states), the adjudged lunatic (the effective legal standing of many disabled people—particularly cognitively disabled people—in modern states)—each of these categories presents a problem for contract, which sustains an island of relational practice (the "Law of Persons").

Maine's model that distinguishes between "status" and "contract" societies is useful for thinking about what kinds of social claims are allowed legitimate standing. "Status" societies are composed of distinct kinds of people (and conglomerates of people): men and women, aristocrats and peasants, warriors and craftsmen, good families and bad families, master races and subject races, high caste members and low caste members. The drawbacks to these kinds of societies are well known, having been the subject of a few hundred years of sustained (and still expanding) critique and reform.

What has replaced status as an organizing social principle is contract. Contract societies are composed of distinct legal bonds among otherwise-undifferentiated, abstractly equal individuals: employment contracts, marriage contracts, property contracts, adoption contracts, citizenship contracts, military service contracts, confidentiality contracts. The focus on contract has opened up tremendous space for struggles for social justice that revolve around contracts and the right to make them, the obligation to fulfill them, and the limits to what might be contractually possible. Anxieties about and punishments for contractual breaches and overreaches (shouldn't employment be open to everyone, regardless of racial status; shouldn't marriage be open to everyone, regardless of sex-gender status; can certain kinds of contracts—to sell sexual services, or body organs—be declared illegitimate or does that limit the ability of individual self-formation via contract?) absorb a lot of social and personal energy. The advantages to these societies are well known, having been the subject of a few hundred years of sustained (and still expanding) praise and struggle.

The drawbacks of contract societies have long concerned status society enthusiasts, generally social conservatives. It is not necessary to rehearse them here. During the latter part of the twentieth century, however, objections to contract and defenses of status have emerged from progressive quarters. These have to do, precisely, with the categories of persons discussed here: indigenous peoples and the disabled (children, too, but they will not form the focus of the discussion to follow). These new modes of argument and mobilization have emerged precisely because those are categories of persons for whom the formulation of contractual relationships presents intractable difficulties.

These difficulties are very varied. In the case of some people with cognitive disabilities and for some indigenous communities, the difficulty is one of competence to understand the terms and implications of forming contracts; the reasons for this are also varied, ranging from intellectual disabilities to language barriers to cultural norms. In the case of some people with physical disabilities, some people with cognitive disabilities, and for some indigenous communities, the difficulty is one of access, for example, with regard to forming employment contracts. In the case of some indigenous communities, the difficulty is one of outcomes—forming contracts about the buying and selling of property in land or forming contracts dependent on particular modes of, for example, education or of family formation, which can be destructive of cultural values and social relations.

In a societies organized around contract, being unable or unwilling to form contracts brings terrible consequences. The ideal life is cobbled together out of successful contract formation: ratification via education to form employment contracts; contacts made via education and employment to form marriage contracts; contracts formed out of education, employment, and marriage to form property contracts; and the production of legitimate contractual heirs to that marriage or, if need be, by the formulation of other contracts: adoption, gamete purchase, surrogacy, and the like. A life of few contracts (education, employment, marriage) can be a lonely and unrewarding one, as many people with disabilities know; a life that forces a choice between contract formation and contract renunciation (as in maintaining some sort of "traditional" cultural existence) can be a very difficult one, as many indigenous people know.

In his celebrated book *The Trouble With Normal* (1999), Michael Warner wrote about the difficulties faced by a different community of contract renouncers: people who don't or won't get married. He writes of the scorn and disbelief reserved for the unmarried, with particular attention to the issue of gay marriage. Gay marriage is a victory for the contract ideal. If everyone is equal before the law, free to form the contracts of their choosing, gays should of course be allowed access to marriage contracts. This formulation champions a contractual (and normal and average, in the senses identified by Lennard Davis) model of personhood. People who are abnormal—who can't or won't avail themselves of the opportunity to form marriage contracts, by default or by choice—produce a kind of existential problem for contract societies. The reactions are varied, but I am interested particularly in the reaction that insists that they are phonies. The attribution of phoniness to them allows two simultaneous propositions to be made about them: one ontological, one moral.

The ontological one is that they cannot exist. This supposes that a satisfying life not made up of contracts is unimaginable. People living without contracts (the unmarried, the unemployed, the unpropertied) do not present an alternative possibility for how life might be lived. They represent failure, not life differently lived but life unlived.

The moral one, not quite the same but closely related, is that they ought not exist. Warner documents the intense moral fury directed at gays and lesbians who are uninterested in marriage even when it is made available to them. The same ruthless attitude, and accompanying policies, have been and continue to be directed at people with disabilities and indigenous peoples who, even when society "bends over backward" (see L. Davis's 2002 dissection of this phrase) to enable them to form contracts, do not do so, or at least not successfully (see also the discussion in S. Taylor 2004). The annihilating response is that it would be better for society if these recalcitrant people did not exist, leading to moral panics about homosexuals, eugenics policies for people with disabilities, or the well-rehearsed argument and language of Baum's editorial—today not expressed directly as genocide but in prim insistence that indigenous people get it together already and get Western educations, jobs, own property, and stop narcissistically insisting everyone indulge their feeble, primitive, infantile difference (Flanagan 2000).

To attribute phoniness to the targets of these discourses and policies is convenient. Lesbians and gay men who don't want to marry are just being perverse; they can't/shouldn't really feel the way they do. Mildly disabled people who don't do well in school or who don't find work are lazy, are malingerers, are trying to pull a fast one; they aren't really disabled at all; people who are really disabled are knowable by the fact that their lives are so sad that they would be better off not existing; that they are allowed to exist makes a mockery of moral life (Singer 1975). Indigenous people who are not participating fully and successfully in the life of contract society despite efforts to encourage or force them to do so are skivers, trying to live off others' hard work, alternatively/simultaneously, the only real indigenous peoples are the ones quarantined from contract society altogether; see, for example, the incredible interest poured into the possible existence of "uncontacted" forest peoples despite the vanishingly low likelihood of such totally isolated communities remaining anywhere in the world (Richard 2008b).

Sham and fakery were central concerns of status societies, too, of course. People pretending to a status category to which they did not belong ("passing" as white, putting on aristocratic airs, denying bastardy, etc.) could and often did get into a lot of trouble. But these were recognized by everyone as perpetual conflicts, ones that might be resolved on the day of Judgment but that would simply have to be managed on Earth. Fakers, in a sense, validated the system. Rooting them out was routine maintenance that reinforced the status society itself. Fakers were perversely helpful to status society realizing its own ideal form on a perpetual basis.

Contract society, however, supposes that it will eventually be possible to get all the contracts right. We were wrong about denying, say, women, or blacks, or homosexuals, access to the free and unfettered formulation of every kind of contract. But eventually, we'll have a system from which status has been eliminated and free, equal, and fully independent individuals will form contracts before the law on an entirely rationalized basis. "Fakers" here—the bad gays and lesbians, the malingering (or too ill) disabled, the recalcitrant indigenes—are threatening and destabilizing. Fakers have to be unreal, morally and ontologically, because if they aren't, society will never be able to realize its ideal form.

This is why narcissism and a passion for vengeance are attributed to these categories of persons. The wounded anger they provoke in contract society by their stubborn existence is attributed to them, as *their* motivating passion. Siebers puts it this way: "While people with disabilities have little power in the social world, their identities possess great theoretical power because they reflect perspectives capable of illuminating the ideological blueprints used to construct social reality" (2004: 8).

As already described, Lennard Davis has documented how high modernist literature has been concerned exactly with imagining that undifferentiated average "everyman" and his inner life. The more he (and it was a he) looked male, straight, able-bodied, and the like, the more realistic he was; he was exactly the sort of person ready willing and able to form the kinds of contracts that constitute a real life in contract society, and the modern novel generally has consisted of an account of one or another he doing exactly that. What proliferated alongside this central, serious canon was "genre literature": chick lit, "ethnic" literature, and gay and lesbian literature, but also children's literature and fantasy and science fiction literature. That many people seemed to take more pleasure in reading this literature—and that it has collectively gained a much larger popular audience than has "serious" fiction—of course presents a direct challenge to the operative assumptions of contract society and is much worried about. Frivolousness, identity politics, "escapism," and general lack of seriousness and realism stand, it is argued, directly in the path of progress—in literary taste and in life.

A potential avenue of reconciliation has been to broaden the remit of the serious canon, to admit what was formerly genre fiction into the ranks of serious fiction, the argument being that either a gay or black or female, say, coming-of-age story in fact is underlain by the sort of universal humanity we already knew about but failed at first to recognize in this guise, or (more sophisticatedly) enables us to improve our imperfect collective notion of what universal humanity consists of, so that—progressively—we will optimize the match between the contracts on offer and the real nature of the human beings making them. Chronologically, these shifts map onto the "realizations" by contract societies about who is entitled to make contracts. Significantly, fantasy and science fiction (both closely affiliated with children's literature) have been less able to break into the serious category.

Lennard Davis writes about the ways that disability plays a role as a foil in the modern, realist novel. This has remained true as women, nonwhites, and homosexuals have gotten the entrée. Where this is less true, I would argue, is in fantasy and science fiction, where disability is more allowable as a central theme rather than as a foil for normalcy.[4] Relative disability is, of course, a central subject matter for children's literature. For all of these reasons, I think Oz is a particularly suggestive case and one that connects for various reasons to the issues treated in the rest of the book: pan-Americana and Indian-settler relations.

SETTLER FANTASY AND AMERINDIAN MYTH

Because of disdain for children's literature, fantasy literature, and science fiction, the comparison I am going to make next—between those genres, and specifically my discussion of the Oz books, and Amerindian myth, particularly as it is treated in the work of A.C. Taylor—will make some readers uncomfortable (very much as the parallels I have also drawn between indigenous peoples and people with disabilities, let alone children, may have done). Consider, for a moment, how the stigma gets passed around like a hot potato: indigenous peoples are "childlike," while bad children behave "like savages"; disabled people (particularly those with cognitive disabilities) are "childlike" or lead infantilized lives, while children are "incapable" of acting and deciding without adult oversight; people with disabilities (again, particularly cognitive ones) have "primitive" intellects, while "primitives" are inherently "less able." Any progressive member of a contract society can adroitly object to any one of these statements, but in every case somebody has to be disavowed, distanced: children, indigenous people, or people with disabilities. But what do these kinds of people really share? I would argue that their real shared quality is that they put the lie to contract society in some way. Each undermines what contract society upholds as its virtuous and ineluctable historical project: the abolition of status, and with it the considerations of relational dependency status societies at least recognize (though, of course, often also institutionalize to exploitative excess).

Oz tells us some noteworthy things about what the narrative imaginary of a society that is wary of status, dependence, and vulnerability looks like. I use the term "wary" advisedly. "Ambivalent" would be too morally neutral in its place. Modern society has formulated effective critiques of social relations formed around status, dependence, and vulnerability, and putting those critiques into lived practice has been achieved through brave social struggle. The wariness is hard won and morally admirable. But it has also meant that certain modes of being and relating are treated as inherently suspect or, alternatively and/or simultaneously, tolerated only when transitory: just as, in the "normal" course of things, children grow up, disabilities ought not to exist, and status-marked peoples (like indigenous peoples) ought not to, either. Childhood, vulnerability, dependence, and status marking, then, are permanent exiles from reality as it is ideally conceived in contract society.

This treatment means that if one wishes to see the themes treated in myth treated in the creative output of contract societies, one has nowhere else to look but in the ghettoized literatures of children's fiction, fantasy, and science fiction. Contract society behaves as if certain aspects of human experience are unreal, but because they can't, really, be gotten rid of it deals with them only in the literature of let's pretend. Oz is a noteworthy and perennially popular example because it returns obsessively to these themes and to the theme of humbug itself. Because those issues and that literature are stigmatized, the conclusion might be that to compare myth to these stigmatized domains is to insult myth. With the respective differences considered, because in contract society for some purposes society children are stigmatized, for other purposes indigenous peoples, and for still others people with disabilities, comparisons among them can be read inevitably to stigmatize somebody.

What I propose to show is that Amerindian myths tell us some noteworthy things about what the narrative imaginary of societies comfortable with status, dependence, and vulnerability looks like. This exercise not to suggest that the Oz books and the collective corpus of Amerindian myth (which I will treat in very tiny part) are equivalent contributions to the collective human heritage. I am not treating them together in order to elevate Oz, still less to denigrate myth. That potential objection seems to me very much an objection of "contract society logic"; that is, to suppose that to compare two things is to equate them. Instead, I ask readers to take what follows as an attempt instead at "the exercise of that 'analogical introspection' that lies at the heart of our discipline" (A. C. Taylor 1996: 212). Every human sociocultural complex makes impossible demands on its natives, be they Trobrianders or Vancouverites. The cry of the Wizard of Oz "how can I help being a humbug, when all these people make me do things that everybody knows can't be done?" is a pretty good key to comparative anthropological analysis via analogical introspection.

FICTIONALITY AND SHAMANISM

I will be drawing in what follows on a pair of essays by Anne-Christine Taylor, who in the rather saturated anthropological scholarship on the analysis of Amerindian myth has managed to make some novel observations indeed. Taylor is a specialist on the Achuar, who live in tropical Ecuador and are a subgroup of the Amazonian indigenous people known in older literature as the Jivaro.

In an essay entitled "Stupefying Ghosts," Taylor argues that certain genres of Achuar narrative offer philosophical perorations on what she terms the problem of "fictionality" (1993a: 440). In a later lecture, she expands this to a broader argument about Amerindian myth. She suggests that the unreal, the counterfactual itself seem in fact to be the point of these narratives: "Certain kinds of myth are in fact anti-causal propositions . . . they describe the world as it is in a highly problematic way, and thus make the obvious paradoxical" (1996: 204). In the one piece Taylor treats certain Achuar forms of narrative, and in the other Amerindian myths, in ways that elaborate on problems of human relations, human capabilities, human intentionality, falsehood, and truth.

In the Achuar narratives dependence, vulnerability, and debility are the focus of considerable elaboration while states of super-ability are treated as suspect—so much so that the more explicitly and clearly the latter are described, the less credible they become. It is the subjective experience of hyper–well-being and hyperpotence that is silenced (or, when too openly expressed, treated as fantastic) here. This is not to say that the situation is "equal and opposite" to the one I have described (or, better, borrowed the description of from Lennard Davis) for modern Western literature. To say ability is normal in modern Western fiction while disability is normal in the narrative oeuvre of Amerindians would be mistaken. Mistaken, because an important aspect of the Amerindian instance is that there is no "normal" in it; social statistical thinking does not haunt it. As Taylor puts it about the Achuar:

> There is no canonical discourse about 'the person' . . . Being a person is thus an array or cline of relational configurations, a set of links in a chain of metamorphoses simultaneously open and bounded . . . being a live self can be defined only by contrast to either a state of being less than alive, in illness, or a state of being more than alive, through the acquisition of arutam. (1996: 210)

Debility is much talked about, but that is because it must continually be accounted for. Among the Achuar, as in many Amerindian societies, no serious illness or death is treated as an outcome of the normal course of things. Even the deaths of very elderly people are attributed ultimately to witchcraft or other supernatural attack. As Taylor puts it,

> anthropological accounts of these groups [specifically, lowland South American] are replete with statements to the effect that Amazonian Indians do not believe death can be caused by natural causes; rather, they view it as due to malignant human agency. (1996: 202)

In an endnote, she amends this to "intentionally evil agency . . . usually anthropomorphized" (212n2). Disability, then, is no more normal than is super-ability in this

Amerindian case. Rather, the point is that vividly imagining and articulating the normal state of being is a contract society sort of narrative enterprise and one for which a perfect counterpart will not be found outside of it.

As Taylor has it, Amerindian myths "describe the world as it is in a highly problematic way" (2004) rather than a commonsensical one. This is perhaps why for an educated reader raised on contract-society-style modern literature—a literature that trains one's sensibilities in a particular way—myths make such odd and discomfiting reads. It also probably helps to explain why contract society readers are always looking for what it is that myth is "really" up to, in a way that is strikingly analogous to the perennial decodings of the "real" (by which is meant, instrumentalist) message of Oz. Myths fail so abjectly at ordinary descriptive tasks that modern readers suppose myths must instead be explanatory, prescriptive (as Taylor 1996: 204 puts it, "justify the world and explain how it came into being or how one should behave") or (in the most famous take on them—that of anthropologist Claude Lévi-Strauss) might even be abstruse logical codes and so should not be looked to for meaning in any direct manner.

The idea that creative narrative must be representational, combined with the self-regard of the cultivated modern reader that she is a sensitive appreciator of finely wrought representation, means that when confronted with myth she cannot but feel that she ought to be able to turn that culturally valorized set of skills on the materials of myth. She should be able to use her sophisticated interiority as an independent interpretive lens, even without much contextual knowledge about the set of relations—that is, the society—from which the myth has been drawn. Myth's famous recalcitrance becomes a kind of challenge. If myth is difficult, this must be a sign of distinction—that one is in the presence of a form of narrative fit only for highly cultivated, highly reflexive minds. The finest kind of mind can appreciate serious modern fiction and can follow the ingenious logical inversions and convolutions in, say, the *Mythologiques'* structuralist decodings and, what is more, find the isolated interior experience of doing so deeply satisfying. Thus, when properly interpreted and appreciated, myth putatively reveals that its originators—Amerindians—have highly cultivated, highly reflexive minds of the exact same kind as those select few modern Western readers who have figured out how to appreciate myth.

What gets lost here is precisely that relationality that status societies spend so much time generating and commenting upon, in which lived activities are produced by and productive of a sensibility that contract societies are at pains to repudiate (often, by dismissing as silly, childish, and fantastical). For all of these reasons, Taylor's insistence that we look seriously at the oddness and paradoxicality of myth is so original, coming as it does in the aftermath of high modern attempts to do so only in the service of decomposing that oddness and paradox and reconstituting it as sleekly machined logic. She has overcome a resistance of which few of us have been aware.

I suspect it was her attentive analysis to several genres of Jivaro stories that prepared her to look anew at myth. In the essay "Stupefying Ghosts," Taylor describes Achuar narratives revolving around encounters with different categories of supernatural beings. I will treat three such encounter-types and consequent narrative-types. Each of the encounters happens to persons who are alone and then is afterward made meaningful through their relations with others.

The first is an encounter—unsought by the potential narrator—with an *iwianch* in the forest. An iwianch is a sort of monstrous ghost that appears to the potential narrator (often, a woman or child; Taylor 1993b: 669) in the guise of a real person. It tricks the potential narrator into engaging with it in conversation. Its aim is to lure the person into a companionship that will palliate its ghostly loneliness. It is only when the potential narrator returns home and encounters a "real real person" (recall the "fake fakes" of Oz . . .) that she becomes aware of what happened and conscious of the horror and risk of the encounter. She is for a time struck dumb, and recovery involves reestablishing ties to real persons. Recuperating from the alienating experience, the imposed silence, and the disconnection from proper relations requires emphasis on, and consciousness of, one's dependence on others. In the aftermath, the potential narrator becomes actually garrulous on the experience, speaking often and at length about what happened to her.

The second is an encounter—sought out by the potential narrator (usually a man, occasionally a woman)—with an *arutam*, or ancestor spirit. This is a process of active questing, involving fasting, ritual prohibitions, and the ingestion of hallucinogenic drugs. True arutam visions are characterized by their overwhelming sensory power and exhilarating or terrifying strangeness, which "produce by an accumulation an unreality which is as close as possible to the experience of reality" (1993a: 443). A successful quester is charged temporarily with a "state of super well-being" (1996: 208) or "state of hyper-selfhood" (1996: 209) that brings with it the potential ability to accomplish a particular future goal (classically, among the Jivaro, vengeance). In the aftermath, the potential narrator is secretive about the arutam vision—"it is strictly prohibited to speak about the message received from the arutam" (1996: 208)—though among Jivaroan groups other than the Achuar, apparently men sometimes do share the content of their visions with one another before raids (1993b: 676n10), and men make claims about the identity of the ancestor that appeared to them though they do not reveal the message conveyed by him (1993b: 666).

The third is an encounter—neither imposed upon nor precisely sought by the potential narrator (always a man)—with a *tsunki*. These are the river-dwelling underwater wives with whom shamans spend time in their dreams. These tsunki dreams come only to select extraordinary persons: real shamans. They are proof of a permanent state of extraordinary ability and radical autonomy that is itself regarded warily by Achuar people. These are also not exceptional, once-in-a-lifetime encounters but the stuff of ongoing domesticity: an intimate home life, lived out nocturnally, of a supernatural kind. One only knows of tsunki dreams from tales told by failed or ex-shamans. Real shamans don't speak of the parallel existences and second families they maintain in their dreams. In the aftermath, for a potential narrator to become an actual narrator, the very import of the story gives the lie to the person telling it: "Intentional creative use of language can produce exactly the same effect as a true story, except it is false" (1993a: 440). The most powerful truth-effect, then, comes of the absence of narration. Such a potential speaker—in practice a nonspeaker—is outside the web of relations that constitutes everyone else's place. While Taylor says that among the Jivaro "subjectivity . . . is primarily a matter of refraction—it takes its source in the sense one has of others' perceptions of self" (1996: 206)—real shamans are exemplars of nonrelation and nondependence and stand in special relation to the debility and vulnerability of their fellows.

Sean Kicummah Teuton says in a recent magisterial recent analysis that in many indigenous American oral traditions, "disability is a paradoxical source of power" (2014: 581). All of this is relevant, of course, to the analysis offered in chapter 4 of the relative shamanic potency of Don Miguel and Don Jorge. Don Miguel was more powerful and the source of his power was more social, such that he also always considered somewhat suspect. Don Jorge was relatively less powerful, the source of his power was extrasocial, and by these tokens he was considered more trustworthy.

The point is not to now draw a synoptic chart of structuralist type showing the tidy arrangement of perfect inverses. A balanced chart of opposites would wrongly suggest that Amerindians never speak of malingering, and that Westerners never doubt claims to extraordinary power, neither of which are the case. The point is that there is a suggestive contrast to be found in what becomes routinized or institutionalized as a mode of discourse in each context. The "marked" and suspect case in modern Western contract society literature is the vulnerable, dependent, disabled one and in the Amerindian status society analog is the invulnerable, independent, super-abled one. That which "officially" cannot be spoken of follows these contrastive emphases. Just as unofficially the Oz stories are superpopular, everyone in Achuar society does seem to know quite a bit about the supposedly secret categories of arutam and tsunki narratives. In Isoso, the shaman of last resort for hard cases was Don Miguel whether or not anybody totally trusted him. Taylor invokes an apposite quote from an anthropologist colleague whose informant had this to say about Jivaro shamans: "There are bad *uwishin* and good *uwishin*, but they are all bad" (Perruchon 2003: 226, cited in Taylor 2014: 101).

FIGURE 6.2. Wovoka
in hat, c. 1900 (courtesy
Nevada Historical Society)

SLANTWISE EFFICACY

What pieces of work are these figures of slantwise efficacy, these pretenders who nevertheless really makes things happen. The most prestigious shamans are highly sought after by patient-supplicants and yet simultaneously subject to lively specula-tion as to the benignity of their power. Yet somehow their dubious qualities work a real charm.

Mutatis mutandis, consider Schultes, the mage of the previous chapter, who inspired so much masculine adoration and who continues to have a youthful fan-base, as does his chief heir and memorialist, Wade Davis. They are phonies who produce genuine enchantment, "fake fakes" par excellence. Take L. Frank Baum, who failed at every hard-nosed entrepreneurial business enterprise he ever tried but made a bonafide fortune when he conjured up the humbug Wizard of Oz. Let us not forget Hernando Sanabria-Fernández, who has been exactly the twentieth-century ventriloquist impresario of Guaraní political unity he "documented" the nineteenth century tumpa to have been.

Apiaguaiki Tüpa, with whom we began, has now in the twentieth and twenty-first centuries, regardless of whether he really did in the nineteenth, a huge indigenous

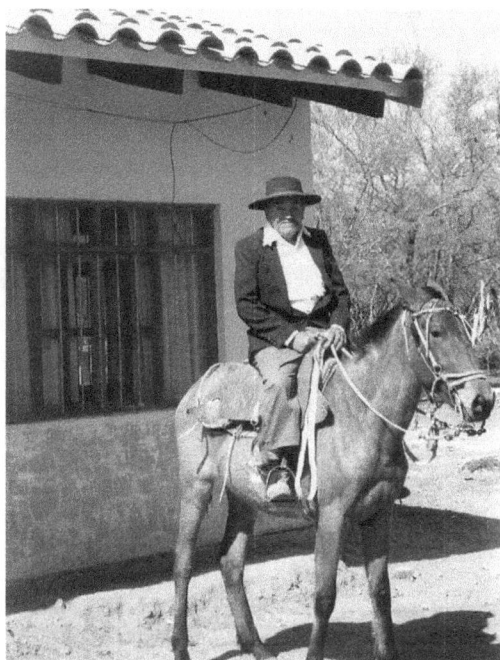

FIGURE 6.3. Don Miguel in hat (photo by author, 1999)

following in Guaraníland. Finally, there is Wovoka—in the historical shadows precisely because he didn't die the martyr's death a "real" messiah ought, hidden by the massive publicity around Wounded Knee (at which he was not present, nor even near) and the fact that he actually spent his life after it as a letter-writing, hat-selling, penny-post-card-posing self-promoter, which he ought not to have done (to be a proper Indian prophet, he surely ought to have died a martyr's death), so we officially don't notice him much at all in the stories we tell now about Wounded Knee. This book has had many sources, including the way Wovoka's deadpan dandyism in photos called to mind another charming black-hatted heartland magic man who was close to my heart.

7

Vulnerability in American Heartlands

The Plains and the Chaco share many features, not least of which is a reputation for free-spirited independence. The Plains: the Old West, the wild frontier, the Marlboro Man herding cattle and the galloping Sioux and the whooping Apache; the "don't mess with Texas" and Alberta as the Texas of Canada. The Chaco: the high boots, broad-brimmed hat, and the plaintive yip of the *macho puestero chaqueño*,[1] so like those of the boots, hat, and plaintive yodel of the macho cowboy; the fearsome mounted Abipones and the raggle-taggle Ayoreos, o; the swagger of smugglers on the lam in this obscure arid interior zone. The Ogallala Aquifer, named for a culturally resonant indigenous group, underlays the arid Great Plains; the Guaraní Aquifer similarly underlays the arid Gran Chaco. For indigenous peoples of the Plains and Prairies before European contact and after it, "mobility constituted a common response to both social and environmental factors" (DeLoria and Riggs 2004: 555); the same is true for the Chaco. Both places are known for their respective developments of colonial-era "horse complexes" in indigenous societies after the European introduction of that animal (Albers 1993; Mitchell 2015; Nichols 1939). Ethnohistorian Branislava Susnik has written of the "conquest by cows" of the Chaco, the way they threatened Chiriguano and Chané farms well in advance of the arrival of white settlers (1968).[2] The explosion of domestic cattle in the Plains and Prairies in the late nineteenth century was similarly transformative. It is said that "perhaps no other activity has so well defined the character of the Great Plains in literature, movies, and the national psyche as cattle ranching" (Dagel 2004: 37),

DOI: 10.5876/9781646420360.c007

and the same is certainly the case for the Gran Chaco in South America. In both places, vast landholdings became features of frontier settlement, with emblematic examples: the 350,000-hectare King Ranch in Texas; the 400,000-hectare Casado Ranch in Paraguay. In another parallelism, Richard King and Carlos Casado were nineteenth-century near-contemporaries and benefited from postcolonial wars in acquiring land, with Mexico in the case of the American King, with Paraguay in the case of the Argentine Casado.

But just as the vaunted independence of the Plains and Prairies, generated in the crucible of the late nineteenth century, relied in large measure on government largesse in the form of railroad building, distribution of land parcels, and provision of military security (and prompted, as we saw in chapter 3, furious lashings-out at Indians who seemed to settlers to be getting too great a share of that largesse), the real history of the Chaco is also one of complex relations of dependence linking its sparsely populated heartland with many outlands and outlanders. Some of this history has already been limned in chapter 4: the way the Chaco became a refuge and an escape from processes under way elsewhere and the way in which its inhabitants were not so much sovereign as subordinate, not so much macho as figured as feminine, as they were pushed (or ran) from elsewhere.

Add to this comparison that just as the Plains got one kind of zealous white settlers escaping contract society strictures—Mormons (in their case, specifically with respect to marriage)—the Chaco got another: Mennonites (in their case, regarding education, military service, and property regimes). The Plains and Prairies got quite a few Mennonites, too, but there are only so many kinds of overlapping parallelisms one little book can manage. In any event, Chaco Mennonites come in here at the close of the book because they provide an important corrective to arguments made throughout the rest of it.

Across the foregoing chapters, evidence has been marshaled to demonstrate that from patriarchy to ableism, Isoseño society specifically and, very often, Amerindian society generally is ordered differently from modern Western society. Thus, the book offers up a tidy inversion of a familiar kind in Americanist anthropology, one that runs in the Americas from the Jesuits to Montaigne to Lévi-Strauss and Clastres through Viveiros de Castro: spiritual/unspiritual, moral/immoral, modern/not, natural/cultural, multinatural/multicultural. Viveiros de Castro both participates in and adroitly traces this tendency (2002). Anne-Christine Taylor's emphasis on puzzlement and ambiguity in handling Americanist material suggests an alternative that was partially explored in the previous chapter. What one finds in Taylor's work—the absence of certainty combined with spirited insight—probably explains its relative (though hardly total) neglect in an anthropological tradition given to breathtakingly confident grand theorizing (that, and sexism).

Absence of certainty appealed to me more the more fieldwork I undertook. Upon landing an academic job in 2005, I embarked on a disastrous attempt at a second project across a national border from my first one. This foray was into a community of indigenous people in the Paraguayan Chaco now usually known as the "Guaraní Occidental." I spent a total of six months working in Paraguay between 2005 and 2009 and established no lasting relationships with Guaraní Occidental people there. In the end, I was asked by Guaraní Occidental leaders not to pursue further research and not to publish verbatim from interviews I did manage to record while in the field there. This experience was traumatic, not least because I had to face up to how tempted I was to find ways to work around this edict in this new community, despite criticisms I had made when outsiders to Isoso declared "unrepresentative" indigenous leaders who manifested uncongenial stances there (Lowrey 2008b). There are historical questions about the Guaraní Occidental community, and its relationship to Isoso, that I hope will someday be answered—perhaps by Bolivian or Paraguayan Guaraní researchers—while at least some of the generation who lived, even as small children, through the relevant events are still among us. That hope seems faint now, though some documentation has been carried out (Riester 2006; Schuchard 1981, 1993).

However, the broad sweep of the historical narrative that brought Isoseño people to Paraguay is a matter of public record and can be told here. The story of the Guaraní Occidental intersects with the history of a community of white settlers in the Paraguayan Chaco—Mennonites. Mennonite history is a product of Western modernity, but at every point in tension with and revolt against that modernity's emergence. This set of facts, and the "structure of the conjuncture" that brought indigenous Guaraní people and white European people together as early twentieth-century settler arrivistes to this part of the Chaco, offers a salutary closing perspective on issues of vulnerability, dependence, indigeneity, and the history of modernity that are at the heart of this book.

RANCHO VIEJO

I have not written much here or anywhere else about Güïrapembïrenda, the third Isoseño village in which I lived during my fieldwork. Most of the book has focused on shamanism, and there was no living shaman in Rancho Viejo (as it is more often called) at the time I did my fieldwork. I did live with a family that included the elderly widow of a very powerful, long-deceased shaman, but not by design. That this family acted as my hosts was merely a product of the way, as I learned with time, most of my time in Isoso was spent circulating among its interrelated **tuicha vae reta** (this family, as I learned after coming to live with them, are distant kin to Don Miguel's family). I have not written more about Rancho Viejo—though the people there taught me how to be comfortable living full time in the Guaraní language, were incredibly kind to me, and were famous throughout Isoso for maintaining the most traditional village way of life—because in terms of the manner in which I originally conceived my research, my sojourn in Güirapembirenda was what a journalist might call "doing background," not a focus in itself. As I now understand Isoso and its history, I accept instead there was much there that I failed to grasp at the time, both in terms of how I understood anthropology and how I understood the place where I was doing ethnographic work. Rancho Viejo is Isoso's most Chané village, its most **tapii** enclave, that is, most "slave" in status. As late as 1908, the Swedish ethnologist Nordenskiöld met living speakers of the Chané language (now entirely extinct) and managed to record a small Chané word list during his time there (Nordenskiöld [1912] 2002: 147n1). Rancho Viejo is Isoso's poorest village and is the Isoseño village that even in the 1990s did not possess clear title to its own land (a process begun elsewhere in Isoso between the 1920s and 1940s and led by Isoseño people themselves). Its villagers always have the least access to external resources and the least reliable representation in internal politics.

My interest in carrying out research in Paraguay arose from the visit by a group of Paraguayan kin while I was living in Rancho Viejo in 1999. It was not clear to me if this was their first visit since the Guerra del Chaco, which ended in 1935, nor if the visitors were from that original generation or were grown offspring of that generation. I didn't meet the visitors myself but only saw them at a distance as they visited other homes. I was then newly arrived to Güirapembirenda and had not yet spent much time with the families with whom they stayed. What made a powerful impression was the swell of emotion when people told me about their presence.

Several years later, after I had defended my doctoral thesis, I thought it would be interesting to see what these kinspeople's lives were like on the other side of what was, in Isoso, a rather fabled frontier: the Bolivia/Paraguay border. I knew men who had worked in the 1980s running contraband across it; I knew many Isoseño people had trekked across it against their will during the Guerra del Chaco in the 1930s and that some of them, in a tragic epic, had also managed to return to Bolivia while others were left behind in Paraguay. I also knew Paraguay had a global reputation for its black market economy, a theme that interested me, along with many anthropologists of my generation, under the very direct spell of Jean and John Comaroffs' hugely influential essay on millennial capitalism (2000). I met a Swedish anthropologist doing doctoral fieldwork among the Bolivian Mennonites (Hedberg 2007) who told me a bit about the Paraguayan Mennonite communities across the border. It sounded perfect: something familiar, but with a manageable tinge of shadiness to give it intrigue. So with my start-up funding from my new academic job, and a few contacts from my old research, off I went.

LITTLE HOUSE ON THE CHACO

After several days in Asunción and the first of what were to become many visits to the friendly Museo Etnográfico Andrés Barbero and its fine library, I took a bus to the Chaco town of Filadelfia. Filadelfia was founded by Mennonites, so I thought I was prepared for what to expect—something like the dusty Old West–style streets of the little town of Charagua in Bolivia, lined with shaded red-tiled verandahs and populated by a mix of criollos, Chaco indigenous people, and traditional Mennonites in their overalls and flowered dresses. I had already been surprised, however, by the fantastic condition of the paved highway between the Paraguayan capital and this provincial town. In Bolivia, even by 2019 the road from Santa Cruz to Charagua has not been paved in its entirety. But my arrival to Filadelfia left me stunned: a piece of the Canadian Prairies plopped down in the Chaco!

Eventually I was to realize how much of the settler-occupied landscape of the American Great Plains, Canadian Prairies, and this bit of the Chaco are all pieces of the Ukrainian steppe plopped down in the New World. In 2005, however, I merely wandered the tidy streets (not yet paved, though the process began around then) and gawped at the suburban house pattern, the North American style grocery store, the car dealership, the gift shop (!), the lending library—which I was allowed to join and which included a Germano-Nordic themed assortment of works in English (including the collected memoirs of Thyra Ferré Björn and those of Maria Von Trapp, all of which I got through during the course of my several months of very unsuccessful fieldwork)—and enjoyed the amenities of the two-story Mennonite-run hotel designed along the lines of an American highway motel of the 1960s and 1970s, complete with pool. And the Mennonites themselves! Most wore contemporary dress, such that I was often mistaken for one—not a local, but perhaps a visiting cousin—and addressed in Plattdeutsch. Many spoke English, ranging from halting to totally fluent, because some Filadelfia Mennonite families migrate back and forth between Paraguay and Canada for work and education, including to what was then newly my own home province, Alberta.

These people seemed to me totally unlike the Mennonites I'd encountered in Bolivia, whose expanding fields bumped up against the downstream, southern limits of Isoso and whose large families could be seen doing their marketing in Charagua. There it was all high-necked dresses, dark stockings, and broad-brimmed straw hats trimmed with ribbon for the women and girls and button-down shirts, overalls, and farmer's caps for the men and boys. Bolivian Mennonites travel by horse-drawn carriage in the Chaco, but on trips to Santa Cruz they travel by bus and train and they sometimes take me in with silent surprise (as I did them, at first) as I use the same modes of transport between Charagua and Santa Cruz on my way in and out of Isoso. We never speak (I did on occasion make overtures when

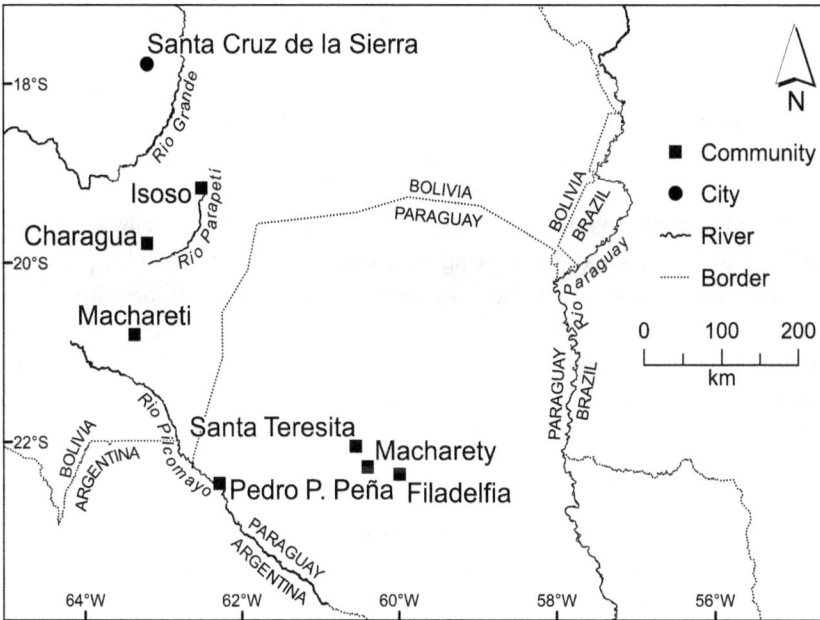

FIGURE 7.1. Cross-border Guaraní communities: Machareti in Bolivia is the namesake of the Guaraní Occidental community Macharety in Paraguay. Filadelfia is a Mennonite town with a sizeable Guaraní Occidental community; other Guaraní Occidental are settled in Santa Teresita and Pedro P. Peña.

seated next to a woman, before I learned most Bolivian Mennonite women speak little Spanish, and once a Mennonite man helped me with a broken armrest). I had lived in Bolivia for years before I had even a single extended conversation with a Mennonite there. By contrast, in Paraguay, I made friends among Mennonites fluent in English or Spanish quickly and easily. One pair of sisters turned out to be the cousins of a professor at the University of Alberta.

As I later learned, the more old-timey-appearing Mennonites of Bolivia were in fact recent pioneers. They were relatively newly arrived to Bolivia from Paraguay (and Belize, and Mexico), fleeing creeping modernism in long-established Mennonite communities elsewhere. This replicative mode has characterized the global Mennonite diaspora across hundreds of years. When not directly driven by external political shifts, it is driven by migratory schisms of more-conservative elements setting out to reestablish a prior, purer hewing to tradition that is perpetually being lost in communities of longer standing (C. Dyck 1993). The innovators stay put, while the conservatives strike out—a pattern that upends conventional modern notions of the establishment and the antiestablishment, modernity and tradition.

All of the themes of this book were, in a way, laid down by my first visit to Isoso in 1997. I came by way of Charagua, a railroad town of dusty streets and adobe construction fronted by those long red-tiled verandahs, of whites in horse-drawn carts wearing Little House on the Prairie garb and of Indians in from the hinterlands. I had no idea, then, what I was looking at, so I got it all geographically and temporally backward. I thought I was seeing some sort of Old West way of life preserved in picturesque amber when in fact I was seeing the leading edge of something novel and still unfolding. Thus this book, written with two decades of hindsight, opened with Bolivian and American wars of the 1890s intended to crush Indians in the name of settler modernity, and it ends treating a group of white settlers who are perpetually attempting to flee modernity itself.

FLEEING FROM CONTRACT

The Mennonites who live in the South American Chaco—12,000 in the Paraguayan Chaco (15,000 live elsewhere in Paraguay) and 70,000 in Eastern Bolivia, including the Bolivian Chaco (Hedberg 2007)—have spent very nearly a half millennium chasing the ragged hem of retreating status society. These Flemish and Frieslander followers of the Anabaptist leader Menno Simons (1496–1561),[3] facing religious persecution in their homeland, took up the offer of the Polish kings in the seventeenth century to drain the swampland around the Vistula and turn it into farms (C. Dyck 1993). At the end of the eighteenth century, when the Prussian state that replaced the Polish kingdom began to implement rationalizing reforms in the realms of education and military service, those Mennonites who were unwilling to conform continued eastward. Czarina Catherine the Great offered them land in the present-day Ukraine that was then recently captured from the Ottoman Empire. The settlement of industrious farmers on this territory was seen by the Czarist administration as a means to strengthen Russian dominion there (Kroeker 2005). Toward the end of the nineteenth century reform regarding, again, education and military service reached even the stubbornly feudal Russian Empire. A group of Mennonites unwilling to adapt departed for the Canadian frontier. They made a deal that was, by then, routinized: hardworking Mennonite farmers promised yet another modernizing state that they would turn a "wasteland" into productive agricultural land in return for exceptional collective status. Across the Canadian Prairies and North American Plains, the railroads "recruited widely for settlers—German Russians were particularly favored, because they had prior experience of how to farm the grasslands—to fill their large government land grants" (Wishart 2004: xv).

However, some Mennonites stayed behind in Russia. Many of those who left for Canada were landless in the Ukraine, such that there was a class as well as religious dimension to their schism (Kroeker 2005). Those who stayed behind in large measure welcomed the modernizing trends reaching prerevolutionary Russia. They expanded their educational institutions and their business interests, becoming patrons and employers to local Slavic peasants. But after the First World War, the creep of modern contract society became intolerable to Mennonites both in Russia and in Canada.

Canada, made self-conscious of its nationhood by the war effort, concluded that an insular system of non-English education (worse yet, German-language education) run by an isolated pacifist community that refused to serve its adopted country in wartime could no longer be tolerated, even in the Manitoba bush. Meanwhile in Russia, after having adapted to alternative military service in forestry and having undergone a renaissance in education—adopting modern pedagogical methods while maintaining German-language instruction—the Mennonites who had stayed behind were abruptly subjected to the discipline of scientific socialism following the Russian Revolution (M. W. Friesen 1997; A. Friesen and Loewen 2001). Prosperous Mennonite estate owners were exemplary enemies of a suddenly modern state, kulaks who had grown fat on feudal privileges offered by the vanquished Czarist regime. Much of the local Slavic peasantry enthusiastically joined in Russian revolutionary efforts to displace and punish sleek Mennonite elites, and some young Mennonite men abandoned pacifism to counterattack (C. Dyck 1993).

These experiences and their aftermath were to inform Mennonite sensibilities about interacting with indigenous communities in the Chaco. Some Mennonites believed they had fallen away from the path of righteousness in the Ukraine, becoming too worldly and treating Slavs not as brothers to be evangelized but servants to be exploited. That some Mennonite men had abandoned their principles of pacifism and engaged in counterreprisals when attacked by Slavic peasants during the Russian Revolution surely added to God's wrath; evidence for this was the fact that these Mennonites had been exiled from their European Eden and forced to settle in the arid Chaco. As a result, many Mennonites urged a different, humbler approach to the local population in Paraguay (Klassen 2004b; Niebuhr 2001).

Many, but far from all. In fact one of the bedeviling problems of the Mennonite arrival to Paraguay in the late 1920s was that the well-educated and worldly Mennonites from the Ukraine, who experienced their arrival to Paraguay as a punitive exile, were forcibly resutured to less educated and more conservative Mennonite brethren from Canada who viewed their own move to Paraguay as part of a continuous historical process of protecting a remnant flame of purity and righteousness (Klassen 2004a). For many years, the two groups of settlers resisted integration and lived in steady conflict. One of the eventual spurs to rapprochement was the emergence of genetic disorders in each insular community.

For both groups, Paraguay was not the first choice of destination. The Canadian Mennonites chose the site, and the Russian Mennonites joined them only when Soviet persecution forced them out of the Ukraine. Both populations faced few remaining options for preserving their special, collective status in a world that was rationalizing, modernizing, and equalizing. Their pacifism was particularly problematic, given that the liberalizing march of progress seemed everywhere to be accompanied by cataclysmic military violence.

To recapitulate themes raised in prior chapters, the Mennonite diaspora has been a flight from contract in pursuit of status. Not "status" in the sense of "high status," of course; a moniker for Mennonites and kindred Anabaptist traditionalists (Amish, Hutterites) is "the Plain People." This term refers to their somber dress, social reticence, and caution about technology. The status they seek is of the legal type described by Sumner Maine: a collectively based relationship to the surrounding social order, not an individually based one. This is much easier in nonmodern settings under the rule of personal sovereigns: kings and empresses do not rule over statistically normal, average, representative citizens but instead hold the supreme position in a social body made of interrelated collective parts (peasants, aristocrats, craftsmen). In such circumstances it doesn't matter if Mennonites are not "normal" and the relationship with them is "special"; there is no normal, and no relationship is average, in status societies. On the other hand, exceptionality is inherently objectionable to modern contract states and is therefore (as the Mennonites know very well) always fragile in these settings in which the standard, average, normal, representative citizen is the proper subject of governance, whether she likes it or not.

Paraguay welcomed Mennonites in the early twentieth century precisely because it was *not* a successful modern state. Paraguay's late nineteenth-century history was marked by fervent and mostly unsuccessful bids to attract immigrants. The devastating War of the Triple Alliance (1864–1870) killed a huge number of Paraguayans (perhaps over 50 percent of the population), and subsequent Paraguayan administrations admitted all comers on abject terms. Brazilian and Argentine absentee landholders took advantage of this state of affairs in ways that continue to impact land tenure in Paraguay to the present day, but few permanent settlers were interested in coming to a landlocked depopulated nation that showed few signs of rallying from its wartime devastation.

It is worth considering the near-simultaneity of the War of the Triple Alliance and the US Civil War. Both were wars marking the transition from status to contract social orders in the Americas. In the case of the US Civil War, the old slave society status order that was abolished was clearly unjust. In the case of Paraguay, what was crushed was an insular protectionist society with a high degree of literacy and industrial development that refused free trade with its larger and more power-ful neighbors, which as a consequence combined to destroy it (Galeano 1973). The violent US war freed people; the violent Paraguayan war freed trade. Because we are used to considering status-to-contract shifts in terms of things such as the abolition of slavery, we don't always consider sufficiently the more dubiously beneficial forms of liberalism that accompanied them.[4]

But to return to our Paraguayan narrative: settlers who came to Paraguay in the late nineteenth and early twentieth centuries were mostly people unable to get a berth elsewhere. Two of the more notorious late nineteenth-century instances were an attempt by a German group that included Friedrich Nietzsche's sister to found a pure Aryan settlement—it failed miserably (Macintyre 2011)—and another by Australians to found a whites-only socialist utopia, which failed slightly less miser-ably (Souter 1968).[5] When Canadian Mennonites came looking in 1921, they were in search of special arrangements only a nation that had difficulty attracting immi-grants would offer (Klassen 2004b). By special legislative decree the Paraguayan Congress under President Eusebio Ayala offered what no other national context (Canada, Mexico, the United States) under consideration would: a "privilegium" that excepted Mennonites from military service and permitted them to orga-nize and run school instruction as they saw fit. Having made this bargain, the Paraguayan state would for two difficult decades leave Mennonite settlers more to their own devices than they ever could have anticipated (Ratzlaff 2008; Stoesz and Stackley 1999).

The agreement the Mennonites made at the start of the otherwise-roaring twen-ties was of a truly feudal type. The land they were to occupy was "ceded" (actu-ally, sold at an outrageously high price) by true South American land barons: the Argentine Casado family, owners of the largest private landholding in the world. The Casados had a hard time of it dragooning sufficient Indian labor to bring que-bracho wood from the Chaco interior to their tannin factory on the Paraguay River. Chaco Indians, true hunter-gatherers, were nomadic, unreliable wage workers and practiced strict family planning (the workers were terrible, and the portions were so small!). What the Casados needed was an apocalyptically desperate population with nowhere else to go, a wildly exponential birthrate, and a proven history of turning badlands into cultivated gardens. They promised the Mennonite advance teams help with land surveying and extension of the rail line into the Chaco interior. They also assured them that there were almost no Indians in the Chaco and that those few Indians who did live there had so much space relative to their popula-tion and were so consumed by wanderlust, Mennonites would hardly ever see them (Klassen 2004a).

NOT SO KAPUTI AFTER ALL

Kaputi menonita (1976) is the title of a regionally famous collection of essays by a Mennonite historian, Peter Klassen, about the Mennonite experience in Paraguay during the War of the Chaco (1932–1935) between Bolivia and Paraguay. Local indigenous people quickly picked up a few useful Plattdeutsch terms, among them *kaput*, which was refashioned as **kaputi** and put to capacious use in communicating with their new neighbors in the Chaco: done, all gone, dead. The Mennonites who had been looking for a feudal agreement resigned themselves to Paraguay as perhaps the only place on earth still backward enough to grant one.

What they did not realize was that Paraguay in fact had modern ambitions for making such an offer—related, unfortunately for the pacifist Mennonites, to war. The Canadian Mennonite contingent arrived in 1927; the Russian contingent followed in 1930. Their unexpectedly numerous Indian neighbors were the first to alert the unsuspecting Mennonites that military troops were on the move from the Bolivian side of the Chaco. Soon enough, Mennonites and Indians alike were overrun by shifting fronts of Bolivian and Paraguayan soldiers in the three-year Guerra del Chaco that left a million dead. Only one Mennonite was among the casualties; indigenous losses were in the thousands, and upwards of 10,000 indigenous persons were displaced by the war (Richard 2008b).

In the lead-up to a war they knew was coming, the Paraguayans had wanted to plant colonies in the Chaco to strengthen their claim to the disputed territory. In 1930, Bolivia, unasked, passed a Mennonite privilegium of its own and insisted that any new Mennonite colonization of the Chaco would have to come through Bolivia rather than through Paraguay (Klassen 2004b). Paraguay won the disputed terrain, and when a third group of Mennonites arrived from Russia (via Germany after the Second World War) to the Chaco—in 1947—they came to the Paraguayan territory. The Bolivian privilegium has since been put to use, however. In the 1950s, conservative Mennonites distressed by the increasing worldliness of colonies in Paraguay and Mexico approached the Bolivian government, pointing out that the legal framework was in place for them to begin farming the Bolivian side of the Chaco. There are now more Mennonites in Bolivia than in Paraguay, operating farms in both Chacoan and Amazonian regions of the country (Hedberg 2007).

Had the Mennonites had any alternatives, the colonies established in Paraguay in 1927 and 1930 would certainly have been completely abandoned. All who could leave did leave in the terrible years between 1927 and the early 1960s. Canada was a favored destination for many, and there is still a lively travel between Manitoba, Alberta, British Colombia, and Paraguay (and now Bolivia). Paraguay was internally in chaos after the Chaco War, wracked by civil wars. The Second World War created serious fissures in the colonies, with some Mennonites hoping an Axis victory would mean a return to their farms in the Ukraine under what they saw as a copacetic German Reich and others deploring the sin of militarism and sympathy to Nazism such hopes bespoke. The 1947 influx of Mennonites from Germany, who had accompanied German forces as they retreated from the Ukraine ahead of the Soviet advance, did nothing to calm this divide (Thiesen 1999).

The Chaco seemed to the Mennonite settlers almost impossible to cultivate, plagued by drought and ants and grasshoppers, and so distant from viable markets as to make anything but subsistence agriculture an exercise in futility. Finally, the Indians were not few, far between, and dying out anyway as the Paraguayan authorities had promised. More turned up every day, curious and often hungry, seeming to incarnate a stern lesson from God about Mennonite failings as missionaries and as willing agents of brotherly love (recapitulating their experience in the Ukraine). Worse yet, as Mennonite families grew and expanded their farms, they had begun to encounter a frightening new tribe—"Moros" (Ayoreo)–who, unlike the friendly Nivaklé and Enhlet peoples, did not hesitate to mount raids and attacks (Bessire 2014; Braunstein and Califano 1978–1979; Combès 2009).

Two factors transformed the situation. First, in 1954, Alfredo Stroessner came to power. The Teuton-friendly son of a German immigrant father, he implemented a dictatorial order in Paraguay that itself represented a kind of neofeudalism particularly amenable to Mennonite interests. He channeled largesse of various kinds, including considerable US loan aid, to Mennonites. Second, in 1961, the Trans-Chaco highway connecting Asunción to Santa Cruz de la Sierra, Bolivia, was completed. Unpaved, but a real all-season road nonetheless. Mennonite products could reach external markets, and the balance of local social power shifted definitively away from Chacoan indigenes. They became the ultimate subvassals, dependent clients in a dictatorial quasi-feudal fiefdom.

THE GUARANÍ OCCIDENTAL

The "Guaraní Occidental" are the descendants of refugees and prisoners fleeing or taken from both Ava and Isoseño communities in Bolivia during and just after the Chaco War. They have used the ethnonym Guaraní Occidental since the early 1970s, when it was suggested by a community member active in Paraguayan indigenous politics to a visiting pair of Austrian anthropologists, Georg and Friedl Grünberg. The Grünbergs chose it for their 1974 monograph about the community, marking its first appearance in the ethnographic literature, and it has replaced a mix of previous terms. The most commonly employed was "Guarayo," which still comes up conversationally in Paraguay but is rejected by the Guaraní Occidental and anthropologists alike because it is properly the ethnonym of an entirely different group living in Amazonian Bolivia. The "Occidental" ("western") part of the label clarifies the fact that these are different indigenous people from the indigenous Guaraní peoples such as the Aché and Mbyá who live in eastern Paraguay. Almost everything about this community, then, is complicated to describe: why they live where they live, why they are called what they are called.

The impact of the war on the indigenous peoples of Bolivia and Paraguay is only now receiving sustained scholarly attention (Chesterton 2016; Richard 2008b). What is clear is that before the war began, both the Bolivian and Paraguayan states viewed the mobile hunter-gatherers of the interior (Enhlet, Manjui, Nivaklé, Ayoreode, and Ishir peoples) to be beneath consideration as national citizens. Nevertheless, these nomads' ease with and familiarity in the disputed terrain meant they were sought after—sometimes forcibly—as guides and trackers during the early stages of troop movements in the interior Chaco. Later in the war, Chaco nomads were regularly shot on sight by both Bolivian and Paraguayan soldiers for fear they would pass information about troop movements (Klassen 1976).

The situation of the Guaraní-speaking peoples living on the northern fringes of the Chaco in Bolivian territory—that is, of the Ava and the Isoseño—was different. Before the war, both nations considered them as actual or at least potential citizens because they were "civilized" sedentary agriculturalists. During the war, they were recruited by both armies to build roads, wash laundry, and do other support work. However, the Bolivian command viewed them warily as possible internal enemies, because they like Paraguayans were Guaraní speakers (Paraguay is the only South American nation in which an indigenous language—Guaraní—is widely spoken across social classes). The Paraguayan command actively courted them as potential allies for the same reason.

Different populations of Bolivian Guaraní reacted in different ways to these expectations. The Parapetí River, and thus Isoso, marked the northernmost extension of the Paraguayan advance into Bolivia during the war. The Isoseño rejected Paraguayan overtures, and the Paraguayan military responded by turning almost the entire population into prisoners of war, marching 2,500 Isoseño people across the Chaco and settling them at what is now Fort Mariscal Estigarribia in present-day Paraguay. It is unclear why Paraguayan authorities chose to carry out such a forced resettlement in the midst of wartime. One likely possibility is that they wanted to increase the nominally "Paraguayan" population of the Chaco, for the same reasons that motivated their welcoming Mennonite settlers from Canada and Russia in the period leading up to the 1932 onset of hostilities. Nomadic Chaco hunter-gatherers wouldn't do; they needed proper farmers such as the Mennonites or the sedentary agriculturalist Isoseño. It is also widely supposed among the contemporary Guaraní Occidental that the major landowner and railway operator in the Paraguayan Chaco, the aforementioned Carlos Casado, needed laborers at his tannin-producing facility on the Paraguay River that marks the eastern border of the Chaco (and Paraguay). Guaraní Occidental also suggest that he used the Paraguayan military (they even name a particular military officer as his agent) to do his armed recruiting. After the war, many desperate Guaraní Occidental refugees did indeed end up accepting work at Puerto Casado to the east and only returned to the Paraguayan Chaco when the tannin factories shut down in the 1960s.

The majority of the Isoseño prisoners returned to Isoso at war's end, but about 700 decided to stay behind for reasons that are not clear (Bossert et al. 2008; Schmidt 1938). It is surely relevant, however, that many if not most of those who either stayed or were left behind were from Güirapembirenda, that is, Isoso's poorest and most Chané village, the one where I did some of my Bolivian fieldwork. Figuring this history out is part of what I hoped to do during my failed Paraguayan fieldwork.

By contrast, Ava Guaraní from the region around the Bolivian Franciscan missions of Macharety and Buena Vista cooperated with the Paraguayan military during the war. These "traitors" to the Bolivian cause were from exactly the region that was at the center of Apiaguaiki Tüpa's movement of some forty years before—the one, recall from the second chapter of this book, that was put down in a brutal massacre by Bolivian soldiers. Nearly two generations had elapsed since, but small wonder that the children and grandchildren of that generation chose a new (and Guaraní-speaking) ally when one arrived at their doorsteps in the form of the Paraguayan Army. As the war drew to a close, these Ava learned from Paraguayan officers that despite considerable Paraguayan territorial gains under the terms of the armistice, their home territory would remain on the Bolivian side of the border. They made the decision to flee Bolivia, fearing postwar reprisals.

This fear of reprisal was well founded. The leader of the Isoseño—who had rejected alliance with the Paraguayans, kept the community unified during the forced exodus to Paraguay, and directed their safe return to Bolivia after the war—was nevertheless executed as a traitor upon his return home (Bossert et al. 2008). Five thousand Ava people abandoned their homes and farms under the auspices of the demobilizing Paraguayan forces. While the majority moved on to Argentina in pursuit of work and better living conditions, about 2,000 Ava settled down among the remnant Isoseño already in Paraguay (Bossert et al. 2008; Fritz 2008). These remaining Isoseño were, keep in mind, the most Chané of the Isoseño, most markedly **tapii** (slave) to Ava ways of seeing.

Like the Mennonites who immediately preceded them, the Ava were let down by the conditions of their settlement in the Paraguayan Chaco. Experienced farmers, they realized that the land they had been promised (but to which they did not receive title) would not in any event be amenable to agriculture, as this Paraguayan part of the Chaco is much drier than is the Bolivian part they had left behind. They felt no affinity at all for the Isoseño remnant already in Paraguay with whom they now had to share their lives. In fact, the two groups had a history of mutual hostility stretching back to the pre-Columbian period (Combès and Lowrey 2006). Unlike the long-missionized Ava Guaraní, Isoseño people remained unchurched at the start of the twentieth century (first Evangelical and then Catholic missions took hold in Isoso only immediately before and after the Chaco war). To be lumped together in Paraguay, then, suited neither group. This put the Ava and Isoseño newcomers in a situation very much like that of the Russian and Canadian Mennonite settlers, in much the same region and at much the same time.

Although Paraguay received the lion's share of territorial concessions after the war, the cost of conducting it had been high in demographic and economic terms and the nation was in a state of continual political turmoil until Alfredo Stroessner seized power in 1954 (Lewis 1980; Miranda 1990; Roett and Sacks 1991). Because of these conditions, the Paraguayan state left this motley crew of Guaraní-speaking arrivistes more or less to its fate for a good twenty years, just as they had the Mennonites. The descendants of these Bolivian Guaraní people now live divided among four communities in the Paraguayan Chaco. In only one do they have much in the way of land title, and everywhere they live their livelihood is precarious and dependent. There is nothing of the cozy disorder of Isoseño social space in this part of the Paraguayan Chaco, only hard-won footholds dependent on the tenuous goodwill of various patrons.

The present-day Guaraní Occidental communities have been shaped by three institutional entities that are hugely important in the Paraguayan Chaco: the Paraguayan military, Catholic missions, and Mennonite colonies (sometimes locally shorthanded as the "three Ms"). Two original Guaraní Occidental settlements were each established near military forts—one at Mariscal Estigarribia in the central Chaco and the second at Pedro P. Peña on the Argentine border. By 1940, the Guaraní people who had previously lived in Franciscan missions in Bolivia requested assistance from the Catholic Church in their new, Paraguayan home. The Missionary Oblates of Mary Immaculate arrived soon after to establish missions in the Paraguayan Chaco. A first mission, Santa Teresita, was set up near Mariscal Estigarribia and a second, San Agustín, near Pedro P. Peña (Fritz 2003; Siffredi 1989). A splinter group from the San Agustín Catholic mission settlement was, at the time I was doing my fieldwork, in the process of establishing a fifth community of Guaraní Occidental people who have converted to evangelical Christianity. Almost all of these evangelical secessionists are, significantly, of Isoseño origin.

The Mennonite authorities purchased land between Filadelfia and Santa Teresita and encouraged its settlement by Guaraní Occidental and Ñandeva (a nomadic Chacoan group that has adopted Guaraní language) people. This new colony is ethnically partitioned, and its Guaraní Occidental quadrant has been christened Macharety after the Ava Bolivian village of ancestral origin of so many Guaraní Occidental people. The new Macharety constitutes the fourth of the four established Guaraní Occidental communities.

FROM STATUS TO CONTRACT AND BACK AGAIN

The main Mennonite town, Filadelfia, used to lock Indian day laborers outside the township gates each night but by the end of the increasingly prosperous 1960s capitalized on the convenience of permitting an indigenous neighborhood within the town limits. Like the rest of Filadelfia, this neighborhood is laid out in strictly demarcated ethnic quadrants: several blocks of Nivaklé, several of Enhlet, and several of Guaraní Occidental residents. By the early 1980s the indigenous neighborhood in Filadelfia was expanding at what Mennonite town authorities considered an alarmingly rapid clip. One of the less-subtle Mennonite responses to this expansion has been to establish a pig farm on the southwestern border of the indigenous quadrant, blocking its growth in a spectacularly awful-smelling fashion.

Filadelfia is designed around a very rigid and explicit apartheid. For many years the role of the Guaraní Occidental in this system was to act as its middle tier, as the "coloreds" to the nomadic Chacoan "blacks." Like South Asians in South Africa, Bolivian Guaraní people are not native to this part of the Chaco; they are from nearby but are not autochthonous to it. As the Mennonites grew prosperous under Stroessner, they recruited Guaraní Occidental who had a background as settled farmers to work as their foremen, as floor supervisors in the agricultural processing plants and as overseers on cattle-ranching and farm operations owned by Mennonites and Mennonite cooperatives. The Guaraní Occidental also had a special relationship with the Stroessner administration. Stroessner solicitously commemorated and acknowledged the wartime services of the Ava. Few outsiders understood or remembered community dynamics well enough to note that the Isoseño remnant had arrived not willingly but as prisoners, and there was nothing to be gained by reminding them. Thus the Guaraní Occidental, though not actually indigenous to Paraguay, were the first Paraguayan indigenous people to be afforded full citizenship status in recognition of their role in the Chaco War (Grünberg and Grünberg 1974). For many years, the Guaraní Occidental explicitly affirmed their similarity to their Mennonite bosses and participated enthusiastically in the denigration of the hunter-gathering peoples indigenous to this part of the Paraguayan Chaco as shiftless primitives. Now, however, Guaraní Occidental react with chagrin to the frequently heard assertion that they "hardly seem Indian at all," a descriptor which they once pursued avidly, according to the Georg and Friedl Grünberg (1974). They are enthusiastic participants in processes of indigenous revitalization, and court alliances both with Chacoan indigenous peoples they once spurned and with Bolivian Guaraní indigenous organizations, both Ava-led and Isoseño (Lowrey 2011).

The change came after a watershed year for contract society: 1989. While the plight of Paraguay's indigenous peoples had received attention from the 1970s on (Chase-Sardi 1971; Meliá and Münzel 1971), it was primarily in terms of their precarious health situation, lack of land rights, poverty, and subjection to human rights violations under the Stroessner regime. Mennonite complicity in all of these issues did not escape notice (Horst 2007). What changed after 1989 was that the pursuit of collective status privileges became a global focus of political mobilization.

From 1945 to 1989, the modern nation-state in both its "socialist" and "capitalist" variants seemed to hew closely to the "from status to contract" arc of history proposed in the nineteenth century by British legal scholar Henry Sumner Maine. Status distinctions of race and gender were everywhere regarded as lamentable atavisms, and contexts such as Paraguay, where feudal-type arrangements were still possible, were taken—even by capitalist allies like the United States—to be historical backwaters. One of the real surprises of the post-1989 era, then, has been the resurgence of status in a world that was supposedly wedded ever more irrevocably to contract.

In South America, indigenous peoples increasingly demand not equal rights but special, collective rights. In the Paraguayan Chaco, this puts indigenous peoples in the position of demanding in a novel political language (indigenous revitalization, ethnic self-determination, identity) something the Mennonites actually possess as an archaic relic (a neofeudal privilegium). The Mennonites, meanwhile, are deeply worried about the eroding of their own status privileges under Paraguay's modernizing, reforming administration. One response to this since the 1990s has been to become part of the government (Bergen 2008), but this sits uneasily with Mennonite strictures regarding worldliness (Bender 1939; Redekop 1973; Wood 2008). The increased emigration of Mennonites from Belize, Mexico, and Paraguay to Bolivia since the 1990s is due in part to the degree to which Bolivia is an exceptional state in the modern world order. Unusual in that it is one of only two majority-indigenous nations in the Americas (the other is Guatemala), it increasingly enfranchises special statuses for indigenous collectivities and was until recently led by a president, Evo Morales, who displayed a charismatic personalism in his ruling style. Bolivia has welcomed the economic dynamism of traditionalist

Mennonite immigrants and has taken to including them in celebratory pastiches of the nation's multicultural identity. Patriotic television ads and posters now have an obligatory smiling blond child in a cap or broad-brimmed hat included with the obligatory smiling Andean child next to a llama and obligatory smiling Camba child holding some tropical flowers.

Back in Paraguay, selectively modernizing Mennonites partially embrace the contract-society discourse of egalitarianism in order to divest themselves of increasingly inconvenient obligations to indigenous denizens of the Chaco. They declare that the era of paternalistic condescension is a now an old-fashioned embarrassment to all involved, that it ought to be left behind, and that Indians are to be encouraged to stand on their own as independent partners to their Mennonite fellow-citizens rather than as humble peons and acolytes to bosses and missionaries (Stahl 2007). The official policy of the Mennonite-run indigenous assistance NGO, Asociación de Servicios de Cooperación Indígena-Menonita (ASCIM, the Association of Indigenous-Mennonite Cooperative Services) has been "decentralization," encouraging self-sufficient indigenous settlement away from colony towns such as Filadelfia. However, the retiring head of the organization conceded to me ruefully that "the trend has been in exactly the opposite direction" (Wilmar Stahl, personal communication, 2008). Non-Mennonite men and women, mostly indigenous (including many Guaraní Occidental) who worked for the Mennonites during the 1970s were actually enrolled in a Mennonite program of social insurance for health and pension benefits. The explosion of the population that has come to Mennonite-dominated regions from elsewhere in Paraguay (including many nonindigenous, criollo migrants), given Mennonite economic success, has caused the Mennonites to discontinue these programs while grandfathering in some earlier enrollees. Thus, some very elderly Guaraní Occidental men receive Paraguayan military pensions and some retirement-age men and women have Mennonite social insurance. The present generation enjoys no such guarantees.

In fact all three of the institutional structures historically shaping indigenous existence in the Paraguayan Chaco—the military, the Mennonites, and the Catholic missions—now speak with a single voice on the theme of "self-determination." Local Indians have not had enough of it, to be sure, but now they are asked to enjoy a surfeit of it whether they will or no. The days of an urban dictator playing benevolent father in rural areas are over. The Mennonites are mechanizing their enterprises, obviating the need to employ as much unskilled and semiskilled indigenous labor. They are also quite clear that the provision of social welfare services they once viewed as part of their divine mandate in the Chaco should be taken over by the Paraguayan state or discontinued altogether. The Catholic Church in Paraguay has received instruction from Rome that it must become self-sustaining. The military is no longer the pillar of social order it once was in Paraguay, part brutal enforcer, part distributor of public largesse.

However, regional indigenous people are vociferously having none of it. What they want from the state, the Catholic Church, the Mennonite cooperatives, and the new-to-the-scene nongovernmental organizations is a set of recognitions and privileges attaching to their collective statuses as indigenous communities. Something along the lines of what the Mennonites have had for the past near-century would do very nicely. The Mennonites are not moving to entirely replace status with contract for themselves, after all; they want their neofeudal Privilegium and their modern citizenship cake too.

DISMODERNISM IN THE CHACO

Whatever their difference, Mennonites and indigenous peoples alike are all now simultaneously claimants to "special" status vis-à-vis the Paraguayan nation-state while also finding the making and substantiating of those claims to be perilously disabling. The Guaraní Occidental make for a very interesting case of betwixt and between in this new situation. There are three instances to be considered here.

First, Mennonites have centuries of experience seeking legal exceptionalism to contract society encroachment, but ascetic religious Teutonic separatism is a hard sell in the modern ecumene, and Mennonites know it. It doesn't help that they adopt bits and patches of contract society ideology when it suits them (as regarding indigenous demands for ongoing patronage) and that one of the persistent dynamics of Mennonite history is wild success with worldly endeavors. If Max Weber had been a mad scientist, you'd think Mennonites had emerged from his laboratory. They become prosperous and then schismatic, over and over. It isn't necessary for outsiders to point out that there is a certain irony to this state of affairs. The cause of their schisms is, inevitably, internal worries and accusations about hypocrisy revolving around precisely this point (C. Dyck 1993). The condemnations heaped upon them from outside and which you can hear in any conversation about Mennonites with Paraguayans (they pretend to love their fellows in a godly fashion, but resist sharing; they pretend to reject the things of the world but are rich) are furiously repeated within, among themselves.

The upshot is always the same: when Mennonites continue to avail themselves of special, protected relationships with the Paraguayan and Bolivian states, *who do they think they are fooling?* Rich, white, and well connected as they are? The old-fashioned garb and rickety wooden vehicles of the "Old Community" Mennonites (who are, in point of fact, always the latest schismatic cutting-edge of Mennonite innovators) become, then, a sort of drag—a performative masquerade about status on the part of contract society's most successful carpetbaggers, a transnational diaspora of jetsetters who can be spotted in airports from Asunción to Santa Cruz to Vancouver to Edmonton. But what are Mennonites supposed to do, in a world where a sustained commitment to unworldliness does really require considerable globe-trotting and sophisticated effort?

Second, indigenous peoples know something about this. One of the ways that the elusive, nomadic, hunter-gathering indigenous peoples of the Chacoan interior press their claims on the Paraguayan state and on the Mennonites in particular is by rooting themselves in spectacularly visible place. In Asunción and Filadelfia a common form of protest takes the form of encampments, squalid tent communities that manifest poverty, lack, and need in their most obvious (and, ideally, inconvenient—usually extending across a well-trafficked central plaza) form. The good burghers are appalled, as they are meant to be, and spurred (sometimes) to action. But this mode of protest is also always condemned as just so much artifice: *who do they think they are fooling?* If they were real nomadic hunter-gathering Indians, they wouldn't be hanging about looking for handouts and press coverage right where you could see them; they'd be slipping elusively through the bush where you couldn't, except for the occasional ambiguous glimpse (see Richard 2008a for a wonderful discussion of "glimpsing" vs. "seeing" as a marker of indigenous authenticity in the Chacoan interior). But what are nomadic hunter-gatherers supposed to do, when that bush and its protective possibilities really have been subjected to exactly the generations of destruction to which they are attempting to draw attention?

Third and finally, the Guaraní Occidental are the worst of all: the fake-fakes, the genuine Indians who hardly seem Indian at all. This used to be one kind of knavery: apostate Bolivian Indians trying to "pass" as regular Paraguayan citizens in Stroessner's neofeudal dictatorial status society. Now it is another: deracinated underemployed proletarians trying to lay claim to special indigenous status protections in a late modern global contract one. *Who do they think they are fooling?* But the Guaraní-Occidental really are just as complicated and strange a case as they seem to be. That they are that impossible thing, nonautochthonous indigenous people, is their true story.

CONCLUSION

Tobin Siebers, writing of the ways that people with disabilities are sometimes forced to exaggerate their very impairments that earn them scorn and exclusion in order to "qualify" for assistance and inclusion, says: "The masquerade produces . . . 'overvisibility,' a term of disparagement aimed at minority groups who appear to be 'too much' for society to bear but also a phenomenon that nevertheless carries potential for political action" (2004: 19). It seems to me that this is not just potentially the case, but already, actually observably in operation.

People who don't fit well into what contract society supposes a human should be are inevitably charged with fakery just for existing. Childhood remains awkwardly but ineluctably a status category because of children's relative incapacity to enter into contract relations. Debates about their contract standing and rights run very hot, as does generalized social anxiety about their special vulnerabilities and powers (expressed in the language of "risk"). Above all, however, one hears lament and mockery about the voracious expansion of childhood: the infantilization of children who ought to be more grown up by age 7 (or 9, or 11) and the phony youth of adolescents and young people who "really" are "perfectly capable" of adult responsibilities. We have too much childhood, all of a sudden. Why is that?

The same is the case for old age. Old age is a status category that the liberations of contract have not been able to abolish. Contract society prides itself on not being "ageist," on the vigor and self-esteem of sexy, active seniors and the hitherto-undreamt-of contributions they can make to society. Nevertheless, fights around raising or lowering the bar for old-age pensions and obligatory retirement are charged, of course, with accusations of fakery: lazy duffers who just want to enter a state of blissful dependency as early as possible, or hangers-on at the workplace who aren't doing anything useful, really, but just want to keep drawing a salary. We have too many old people, as we all hear all the time. Why is that?

Childhood, old age, disability, indigeneity—growth in these status categories represents, I think, an inarticulate form of political critique of contract society. I say inarticulate because it cannot but be inarticulate in a world in which the language of politics is all the other way, revolving as it does around liberation, independence, and autonomy. But inarticulate does not mean apolitical. As Eva Feder Kittay has it, "the subjective conditions resulting from inevitable human dependencies, like the fact of differing conceptions of the good, are at the heart of considerations that propel us into social and political associations" (1999: 84).

Now, just because several of these conditions (childhood, old age, disability) are universal does not mean they do not intersect with history and do not fluctuate demographically; of course they do. And just because modern Western society has tended to handle this whole set of considerations one way does not mean that traditional, indigenous society is modern Western society stood on its head (though I do think the growth of self-ascription to indigeneity has something to do with an understandable desire to do just that). I have hoped to show this in two ways—first, through the rich particularity of the Isoseño case and second, through the small counterexample of the Mennonites, which is a product of modern contract history

as much as it is a counterpoint to it. These things are neither parallel nor perpendic-
ular to one another. Willy-nilly they jumble through time and the world together:
something the mixed-up case of the Guaraní Occidental illustrates particularly
acutely.

In juxtaposing these instances here at the end, I am not trying to arrive at perfect
schemas of inversion but instead to generate a sense of roughly sympathetic patterns. Two of the analysts I've found most helpful as guides in thinking through all
of this have put it surprisingly similarly:

> The role of analogical thinking seems crucial to the concept of equality-in-connection.
> The procedure by which we go from one situation to another is not a procedure
> of generalization or universalization, nor is it a deduction from a general rule. It is
> instead a process of analogical extension. (Eva Feder Kittay 1999: 69)

> We must, in other words, treat the net of often inexplicit and unelaborated assump-
> tions that is constitutive of culture *as if* it were a metaphysics, because this fictional
> construct is of necessity our essential, indeed our only, procedure for bringing to
> light and verifying the necessary circularity of the combination of premises found
> in any given culture, as well as our only way of allowing for the exercise of that
> "analogical introspection" that lies at the heart of our discipline. (Anne-Christine
> Taylor 1996: 212)

This emphasis on analogy, likeness, inexplicitness, extension, even circularity—and
allowing for a bit of acknowledged humbug along the way—are ways of thinking and relating that are full of what disability activist Harriet McBryde Johnson
once called the "corruption that comes from interconnectedness" (Johnson 2003,
n.p.). The "corruption that comes from interconnectedness": an apt summary of
the absorbing concerns at the heart of shamanism, of anthropology, and of so
much daily human life.

Notes

CHAPTER 1: NO PLACE LIKE HOME

1. To note a Plains/Chaco parallel: at least one Chaco Indian group, the Tapiete, also utilized a routinized sign language (Erland von Nordenskiöld [1912] 2002: 285–290).

2. Among the reasons the feminist theorist Shulamith Firestone (1970) is so neglected nowadays is probably because she acted as the unspeakable mad scientist of modernity and proposed electrifying the massive, slab-like, unacknowledged body of dependency work with the lightning bolt of progressivist technological utopianism, managing thereby to please no one.

3. Charles II of Spain's multiple impairments did not preclude him from marrying twice and presiding over the Spanish Empire for thirty-five years, from the time he was a child until his death. For the purposes of this book, it is interesting that he was nicknamed "El Hechizado," the Bewitched.

CHAPTER 2: THE CHACO PROPHET

1. The consensus result from my own literature searches and consultation with colleagues is that the various kinds of arrows in historical use in lowland South America (with the exception of curare darts in the Amazon) would all be too long to be carried comfortably in a back quiver (thanks to respondents to a query sent to the Society for the Anthropology of Lowland South Americanists listserv: Manuel Arroyo-Kalin, Diego Villar, Anthony Seeger, Katherine Milton, William Crocker, Fernando Santos-Granero, Peter Riviere, and

Philippe Erickson for fascinating and detailed answers; thanks also to my University of Alberta Plains specialist colleague John Ives for a similar response).

2. I sometimes use the old-fashioned term "Sioux" rather than "Lakota" advisedly, as a counterpart to "Chiriguano."

3. The orthography used in Sanabria's title is partially consistent with older conventions for Guaraní and partially idiosyncratic.

4. Rumor has it he subtracted three years from his real age, in order to date his birth to after his parents' marriage (Combès, personal communication).

5. The Guaraní word **tumpa** (according to official present-day orthography, **tüpa**, but still almost always rendered **tumpa**) is not easy to translate. It is used in Guaraní to describe the Christian god; **ñanderu tumpa** translates as "God Our Father." But there are other kinds of tumpa: **tatu tumpa** and **aguara tumpa** are characters in important myths but also in comic stories. I have translated these as "Lord Armadillo" and "Lord Fox" (Lowrey 2003), but they might be better captured by "Extraordinary Armadillo" and "Extraordinary Fox." Tatu Tumpa is hardworking, honest, upstanding; Aguara Tumpa is a trickster. A "tumpa," then, is something unusual and powerful but not precisely divine in the Western sense, nor always benevolent. Isabelle Combès and Alba van der Valk have kindly shared with me an 1869 letter written by the Franciscan missionary Doroteo Giannechini that sums up the complexity of the term **tumpa** very well. It is too long to quote here, but I mention it for the sake of interested specialists (Giannechini 1869).

6. Isn't this the only possible use that occurs to anyone vis-à-vis forks?

7. I am indebted to Combès for providing me with this source.

8. Jane Tompkins's description of *Last of the Mohicans*, and her own ambivalent sympathy for that much-maligned text, reminded me powerfully of Sanabria Fernández's literary style when I came across it: "This incredible sequence of events violates every conceivable standard of common sense, not to mention principles of formal economy or thematic relevance . . . Cooper's plots substitute the elaborate for the economical, the extraneous for the relevant, the gratuitous for the necessary, and the impossible for the probable" (1985: 113–114).

9. Sanabria's text is difficult to render in English because it is so studiedly archaicized. It is insistently purple and Victorian; he obscures the conditions of production of his book not only in his vagueness as to source material but also in the way his prose style formally erases its own historical context of writing—the late 1960s—and places it in the century of the material it treats—the early 1890s.

10. The story continues to become more pathetic with each retelling: the Spanish language Wikipedia entry for Apiaguaiki Tumpa [*sic*] has him discovered as a baby, orphaned, on a battlefield (date and location unspecified), from whence he was delivered to be raised by the "shaman Machirope." The English-language entry on him is less bathetic but more incorrect: it describes him as Paraguayan and dates his life to the years 1844–1872.

11. Ominously, he says in this 1986 talk that the letter from Ayemoti was written to a "padre Vitali" (1992: 22) rather than to "padre Dambroggi" as in the 1972 book. This claim is worrisome because the only copy of Ayemoti's letter is the one published in Sanabria's 1972 book. He says he copied it out, by hand, from the Archives of the Apostolic Vicarage of Cuevo. These archives have since been moved, and the original letter seems to have disappeared (Combès, personal communication).

12. Chapiaguasu means "big young fellow." My colleague Isabelle Combès has found conflicting newspaper reports regarding the tumpa and his—by most reports older—companion Ayemoti (a name meriting further consideration in its own right, as it means "I have turned myself white," Gustafson 2009: 35): at least one suggests that it was instead the **tumpa** who was the elder of the two. There are also notices of more than one tumpa having been active at around the same time, all suggesting that our present grasp of the events of 1891–1892 is very approximate. For more on this, see Combès 2014.

13. It appears to be a lurid and individualized retelling of a claim made by anthropologist Nordenskiöld ([1912] 2002: 208) that criollo authorities were supposed to use enemas as a punishment to humiliate Chiriguano men. Sanabria was amazingly well read but also very inventive (and never much given to crediting prior authors).

14. I shared this systematic critical analysis of the numbers cited and order of battle I make here with Combès in 2012; much of it appears as if it were her own original work in her 2014 book.

15. The military commander Chavarría gives some very contradictory numbers in an appendix to his report (1892: 30–31) that do not help to clarify matters. There are some basic (and very large) mathematical errors, and he conflates dead, wounded, and prisoners taken on all occasions (including the lead-up and aftermath to Kuruyuki). One could perhaps say that 5,000 or 6,000 Bolivian Guaraní people ended up in one or more of these categories in the time period around Kuruyuki. Chavarría is in contrast perfectly clear as to the number of whites killed in association with these events: 30; "allied Indian" deaths came in at 50 (32).

16. Utley wrote his book while in the Historical Section of the Joint Chiefs of Staff in the Pentagon.

CHAPTER 3: THE PLAINS PROPHET

1. Richard Jensen et al. (1991: 135) offer a different, and even sadder, account of this adoption.

2. The specifics of the Ghost Dance prophecy and prescriptions for behavior, and their particular receptions in different Amerindian communities, are treated carefully in Gregory Smoak (2006: 165–171).

3. Utley makes clear he finds their self-exculpatory testimony plausible: "They did not deliberately kill women and children, although in a few instances more caution might have

been exercised. Women and children were mixed with men, and smoke and dust obscured the battlefield. It was inevitable that, in the excitement of combat, the troops would shoot noncombatants. Indeed, as we have seen, the warriors themselves upon one occasion poured a destructive fire into their own families" (1963: 230). And "It is time that Wounded Knee be viewed for what it was—a regrettable, tragic incident of war that neither side intended, and that called forth behavior for which some individuals on both sides, in unemotional retrospect, may be judged culpable, but for which neither side as a whole may be properly condemned" (230). Mistakes were made.

4. On December 22, a white man, Albert Hopkins, turned up in Pine Ridge, "wearing a blanket and claiming to be the Indian messiah, and announced his intention of going alone into the Bad Lands to the Indians, who were expecting his arrival, with the 'Pansy Banner of Peace'" (Mooney [1896] 1973: 893). He was promptly arrested. Hopkins turned up again in 1893, in Washington, asking permission to return to the Sioux reservations to encourage them to "accept the teaching of the pansy and its motto, which now they only partially or very doubtfully accept" (894).

5. Many aspects of Allan Young's influential critique of the "stress discourse" are pertinent here, despite the fact that Young himself excepts Wallace's "idiosyncratic" treatment of stress from his analysis (1980: 134). Notwithstanding, arguments such as Young's formed an important part of the armature of critique that eroded disciplinary interest in the "culture and personality" approach to which Wallace's 1956 article contributed.

CHAPTER 4: SHAMANS AND WIVES

1. Apoyo Para el Campesino-Indígena del Oriente Boliviano (Support for the Peasant-Indigene of Eastern Bolivia: APCOB) is headed by a German anthropologist, Jürgen Riester, who first visited Isoso in the early 1970s and who founded APCOB in 1980 (see Riester 1985).

2. This can be translated as "Great Festival" but **Ara-ete** literally means an "exemplary day or atmosphere" that is a supreme or perfect example of its type.

3. This was not a fluke of timing: Nordenskiöld during his 1908 sojourn among the "Chané of the Parapetí River" (the Isoseño) records several animal remedies—rhea, iguana, and chicken fat—and among the related "Chané of Itiyuro" (a group still extant in Argentina) he says stork, jaguar, and peccary fat, along with the beak of the toucan, are used in medicinal practice. He says, "although they also prepare remedies from certain plants" (he does not name any), they primarily use medicines of animal origin. According to him, this was not at all due to being relatively medically backward; in fact, they surprised him by cleaning wounds with water that had been boiled—a much sounder method than that used by their criollo counterparts in the region ([1912] 2002: 200).

4. Usually translated into Spanish as *bicho*, or "bug," "creature" (see Lowrey 2003: 183n11 for possible etymologies).

5. The **paye** is a thing one has and a thing one is; it is often written **ipaye** ("his/her paye"), which is, according to modern Guaraní orthography, more correct. I use **paye** because this accords better with daily use as I heard it and with most of the renderings in the historical literature. Although I have never seen the object in question myself, I have read and been told accounts of occasions upon which the paye is actually produced from the shaman's body (see Lowrey 2003: 184n14).

6. Nordenskiöld ([1912] 2002: 199) writes of the distinction reported to him by "Chané and Chiriguano" between **ipaye**, "who are good and annul bewitchments" and **ipayepotchi**, "who can annul bewitchments but can also bewitch." Although he does not give the translation, the latter would simply mean "bad (in the sense of ill-humoured or malevolent) paye."

7. Quite a bit of evidence suggests that this replicative process continued right into the Chaco proper, producing, for example, the Guaraní-speaking **Ñañaigua** (wilderness dwellers) or **Tapiete** ("true" or "paradigmatic" slaves—essentially, the slaves of slaves, the subordinates to the tapïi) who manifest the nomadic, hunter-gathering way of life of true Chacoan people and yet speak Guaraní (see Combès 2008).

8. In a rather delightful Freudian slip, in the first writing of this passage I wrote "willy" for "silly" here.

9. The Parapetí River flows east and north out of the Andes; it peters out in swamps at the edge of the arid Chaco. Unlike in the case of tributaries of the Amazon, where "upstream" means "more remote" and "downstream" means "toward the mouth and bigger towns," in the case of the Parapetí "upstream" means "toward bigger towns in the foothills of the Andes" and "downstream" means "as the river becomes a seasonal trickle that disappears into the Chaco swamps."

CHAPTER 5: SHAMANS AND SPIES

1. A recent PhD from the University of Kent told me that in his fieldwork among the Colombian Kofán—the very community to which Schultes was supposed to have been so close—no memory of his having visiting exists even among elderly people (J. Carrizosa, personal communication, 2015).

2. Davis has this to say about the posts in the later, even more hagiographic book he edited of Schultes's photographs: "He became so trusted that he was able to establish profitable rubber depots both at Soratama and Jinogojé on the Río Apaporis a mere thirty years after the worst of the trade's ravages. Only for Schultes would the Barasana, Tatuyo, Makuna, Yukuna, and all the other peoples of the Anaconda return to the gather the latex known to them as the white blood of the forest" (2004: ix–x). One of the photos published in the book, which shows Schultes dressed for the "Kai-ya-ree" dance, Davis captions as being of "Schultes and two Tanimuka dancers" (105). In fact, the photo is of Isidoro Cabrera (also dressed in dance regalia), a presumably Indian man in regalia, and Schultes. Cabrera's family

worked as foremen for notorious Peruvian rubber baron Julio César Arana and remained involved in rubber exploitation in the area after it was ceded to Colombia in 1927 (Augusto Oyuela-Caycedo, personal communication, 2017).

3. In response to a set of queries I sent about *One River*, Davis replied (in part): "He was conservative in terms of his notion of the role of government in the lives of people. But he was a total libertarian who far before his time could care less about someone's sexual orientation or interest in drugs. He was one of the most inspiring explorers of the century. What he accomplished ought to make all of us feel very humble indeed."

4. For a fascinating general account of the intersection of Western "seekers" and Mexican mushrooms in the Mazatec, see Feinberg (2003).

5. It's a problem unlikely to find definitive resolution—John Marks wrote his book on MKULTRA using the available sources; most of the files relating to the program were destroyed in 1973 on the initiative of its director Sidney Gottlieb and the man who was then stepping down as director, Richard Helms, in part because of Gottlieb's desire to "protect the reputations of the researchers with whom he had collaborated on the assurance of secrecy" (Marks 1979: 220).

6. Gillmore in his book compares the rather sinister Cameron to . . . a shaman (1987: 123).

7. A photo of the two men together can be found http://www.huntglobalpartnerships .com, accessed October 10, 2019.

8. Guaraní for liver, the seat of many thoughts and emotions.

9. LaBarre dismisses this inconvenient circumstance by asserting that though peyote usage did not spread to the North American plains and prairies until after the 1880s, the indigenous people there were "aboriginally pre-adapted to peyotism" (1972: 277).

10. There is, in fact, a fascinating investigative project to be had here, taking the cases of peyote, ayahuasca and cannabis and their respective associations with anticolonial religious movements (Rastafarianism in the last case).

11. Hee hee.

12. A story about Schultes being forced to play endless rounds of chess with an isolated military commander in the Colombian Amazon that appears in both books suggests Schultes himself was not above plagiarism in telling the story of his own life—this incident is inescapably reminiscent of one that appears in Evelyn Waugh's novel *A Handful of Dust*.

13. Halstead's dog, which survived him, was named Toto. See the next chapter for why this is delightful.

14. He repeats this story on a fundraising website: "In December of 1982, an American graduate student fleeing a South American civil war ['civil war' is a strangely even-handed way to phrase the murderous persecution of civilians by a military dictatorship—KL] paid a bush pilot to drop him on the most remote airstrip in the rainforests of the northeast Amazon. There, Mark Plotkin was met by the Trio Indians, none of whom he knew and whose language he did not speak" (https://www.indiegogo.com/projects/saving-the-rainforest

-shamans-at-sixty#/story). He also claims on the same website that his Amazon Conservation Team is in contact with an extraordinary "14" uncontacted groups in the NW Amazon.

CHAPTER 6: WIZARDS AND GHOSTS

1. Of which there are fourteen, beginning with the Wonderful Wizard of Oz that went on to cinematic fame. After Baum's death, Ruth Plumly Thompson was contracted by Baum's publisher to continue the Oz series and wrote a further twenty-one books.

2. Given Baum's simultaneous connection to every possible position on the contentious issues of his age, it is somehow not surprising that his mother-in-law was Matilda Gage, a famous feminist and great supporter of American Indian rights—albeit on the basis of a rather potted Bachofian set of ideas about Iroquois social organization. She believed American Indian societies to maintain elements of a primordial Matriarchate. She wrote admiringly of the Iroquois Confederacy, and because of her favorable written portrayals the Mohawk adopted her into their Wolf Clan (Lurie 2000).

3. This sentimental beast, who thinks terrible thoughts but performs only good actions, is a funhouse reflection of the modern history of contract society liberalism.

4. As I was finishing the writing of this book, it struck me that as the "flight from contract" I suggest is becoming a widespread contemporary sociopolitical phenomenon, fantasy and science fiction are now being taken seriously as important forms of fiction; in light of the points I make about disability and indigeneity, it is interesting that the wildly popular television series *Game of Thrones* features disabled characters prominently within a status society setting.

CHAPTER 7: VULNERABILITY IN AMERICAN HEARTLANDS

1. Examples of the *chacarera* musical genre can be heard by web-searching Dalmiro Cuéllar Ayala ("Chaco sin fronteras," "La huella y vaca"), El Negro Palma ("Puestero tejada," "Homenaje a las coplas"), or Los Canarios del Chaco ("La llorona abajeña"); listen for the laughing staccato yip.

2. For the purposes of the argument about kinship made in chapter 4, it is interesting that David Aberle (1961) said, "The cow is the enemy of matriliny, the friend of patriliny"; see also Clare Janaki Holden and Ruth Mace (2003).

3. Considered only as a religious denomination, Mennonites today include among their numbers people of many different ethnic origins, including some indigenous people in Paraguay. Evangelical efforts by Mennonites map in complicated ways on to splits between traditionalists and modernizers. The usage here follows everyday usage in the Chaco, where "Mennonite" is as much an ethnonym as a religious denomination and specifies people whose ancestry is traceable to Anabaptist followers of Menno Simons in the Low Countries of Europe.

4. There is a large scholarly literature on the US Civil War that does consider it from an economic point of view, so here I am referring to the popular imagination.

5. Renowned Paraguayan ethnologist León Cadogan (1899–1973) was the son of two founders of "Nueva Australia."

References

Aberle, David F. 1961. "Matrilineal Descent in Cross-Cultural Comparison." In *Matrilineal Kinship*, ed. David Schneider and Kathleen Gough, 655–730. Berkeley: University of California Press.

Abu-Lughod, Lila. 1990. "The Romance of Resistance: Tracing Transformations of Power through Bedouin Women." *American Ethnologist* 17 (1): 41–55.

Albarelli, Henry P., Jr. 2005. *A Terrible Mistake: The Murder of Frank Olson and the CIA's Secret Cold War Experiments*. Chicago: Independent Publishers Group.

Albers, Patricia. 1993. "Symbiosis, Merger, and War: Contrasting Forms of Intertribal Relationship among Historic Plains Indians." In *The Political Economy of North American Indians*, ed. J. H. Moore, 94–132. Norman: University of Oklahoma Press.

Albers, Patricia, and William James. 1986. "Historical Materialism versus Evolutionary Ecology: A Methodological Note on Horse Distribution and American Plains Indians." *Critique of Anthropology* 6 (1): 87–100.

Albó, Xavier. 1990. *Los guaraní-chiriguano*. Vol. 3, *La comunidad hoy*. La Paz, Bolivia: CIPCA Cuadernos de Investigación 32.

Bailey, Paul. 1957. *Wovoka, the Indian Messiah*. Tucson, AZ: Westernlore Press.

Barker, Michael James. 2013. "Royal Alternative Medicine." July 28. Blog post on *Thoughts of a Leicester Socialist*. https://thoughtsofaleicestersocialist.wordpress.com/2013/07/28/royal-alternative-medicine/.

Barker, Michael James. 2009. "When Environmentalists Legitimize Plunder." January 26. *Swan's Commentary*. http://www.swans.com/library/art15/barker12.html.

Barker, Michael James. 2008. "The Philanthropic Roots of Corporate Environmentalism." November 3. *Swan's Commentary*. http://www.swans.com/library/art14/barker07 .html.

Baum, L. Frank. 1906. *John Dough and the Cherub*. Chicago: Reilly and Britton.

Baum, L. Frank. 1905. *The Woggle-Bug Book*. Chicago: Reilly and Britton.

Baum, L. Frank. 1904. *The Marvelous Land of Oz*. Chicago: Reilly and Britton.

Baum, L. Frank. 1900. *The Wonderful Wizard of Oz*. Chicago: Reilly and Britton.

Baynton, Douglas. 2001. "Disability and the Justification of Inequality in American History." In *The New Disability History: American Perspectives*, ed. Longmore and Umansky, 33–57. New York: New York University Press.

Baynton, Douglas. 1996. *Forbidden Signs: American Culture and the Campaign against Sign Language*. Chicago: University of Chicago Press.

Beckwith, Osmond. 1961. "The Oddness of Oz." *Kulchur* 1 (4): 19–34.

Bender, Harold S. 1939. "Church and State in Mennonite History." *Mennonite Quarterly Review* 13 (2): 83–103.

Bergen, Ernst. 2008. *Jumping into Empty Space: A Reluctant Mennonite Businessman Serves in Paraguay's Presidential Cabinet*. Intercourse, PA: Good Books.

Bessire, Lucas. 2014. *Behold the Black Caiman: A Chronicle of Ayoreo Life*. Chicago: University of Chicago Press.

Bolpress. 2009. "Legislador de Podemos negocio tierras con Menonitas." https://boliviasol .wordpress.com/2009/01/21/legislador-de-podemos-negocio-tierras-guaranies-con -menonitas/.

Bonilla, Oiara. 2013. "Be My Boss! Comments on South African and Amerindian Forms of Subjection." *Journal of the Royal Anthropological Institute (N.S.)* 19 (2): 246–247.

Bonilla, Oiara. 2005. "O bom patrão e o inimigo voraz: Predação e comercio na cosmologia Paumari." *Mana* 11 (1): 41–66.

Booth, William. 1988. "Voodoo Science." *Science* 240 (April 15, 4850): 274.

Bossert, Federico, Isabelle Combès, and Diego Villar. 2008. "La Guerra del Chaco entre los chané e isoseños del Chaco Occidental." In *Mala guerra: Los indígenas en la Guerra del Chaco, 1932–1935*, ed. Nicolás Richard, 203–234. Asunción and Paris: ServiLibro–Museo del Barro–CoLibris.

Braunstein, José and Mario Califano. 1978–1979. "Los grupos ayoreo: Contribución para el conocimiento de gentilicios y toponímicos del Chaco boreal." *Scripta Etnológica* 5 (1): 92–101.

Canessa, Andrew. 2012. *Intimate Indigeneities: Race, Sex, and History in the Small Spaces of Andean Life*. Durham, NC: Duke University Press.

Chagnon, Napoleon. 1968. *Yanomamo: The Fierce People*. New York: Holt McDougal.

Chamberlain, Kathleen P. 2007. *Victorio: Apache Warrior and Chief.* Norman: University of Oklahoma Press.

Chase, Alston. 2002. *Harvard and the Unabomber: The Education of an American Terrorist.* New York: W. W. Norton and Company.

Chase-Sardi, Miguel. 1971. "La situación actual de los indígenas del Paraguay." *Suplemento Antropológico* 6 (1–2): 9–98.

Chavarría, Melchor. 1892. *Informe que presenta al Señor Ministro de Gobierno, el delegado en las Provincias de Tomina, Azero y Cordillera.* Sucre, Bolivia: Tipografía del Cruzado.

Chesterton, Bridget, ed. 2016. *The Chaco War: Environment, Ethnicity, and Nationalism.* London: Bloomsbury Academic Publishing.

Clastres, Hélène. (1975) 1995 *The Land without Evil: Tupí-Guaraní Prophetism.* Trans. from the French by Jacqueline Grenez Brovender, with an introduction by Jonathan Hill. Urbana-Champaign: University of Illinois Press.

Clastres, Pierre. (1974) 1977. *Society against the State.* New York: Zone Books.

Colby, Gerard, and Charlotte Dennet. 1995. *Thy Will Be Done: Nelson Rockefeller and Evangelism in the Age of Oil.* New York: Harper Collins.

Colker, Ruth. 1999. "The Americans with Disabilities Act: A Windfall for Defendants." *Harvard Civil Rights—Civil Liberties Review* 34 (1): 99–163.

Comaroff, Jean, and Comaroff, John. 2000. "Millennial Capitalism: First Thoughts on a Second Coming." *Public Culture* 12 (2): 291–343.

Combès, Isabelle. 2014. *Kuruyuki.* Cochabamba, Bolivia: Instituto de Misionología, Colección Scripta Autochtona (n. 12).

Combès, Isabelle. 2009. *Zamucos.* Cochabamba, Bolivia: Instituto de Misionología, Colección Scripta Autochtona (n. 1).

Combès, Isabelle. 2008. "Los fugitivos escondidos: Acerca del 'enigma' tapiete." *Boletín del Instituto Francés de Estudios Andinos* 37 (3): 511–533.

Combès, Isabelle. 2005a. *Etno-historias del Isoso: Chané y chiriguanos en el Chaco boliviano (siglos XVI a XX).* Santa Cruz de la Sierra, Bolivia: Instituto Francés de Estudios Andinos / Fundación PIEB.

Combès, Isabelle. 2005b. "Las batallas de Kuruyuki: Variaciones sobre una derrota chiriguana." *Bulletin de l'Institut Français d'Études Andines* 34 (2): 221–233.

Combès, Isabelle. 2004. "Tras la huella de los ñanaigua: De tapii, tapiete y otros salvajes en el Chaco boliviano." *Boletín del Instituto Francés de Estudios Andinos* 33 (2): 255–269.

Combès, Isabelle. 1999. *Arakae: Historia de las comunidades izoceñas.* Santa Cruz de la Sierra, Bolivia: Capitanía del Alto y Bajo Isoso / Wildlife Conservation Society Bolivia.

Combès, Isabelle, and Kathleen Lowrey. 2006. "Slaves without Masters? Arawakan Dynasties among the Chiriguano (Bolivian Chaco, XVI–XX centuries)." *Ethnohistory* 53 (4): 689–714.

Combès, Isabelle, and Diego Villar. 2007. "Os mestiços mais puros: Representações chiriguano e chané da mestiçagem." *Mana* 13 (1): 41–62.

Combès, Isabelle, and Diego Villar. 2004. "Aristocracias chané: 'Casas' en el Chaco argentino y boliviano." *Journal de la Société des Américanistes* 90 (2): 63–102.

Combès, Isabelle, Diego Villar, and Kathleen Lowrey. 2009. "Comparative Studies and the South American Gran Chaco." *Tipití: Journal of the Society for the Anthropology of Lowland South America* 7 (1–2): 69–102.

Corrado, Alejandro. 1884. "Continuación de la historia del Colegio Franciscano de Tarija." In *El colegio franciscano de Tarija y sus misiones: Noticias históricas recogidas por dos misioneros del mismo colegio*, ed. Antonio Camajuncosa and Alejandro Corrado, 279–503. Quaracchi: College of St. Bonaventure.

Culver, Stuart. 1988. "What Manikins Want: *The Wizard of Oz* and *The Art of Decorating Dry Goods Windows*." *Representations* 21 (Winter): 97–116.

Dagel, Kenneth C. 2004. "Cattle Ranching." In *Encyclopedia of the Great Plains*, ed. David J. Wishart, 37–38. Lincoln: University of Nebraska Press.

Dalton, Rex. 2004. "Natural Resources: Bioprospects Less than Golden." *Nature* 429: 598–600.

Davis, Lennard. 2002. *Bending over Backwards: Essays on Disability and the Body*. New York: New York University Press.

Davis, Lennard. 1995. *Enforcing Normalcy: Disability, Deafness, and the Body*. London: Verso.

Davis, Wade. 2004. *The Lost Amazon: The Photographic Journey of Richard Evans Schultes*. With a foreword by Andrew Weil. Vancouver/Toronto: Douglas and McIntyre.

Davis, Wade. 1997. *One River: Explorations and Discoveries in the Amazon Rainforest*. New York: Simon and Schuster.

Davis, Wade. 1987. *The Serpent and the Rainbow: A Harvard Scientist Uncovers the Startling Truth about the Secret World of Haitian Voodoo and Zombis*. New York: Warner.

Davis, Wade. 1986. "The Ethnobiology of the Haitian Zombie (Ethnobotany, Vodoun, Tetrodotoxin)." PhD diss., Cultural Anthropology, Harvard University.

DeLoria, Philip, and Christopher Riggs. 2004. "Native Americans." In *The Encyclopedia of the Great Plains Indians*, ed. David J. Wishart, 555–561. Lincoln: University of Nebraska Press.

DeMallie, Raymond. 1982. "The Lakota Ghost Dance: An Ethnohistorical Account." *Pacific Historical Review* 51 (4): 385–405.

Dighe, Ranjit S. 2002. *The Historian's Wizard of Oz: Reading L. Frank Baum's Classic as a Political and Monetary Allegory*. Santa Barbara, CA: Praeger.

Dyck, Cornelius J. 1993. *An Introduction to Mennonite History: A Popular History of the Anabaptists and the Mennonites*. Waterloo, ON: Herald Press.

Dyck, Erika. 2007. *Psychedelic Psychiatry: LSD from Clinic to Campus*. Baltimore: Johns Hopkins University Press.

Eastman, Charles. (1916) 1977. *From the Deep Woods to Civilization*. Lincoln: University of Nebraska Press.

Erickson, Clark. 2010. "The Transformation of Environment into Landscape: The Historical Ecology of Monumental Earthwork Construction in the Bolivian Amazon." *Diversity* 2 (4): 618–652.

Estes, J. Worth. 1994. "A Quixotic Search for New Drugs." *Natural History* 103 (3, March 19): 62.

Estrada, Víctor R. 2010. "Evaluación sobre la administración compartida del Parque Nacional y Área Natural de Manejo Integral Kaa-Iya del Gran Chaco, por los periodos 1995–2005 y adenda 2006." Unpublished report.

Estrella del Oriente. 1892. No. 1451, May 3, 2 (Santa Cruz de la Sierra, Bolivia).

Evans-Pritchard, Edward E. 1937. *Witchcraft, Oracles, and Magic among the Azande*. Oxford: Clarendon Press.

Fausto, Carlos. 2012. *Warfare and Shamanism in Amazonia*. Cambridge: Cambridge University Press.

Fausto, Carlos. 2007. "Feasting on People: Eating Animals and Humans in Amazonia." *Current Anthropology* 48 (4): 497–530.

Fausto, Carlos. 2000. "Of Enemies and Pets: Warfare and Shamanism in Amazonia." *American Ethnologist* 26 (4): 933–956.

Feinberg, Benjamin. 2003. *The Devil's Book of Culture: History, Mushrooms, and Caves in Southern Mexico*. Austin: University of Texas Press.

Ferguson, James. 2013. "Declarations of Dependence: Labour, Personhood, and Welfare in Southern Africa." *Journal of the Royal Anthropological Institute (N.S.)* 19 (2): 223–242.

Ferraro, Armando and Leon Roizin. (1949). Cerebral morphologic changes in monkeys subjected to a large number of induced convulsions (32-100). *American Journal of Psychiatry*, 106, 278–284.

Firestone, Shulamith. 1970. *Dialectic of Sex: The Case for Feminist Revolution*. New York: Morrow.

Flanagan, Tom. 2000. *First Nations? Second Thoughts*. Montreal and Kingston: McGill-Queens University Press.

Flood, Renée Sansom. 1995. *Lost Bird of Wounded Knee: Spirit of the Lakota*. New York: Scribner.

Fowler, Loretta. 2003. *The Columbia Guide to American Indians of the Great Plains*. New York: Columbia University Press.

Fraser, Nancy, and Linda Gordon. 1994. "A Genealogy of Dependency: Tracing a Keyword of the U.S. Welfare State" *Signs* 19 (2): 309–336.

Friesen, Abram, and Abram J. Loewen. 2001. *Escape across the Amur River*. Winnipeg, Canada: CMBC Publications and Manitoba Mennonite Historical Society.

Friesen, Martin W. 1997. *New Homeland in the Chaco Wilderness*. Trans. Jake Balzer. Loma Plata, Paraguay: Cooperativa Chortitzer.

Fritz, Miguel. 2008. "Indígenas y la Guerra del Chaco. El impacto de lo indicible." In *Mala guerra: Los indígenas en la Guerra del Chaco, 1932–1935*, ed. Nicolás Richard, 149–170. Asunción and Paris: ServiLibro–Museo del Barro–CoLibris.

Fritz, Miguel. 2003. "Y así empezó nuestra comunidad: Historia de las comunidades del Vicariato Apostólico del Pilcomayo." *Suplemento Antropológico* 38 (2): 205–290.

Galeano, Eduardo. 1973. *The Open Veins of Latin America*. New York: Monthly Review Press.

Gallo Toro, Victor. 1996. *Plantas medicinales de los guaraníes: Aporte al conocimiento de la etnobotánica en relación a su flora medicinal*. La Paz, Bolivia: Ediciones Fondo Editorial FIA–SEMILLA–CEBIAE Serie: Producción Agropecuaria.

Gardner, Martin. 1962. "Why Librarians Dislike Oz." *The American Book Collector* 13 (December): 14–16.

Gillmore, Don. 1987. *I Swear by Apollo: Dr. Ewen Cameron and the CIA-Brainwashing Experiments*. Montreal: Eden Press.

Giannechini, Doroteo. 1869. "Carta." Archivo Franciscano de Tarija, Carpeta 878, 26.VI.

Goffman, Erving. 1963. *Stigma: Notes on the Management of Spoiled Identity*. New York: Simon and Schuster.

Gorman, Peter. January 1995. "Ethnobotanist and Psychedelic Pioneer: Interview with Richard Evans Schultes." *High Times*, no. 233: 58–61.

Gough, Kathleen. 1971. "Nuer Kinship: A Re-examination." In *The Translation of Culture: Essays to E.E. Evans-Pritchard*. ed. T.O. Biedelman, 79–121. London: Routledge.

Gow, Peter. 2014. "Levi-Strauss's 'Double Twist' and Controlled Comparison: Transformational Relations between Neighboring Societies." *Anthropology of This Century*, no. 10, May. http://aotcpress.com/articles/lvistrausss-double-twist-controlled-comparison-transformational-relations-neighbouring/.

Gow, Peter. 1996. "River People: Shamanism and History in Western Amazonia." In *Shamanism, History, and the State*, ed. Nicholas Thomas and Caroline Humphrey, 90–103. Ann Arbor: University of Michigan Press.

Gow, Peter. 1991. *Of Mixed Blood: Kinship and History in the Peruvian Amazon*. Oxford: Oxford University Press.

Graeber, David. 2004. *Fragments of an Anarchist Anthropology*. Chicago: Prickly Paradigm Press.

Grünberg, Georg, and Friedl Grünberg. 1974. "Los chiriguanos (guaraníes occidentales) del Chaco central paraguayo." *Suplemento Antropológico* 9 (1–2): 1–109.

Gunder Frank, Andre. 1967. *Capitalism and Underdevelopment in Latin America*. New York: Monthly Review Press.

Gustafson, Bret. 2009. *New Languages of the State: Indigenous Resurgence and the Politics of Knowledge in Bolivia*. Durham, NC: Duke University Press.

Guthrie, Thomas. 2007. "Good Words: Chief Joseph and the Production of Indian Speech(es), Texts, and Subjects." *Ethnohistory* 54 (3): 510–546.

Gutstein, Donald. 2005. "Who Funds the Fraser Institute?" British Columbia Teachers' Federation *Teacher Newsmagazine* 17 (4, January/February): 11.

Hagenbach, Dieter, and Lucius Werthmüller. 2011. *Mystic Chemist: The Life of Albert Hofmann and His Discovery of LSD*. Santa Fe: Synergetic Press.

Hampson, Sarah. 2012. "Everest, Mallory—and Canada's Indiana Jones." *The Globe and Mail*, January 2.

Harkin, Michael, ed. 2004. *Reassessing Revitalization Movements: Perspectives from North America and the Pacific Islands*. Lincoln: University of Nebraska Press.

Hartsock, Nancy. 1987. "Rethinking Modernism: Minority vs. Majority Theories." *Cultural Critique* 7 (Autumn): 187–206.

Hastings, A. Waller. n.d. "L. Frank Baum's Editorials on the Sioux Nation." Unpublished manuscript.

Heckenberger, Michael J., Christian Russell, Carlos Fausto, Joshua R. Toney, Morgan J. Schmidt, Edithe Pereira, Bruna Franchetto, and Afukaka Kuikuro. 2008. "Pre-Columbian Urbanism, Anthropogenic Landscapes, and the Future of the Amazon." *Science* 29, vol. 321 (5893): 1214–1217.

Hedberg, Ana Sofia. 2007. *Outside the World: Cohesion and Deviation among Old Colony Mennonites in Bolivia*. Uppsala: Uppsala Studies in Cultural Anthropology 42.

Hill, Jonathan D., and Fernando Santos-Granero. 2002. *Comparative Arawakan Histories: Rethinking Language Family and Culture Area in Amazonia*. Urbana: University of Illinois Press.

Hindery, Derrick. 2013. *From Enron to Evo: Pipeline Politics, Global Environmentalism, and Indigenous Rights in Bolivia*. Tucson, AZ: University of Arizona Press.

Hirsch, Silvia. 1991. *Political Organization among the Izoceño Indians of Bolivia*. PhD dissertation, Department of Anthropology, University of California–Los Angeles.

Hirsch, Silvia, and Alexander Zarzycki. 1993. "Ipayereta, imbaekuaareta y evangelistas: Cambios y continuidades en la sociedad izoceña." In *Chiriguano*, ed. Jürgen Riester, 513–540. Santa Cruz de la Sierra, Bolivia: APCOB.

Hittman, Michael. 1990. *Wovoka and the Ghost Dance*. Lincoln: University of Nebraska Press.

Holden, Clare Janaki, and Ruth Mace. 2003. "Spread of Cattle Led to the Loss of Matrilineal Descent in Africa: A Coevolutionary Analysis." *Proceedings of the Royal Society of London B* 270 (1532): 2425–2433.

Hornborg, Alf. 2005. "Ethnogenesis, Regional Integration, and Ecology in Prehistoric Amazonia." *Current Anthropology* 46 (4): 589–620.

Horst, René Harder. 2007. *The Stroessner Regime and Indigenous Resistance in Paraguay*. Gainesville: University of Florida Press.

Hugh-Jones, Stephen. 1994. "Shamans, Prophets, Priests, and Pastors." In *Shamanism, History, and the State*, ed. Nicholas Thomas and Caroline Humphrey, 32–75. Ann Arbor: University of Michigan Press.

Huismann, Wilfried. 2012. *Pandaleaks: The Dark Side of the WWF*. Trans. Ellen Wagner. New York: CreateSpace Independent Publishing Platform.

Hutton, Ronald. 2001. *Shamans: Siberian Spirituality and the Western Imagination*. London: Hambledon and London.

Jensen, Richard E., R. Eli Paul, and John E. Carter, eds. 1991. *Eyewitness at Wounded Knee*. Lincoln: University of Nebraska Press.

Johnson, Harriet McBryde. 2003. "Unspeakable Conversations." *New York Times*, February 16.

Julien, Catherine. 2007. "Kandire in Real Time and Space: Sixteenth-century Expeditions from the Pantanal to the Andes." *Ethnohistory* 54 (2): 245–272.

Kao, C. Y., and T. Yasumoto. 1990. "Tetrodotoxin in 'Zombie Powder.'" *Toxicon* 28 (2): 129–132.

Kehoe, Alice Beck. 1989. *The Ghost Dance: Ethnohistory and Revitalization*. Long Grove, IL: Waveland Press.

Kittay, Eva Feder. 1999. *Love's Labour: Essays on Women, Equality, and Dependency*. New York: Routledge.

Klassen, Peter. 2004a. *The Mennonites in Paraguay*. Vol. 2, *Encounter with Indians and Paraguayans*. Trans. Gunther H. Schmitt. Kitchener, ON: Pandora Press.

Klassen, Peter. 2004b. *The Mennonites in Paraguay*. Vol. 1, *Kingdom of God and Kingdom of this World*. Trans. Gunther H. Schmitt. Hillsboro, KS: Print Source Direct.

Klassen, Peter. 1976. *Kaputi Menonita: Arados y fusiles en la Guerra del Chaco*. Asunción, Paraguay: Imprenta Modelo, S.A.

Koupal, Nancy Tystad. 2000. "On the Road to Oz: L. Frank Baum as Western Editor." In *Baum's Road to Oz: the Dakota Years*, ed. Nancy Tystad Koupal, 49–106. Pierre, SD: South Dakota State Historical Society Press.

Krieger, Linda Hamilton. 2003. *Backlash against the ADA: Reinterpreting Disability Rights*. Ann Arbor: University of Michigan Press.

Johnson, W. Fletcher. 1891. *Life of Sitting Bull and History of the Indian War*. Philadelphia: Edgewood Publishing.

Krieg, Margaret B. 1964. *Green Medicine: The Search for Plants that Heal*. Chicago: Rand McNally and Company.

Kroeker, Wally. 2005. *An Introduction to the Russian Mennonites*. Intercourse, PA: Good Books.

LaBarre, Weston. 1972. "Hallucinogens and the Shamanic Origins of Religion." In *Flesh of the Gods: The Ritual Use of Hallucinogens*, ed. Peter T. Furst, 261–278. Long Grove, IL: Waveland Press.

LaBarre, Weston. 1970. *Ghost Dance: The Origins of Religion*. London: Allen and Unwin.

LaBarre, Weston. 1941. Review of *White Water, Black Magic* by Richard Gill. *American Anthropologist* 43 (1): 103–104.

Lafone Quevedo, Samuel. 1919. "Guarani Kinship Terms as Index of Social Organization." *American Anthropologist* 21 (4): 421–440.

Langer, Erick. 2009. *Expecting Pears from an Elm Tree: Franciscan Missions on the Chiriguano Frontier in the Heart of South America, 1830–1949*. Durham, NC: Duke University Press.

Lee, Martin A., and Bruce Shlain. 1985. *Acid Dreams: The Complete Social History of LSD—the CIA, the Sixties, and Beyond*. New York: Grove Press.

Lévi-Strauss, Claude. 1963. "Do Dual Organizations Exist?" In *Structural Anthropology*, trans. Claire Jacobson and Brooke Grundfest Schoepf, 132–163. New York: Basic Books.

Lévi-Strauss, Claude. (1955) 1961. *Tristes tropiques*. New York: Hutchison and Company.

Lewis, Paul H. 1980. *Paraguay under Stroessner*. Chapel Hill: University of North Carolina Press.

Littlefield, Henry M. Spring 1964. "The Wizard of Oz: Parable on Populism." *American Quarterly* 16 (1): 47–58.

Loncraine, Rebecca. 2009. *The Real Wizard of Oz: The Life and Times of L. Frank Baum*. New York: Gotham Books.

Lone Hill, Dana. 2013. "The Wounded Knee Medals of Honor Should be Rescinded." February 18. *The Guardian* online. http://www.theguardian.com/commentisfree/2013/feb/18/massacre-wounded-knee-medals-honor-rescinded.

Lowrey, Kathleen Bolling. 2011. "Ethics, Politics, and Host Space: A Comparative Case Study from the South American Chaco." *Comparative Studies in Society and History* 53 (4): 882–913.

Lowrey, Kathleen Bolling. 2008a. "Incommensurability and New Economic Strategies among Indigenous and Traditional Peoples." *Journal of Political Ecology* 15: 61–74.

Lowrey, Kathleen Bolling. 2008b. "Liderazgo entre los guaraníes occidentales del Chaco paraguayo." In *Liderazgo, representatividad y control social en el Gran Chaco Sudamericano y zonas adyacentes*, ed. José Braunstein and N. Meichtry, 269–274. Corrientes, Argentina: Editorial Universitaria de la Universidad Nacional del Nordeste.

Lowrey, Kathleen Bolling. 2007. "Witchcraft as Metaculture in the Bolivian Chaco." *Journal de la Société des Américanistes* 93 (2): 121–152.

Lowrey, Kathleen Bolling. 2006a. "Entre estructura e historia: El Chaco." In *Definiciones étnicas, organización social y estrategias políticas en el Chaco y la Chiquitanía*, ed. Isabelle Combès, 25–31. Santa Cruz de la Sierra, Bolivia: Institut Français d'Études Andines—SNV—El País.

Lowrey, Kathleen Bolling. 2006b. "Bolivia multiétnico y pluricultural, Ten Years Later: White Separatism in the Bolivian Lowlands." *Latin American and Caribbean Ethnic Studies Journal* 1 (1): 63–84.

Lowrey, Kathleen Bolling. 2006c. "Salamanca and the City: Culture Credits, Nature Credits, and the Modern Moral Economy of Indigenous Bolivia." *Journal of the Royal Anthropological Institute* 12 (2): 275–292.

Lowrey, Kathleen Bolling. 2003. "Enchanted Ecology: Magic, Science, and Nature in the Bolivian Chaco." PhD diss., Department of Anthropology, University of Chicago.

Lurie, Alison. 2000. "The Oddness of Oz." *New York Review of Books*, December 21.

Macdonald, Nancy. 2014. "Renowned Anthropologist on a New Adventure—Academia." September 6. *Maclean's*. https://www.macleans.ca/society/renowned-anthropologist -wade-davis-begins-a-new-adventure-academia/.

MacIntyre, Ben. 2011. *Forgotten Fatherland: The True Story of Nietzsche's Sister and Her Lost Aryan Colony*. New York: Broadway Books.

Mahmood, Saba. 2005. *The Politics of Piety: The Islamic Revival and the Feminist Subject*. Princeton, NJ: Princeton University Press.

Maine, Henry Sumner. 1861. *Ancient Law: Its Connection to the Early History of Society, and Its Relation to Modern Ideas*. London: John Murray.

Mancuso, Alessandro. 2008. "Descent among the Wayú: Concepts and Social Meanings." *Journal de la Société des Américanistes* 94 (1): 99–126.

Mann, Charles C. 2005. *1491: New Revelations of the Americas before Columbus*. New York: Knopf.

Marks, John D. 1979. *The Search for the Manchurian Candidate: The CIA and Mind Control, the Secret History of the Behavioral Sciences*. New York: W.W. Norton and Company.

Martarelli, Angelico. 1892. *Sublevación de los indios chiriguanos en las provincias de Azero y Cordillera*. Potosí, Bolivia: El Porvenir.

Massumi, Brian. 2002. *Parables for the Virtual: Movement, Affect, Sensation.* Durham: Duke University Press.

Maurer, Bill. 2006. "The Anthropology of Money." *Annual Review of Anthropology* 35 (1): 15–36.

Maxwell, Nicole. 1961. *Witch Doctor's Apprentice: Hunting for Medicinal Plants in the Amazon.* New York: Citadel Press.

McGillycuddy, Julia. 1941. *McGillycuddy, Agent.* Oxford: Oxford University Press.

Meliá, Bartomeu. 1988. *Los guaraní chiriguano.* Vol. 1, *Nuestro modo de ser.* La Paz, Bolivia: CIPCA Cuadernos de Investigación 30.

Meliá, Bartomeu, and Christine Münzel. 1971. "Ratones y jaguares: Reconstrucción de un genocidio a la manera del de los Axé-Guayakí del Paraguay oriental." *Suplemento Antropológico* 6 (1–2): 101–147.

Métraux, Alfred. 1946a. "Ethnography of the Chaco." In *Handbook of South American Indians.* Vol. 1, ed. Julian Steward, 197–130. Washington, DC: Smithsonian Institution.

Métraux, Alfred. 1946b. "Chiriguano and Chané." In *Handbook of South American Indians.* Vol. 3, ed. Julian Steward, 465–485. Washington, DC: Smithsonian Institution.

Métraux, Alfred. 1931. "Les hommes-dieux chez les Chiriguano et dans l'Amérique du Sud." *Revista del Instituto de Etnología de la Universidad Nacional de Tucumán* 2 (1): 61–91.

Miranda, Carlos. 1990. *The Stroessner Era: Authoritarian Rule in Paraguay.* Boulder, CO: Westview Press.

Mitchell, Peter. 2015. *Horse Nations: The Worldwide Impact of the Horse on Indigenous Societies Post-1492.* Oxford: Oxford University Press.

Mooney, James. (1896) 1973. *The Ghost-Dance Religion and the Sioux Outbreak of 1890.* Unabridged republication of the Fourteenth Annual Report (Part 2) of the Bureau of Ethnology to the Smithsonian Institution, 1892–1893. New York: Dover Publications.

Morgan, Henry Lewis. 1871. *Systems of Consanguinity and Affinity of the Human Family.* Washington, DC: Smithsonian Institution.

Murdock, George P. 1957. "World Ethnographic Sample" *American Anthropologist* 59 (4): 664–687.

Nichols, Madeleine. 1939. "The Spanish Horse of the Pampas." *American Anthropologist* 41 (1): 119–129.

Niebuhr, Gundolf. 2001. "Logros y desafíos en la convivencia multicultural." *Suplemento Antropológico* 36 (2): 451–463.

Nino, Bernardino, and Angelico Martarelli. (1918) 2006. *El Colegio Franciscano de Potosí y sus misiones en el Chaco: Noticias históricas recogidas por dos misioneros del mismo Colegio.* Cochabamba, Bolivia: Talleres gráficos Kipus.

Nordenskiöld, Erland von. (1912) 2002. *La vida de los indios.* Santa Cruz de la Sierra, Bolivia: APCOB.

Oakdale, Suzanne. 2005. *I Foresee My Life: The Ritual Performance of Autobiography in an Amazonian Community*. Lincoln: University of Nebraska Press.

Oliver, Mike. 2013. "The Social Model of Disability, Thirty Years on." *Disability and Society* 28 (7): 1024–1026.

Organization for Economic Cooperation and Development (OECD). 2012. *Development Cooperation Report*. https://www.oecd.org/development/dcr2012.htm.

Orlove, Benjamin, John C. H. Chiang, and Mark A. Cane. 2000. "Forecasting Andean Rainfall and Crop Yield from the Influence of El Niño on Pleiades Visibility." *Nature* 403 (6765): 68–71.

Overing, Joanna. 2003. "In Praise of the Everyday: Trust and the Art of Social Living in an Amazonian Community." *Ethnos* 68 (3): 293–316.

Overing, Joanna. 1988. "Styles of Manhood: An Amazonian Contrast in Tranquility and Violence." In *Societies at Peace*, ed. S. Howell and R. Willis, 79–99. London: Tavistock Publications.

Overing, Joanna. 1975. *The Piaroa: a People of the Orinoco Basin/ A Study in Kinship and Marriage*. Oxford: Clarendon Press.

Overing, Joanna, and Alan Passes. 2000. *The Anthropology of Love and Anger: The Aesthetics of Conviviality in Native Amazonia*. London: Routledge.

Pérez Fernández, Marcelino. 1995. *Hernando Sanabria Fernández, 1909–1986: Inventario bibliográfico*. Santa Cruz de la Sierra, Bolivia: UPSA.

Pifarré, Francisco. 1989. *Los guaraní-chiriguano*. Vol. 2, *Historia de un pueblo*. La Paz, Bolivia: CIPCA Cuadernos de Investigación 31.

Plotkin, Mark. 1993. *Tales of a Shaman's Apprentice: An Ethnobotanist Searches for New Medicines in the Amazon Rain Forest*. New York: Penguin.

Prudén, Hernán. 2003. "Santa Cruz entre la post-guerra del Chaco y las postrimerías de la revolución nacional: Cruceños y cambas." *Historias: Revista de la coordinadora de historia (La Paz, Bolivia)* 6: 41–61.

Rahn, Suzanne, ed. 2003. *L. Frank Baum's World of Oz: A Classic Series at 100*. Children's Literature Association Centennial Studies, no. 2. Lanham, MD: Scarecrow Press.

Rapp, Rayna, and Faye Ginsburg. 2010. "The Human Nature of Disability." *American Anthropologist* 112 (4): 517.

Ratzlaff, Gerhard. 2008. *One Body, Many Parts: The Mennonite Churches in Paraguay*. Trans. Jake Balzer. Asunción: Evangelical Mennonite Association of Paraguay.

Reaume, Geoffrey. 2008. "Introduction to Disability Studies Quarterly Theme Issue on Disability in Canada." *Disability Studies Quarterly* 28 (1). https://dsq-sds.org/article/view/63/63.

Redekop, Calvin. 1973. "Religion and Society: A State within a Church." *Mennonite Quarterly Review* 48 (4): 339–357.

Reichel-Dolmatoff, Gerardo. 1975. *The Shaman and the Jaguar: A Study of Narcotic Drugs among the Indians of Colombia*. With an introduction by Richard Evans Schultes. Philadelphia: Temple University Press.

Renard-Casevitz, France-Marie. 2002. "Social Forms and Regressive History: From the Campa Cluster to the Mojos and from the Mojos to the Landscaping Terrace-Builders of the Bolivian Savanna." In *Comparative Arawakan Histories: Rethinking Language Family and Culture Area in Amazonia*, ed. Jonathan D. Hill and Fernando Santos-Granero, 123–146. Urbana: University of Illinois Press.

Richard, Nicolas. 2008a. "Les chiens, les hommes et les étrangers furieux: Archéologie des identités indiennes dans le Chaco boréal." PhD diss, EHESS, Paris.

Richard, Nicolas, ed. 2008b. *Mala guerra: Los indígenas en la Guerra del Chaco, 1932–1935*. Asunción and Paris: ServiLibro–Museo del Barro–CoLibris.

Riedlinger, Thomas J. 1990. "A Latecomer's View of R. Gordon Wasson." In *The Sacred Mushroom Seeker: Essays for R. Gordon Wasson*, ed. T. J. Riedlinger, 205–220. Portland, OR: Discorides Press.

Riester, Jürgen. 2006. "Iyambae—Ser Libre: La Guerra del Chaco en la memoria indígena isoseña." February 1. *Nuevo Mundo Mundos Nuevos*. https://nuevomundo.revues.org /1635.

Riester, Jürgen. 1985. "CIDOB's Role in the Self-Determination of the Eastern Bolivian Indians." In *Native Peoples and Economic Development: Six Case Studies from Latin America*, ed. Theodore MacDonald, 55–74. Cambridge: Cultural Survival.

Ritter, Gretchen. 1997. "Silver Slippers and a Golden Cap: L. Frank Baum's 'The Wonderful Wizard of Oz' and Historical Memory in American Politics." *Journal of American Studies* 31 (2): 171–202.

Rockoff, Hugh. 1990. "The 'Wizard of Oz' as a Monetary Allegory." *Journal of Political Economy* 98 (4): 739–760.

Roett, Riordan, and Richard S. Sacks. 1991. *Paraguay: The Personalist Legacy*. Boulder, CO: Westview Press.

Rogers, Katherine. 2002. *L. Frank Baum: Creator of Oz*. Boston: Da Capo Press.

Rossum, Sonja, and Stephen Lavin. 2000. "Where Are the Great Plains? A Cartographic Analysis." *Professional Geographer* 52 (3): 543–552.

Rouse, Irving. 1948. "The Arawak." In *Handbook of South American Indians*. Vol. 4, ed. Julian Steward, 507–546. Washington, DC: Smithsonian Institution.

Rutherford, Danilyn. 2016. "Affect Theory and the Empirical." *Annual Review of Anthropology* 45 (1): 285–300.

Sahlins, Marshall. 1996. "The Sadness of Sweetness: The Native Anthropology of Western Cosmology." *Current Anthropology* 37 (3): 395–428.

Sahlins, Marshall. 1985. *Islands of History*. Chicago: University of Chicago Press.

Saignes, Thierry. 1980. "Indios de Abajo, ideología e historia: Los Chiriguanos en los ojos del otro." *Revista del Instituto Nacional de Antropología* 2: 78–120.

Saignes, Thierry. 1990. *Ava y Karai: Ensayos sobre la frontera chiriguana, siglos XVI–XX*. La Paz, Bolivia: Hisbol.

Salomon, Frank. 2004. *The Cord Keepers: Khipus and Cultural Life in a Peruvian Village*. Durham, NC: Duke University Press.

Salomon, Frank, and Stuart Schwartz, eds. 1999. "Introduction." In *The Cambridge History of the Native Peoples of the Americas*. Vol. 3. Cambridge: Cambridge University Press.

Sanabria Fernández, Hernando. (1972) 2008. *Apiaguaiqui Tumpa: Biografía del Pueblo Chiriguano y de Su último caudillo*. Santa Cruz de la Sierra, Bolivia: La Hoguera.

Sanabria Fernández, Hernando. 1992. *Apiaguaiqui Tumpa: Conferencia dictada en la Colonia Piraí en 1986*. Santa Cruz de la Sierra, Bolivia: CEJIS.

Santos-Granero, Fernando. 2016. "Masters, Slaves, and Real People: Native Understandings of Ownership and Humanness in Tropical American Capturing Societies." In *Ownership and Nurture: Studies in Native Amazonian Property Relations*, ed. Marc Brightman, Carlos Fausto, and Vanessa Grotti, 36–62. New York: Berghahn.

Santos-Granero, Fernando. 2002. "The Arawakan Matrix: Ethos, Language, and History in Native South America." In *Comparative Arawakan Histories: Rethinking Language Family and Culture Area in Amazonia*, ed. Jonathan D. Hill and Fernando Santos-Granero, 25–50. Urbana: University of Illinois Press.

Schindler, H. 1985. "Equestrian and Non-equestrian Indians of the Gran Chaco during the colonial period." *Indiana* 10: 451–464.

Schmidt, Max. 1938. "Los chiriguanos e izozós." *Revista de la Sociedad Científica del Paraguay* 5 (3): 1–115.

Schuchard, Barbara. 1981. "The Chaco War: An Account from a Bolivian Guaraní." *Latin American Literatures* 5 (2): 47–58.

Schuchard, Barbara. 1993. "La conquista de la tierra: Relatos guaraníes de Bolivia acerca de experiencias guerreras y pacíficas recientes." In *Chiriguano*, ed. Jürgen Riester, 421–476. Santa Cruz de la Sierra, Bolivia: Apoyo Para el Campesino-Indígena del Oriente Boliviano.

Schultes, Richard Evans. 1973. "Man and Marihuana." *Natural History* 82 (7): 59–65.

Schultes, Richard Evans, and Albert Hoffman. (1973) 1980. *The Botany and Chemistry of Hallucinogens*. 2nd ed. Springfield, IL: Charles C. Thomas Publishers.

Schultes, Richard Evans, Albert Hoffman, and Christian Rätsch. 1992. *Plants of the Gods: Their Sacred, Healing, and Hallucinogenic Powers*. Rochester, VT: Healing Arts Press.

Schultes, Richard Evans, and Robert F. Raffauf. 1990. *The Healing Forest: Medicinal and Toxic Plants of the Northwest Amazon*. Portland, OR: Discorides Press.

Sheldrake, Merlin. n.d. "Heroes and Visions in Amazonian Ethnobotany." Unpublished ms.

Shulgin, Alexander. 2001. "A Tribute to Richard Evans Schultes." April 13. The Vaults of Erowid. https://www.erowid.org/culture/characters/schultes_richard/schultes_richard _tribute1.shtml.

Siebers, Tobin. 2004. "Disability as Masquerade." *Literature and Medicine* 23 (1, Spring): 1–22.

Siebers, Tobin. 2002. "Tender Organs, Narcissism, and Identity Politics." In *Disability Studies: Enabling the Humanities*, ed. and introduction by Sharon L. Snyder, Brenda Jo Brueggemann, and Rosemarie Garland Thomson, 34–52. Afterword by Michael Bérubé. New York: Modern Language Association of America.

Siffredi, Alejandra. "Un encuadre articulatorio de las relaciones interétnicas: El caso de la misión multiétnica Santa Teresa (Chaco Boreal)." *Cuadernos de Antropología* 2 (3): 110–126.

Singer, Peter. 1975. *Animal Liberation: A New Ethics for Our Treatment of Animals*. New York: Harper Collins.

Smoak, Gregory. 2006. *Ghost Dances and Identity: Prophetic Religion and Indian Ethnogenesis in the Nineteenth Century*. Berkeley: University of California Press.

Souter, Gavin. 1968. *A Peculiar People: The Australians in Paraguay*. Sydney: Angus and Robertson.

Sprague, Jeb. 2012. *Paramilitarism and the Assault on Democracy in Haiti*. New York: Monthly Review Press.

Stahl, Wilmar. 2007. *Culturas en interacción: Una antropología vivida en el chaco paraguayo*. Asunción, Paraguay: Editorial El Lector.

Stevenson, Robert Louis. (1896) 1998. *In the South Seas*. London: Penguin.

Stoesz, Edgar, and Muriel T. Stackley. 1999. *A Garden in the Wilderness: Mennonite Communities in the Paraguayan Chaco, 1927–1997*. Winnipeg: Canadian Mennonite Bible College Publications.

Strathern, Marilyn. 1987. "An Awkward Relationship: The Case of Feminism and Anthropology." *Signs* 12 (2): 276–292.

Surralles, Alexandre. 2009. *En el corazón del sentido: Afectividad, percepción, acción en los candoshi*. Lima: Institut Français d'Études Andines.

Susnik, Branislava. 1968. *Chiriguanos I: Dimensiones etnosociales*. Asunción, Paraguay: Museo Etnográfico Andrés Barbero.

Swazey, Judith. 1974. *Chlorpromazine in Psychiatry: A Study of Therapeutic Innovation*. Boston: MIT Press.

Taussig, Michael. 1987. *Shamanism, Colonialism, and the Wild Man: A Study in Terror and Healing*. Chicago: University of Chicago Press.

Taussig, Michael. 1984. "Culture of Terror, Space of Death: Roger Casement's Putumayo Report and the Explanation of Torture." *Comparative Studies in Society and History* 26 (3): 467–497.

Taylor, Anne-Christine. 2014. "Healing Translations: Moving between Worlds in Achuar Shamanism." *Hau* 4 (2): 95–118.

Taylor, Anne-Christine. 1996. "The Soul's Body and Its States: An Amazonian Perspective on the Nature of Being Human." *Journal of the Royal Anthropological Institute* (n.s.) 2 (2): 201–215.

Taylor, Anne-Christine. 1993a. "Des fantômes stupéfiants: Langage et croyance dans la pensée achuar." *L'Homme* 33 (126/128): 429–447.

Taylor, Anne-Christine. 1993b. "Remembering to Forget: Identity, Mourning, and Memory Among the Jivaro." *Man* 28 (4): 653–678.

Taylor, Sunny. March, 2004. "The Right Not to Work: Power and Disability." *Monthly Review* 55 (10): 30–44.

Teuton, Sean Kicummah. 2014. "Disability in Indigenous North America." In *The World of Indigenous North America*, ed. Robert Warrior, 569–593. New York: Routledge.

Thiesen, John D. 1999. *Mennonite and Nazi: Attitudes Among Mennonite Colonists in Latin America, 1933–1945*. Kitchener: Pandora Press.

Thornton, Russell. 2006. *We Shall Live Again: The 1870 and 1890 Ghost Dance Movements as Demographic Revitalization*. Cambridge: Cambridge University Press.

Tompkins, Jane. 1985. *Sensational Designs: The Cultural Work of American Fiction, 1790–1860*. Oxford: Oxford University Press.

Trautmann, Thomas R., and Peter M. Whiteley. 2012. *Crow-Omaha: New Light on a Classic Problem of Kinship Analysis*. Tucson: University of Arizona Press.

Turner, Terence S. 2013. "Schemas of Kinship Relations and the Construction of Social Categories among the Mebêngôkrê Kayapó." Unpublished manuscript.

Turner, Terence S. 2003. "The Beautiful and the Common: Inequalities of Value and Revolving Hierarchy among the Kayapó." *Tipití: Journal of the Society for the Anthropology of Lowland South America* 1 (1): 11–26.

Turner, Terence S. 2002. "Representation, Polyphony and the Construction of Power in a Kayapo Video." In *Indigenous Self-Representation in South America*, ed. Kay Warren and Jean Jackson, 229–250. Austin: University of Texas Press.

Turner, Terence S. 1996. "An Indigenous Amazonian People's Struggle for Socially Equitable and Ecologically Sustainable Production: The Kayapo Revolt against Extractivism." *Journal of Latin American Anthropology* 1 (1): 98–121.

Turner, Terence S. 1993. "The Role of Indigenous Peoples in the Environmental Crisis: The Case of the Brazilian Kayapo." *Perspectives in Biology and Medicine* 36 (3): 526–545.

Turner, Terence S. 1991. "Representing, Resisting, Rethinking: Historical Transformations of Kayapo Culture and Anthropological Consciousness." In *Colonial Situations: Essays on the Contextualization of Ethnographic Knowledge*. History of Anthropology, vol. 7, ed. George W. Stocking Jr., 285–313. Madison: University of Wisconsin Press.

Turner, Terence S. 1984a. "Dual Opposition, Hierarchy, and Value: Moiety Structure and Symbolic Polarity in Central Brazil and Elsewhere." In *Différances, valeurs, hiérarchie: Textes offerts à Louis Dumont*, ed. Jean-Claude Galey, 335–370. Paris: Éditions de l'École de Hautes Études en Sciences Sociales.

Turner, Terence S. 1984b. "Production, Value and Exploitation in Simple Societies." Unpublished manuscript.

Turner, Terence S. 1980. "The Social Skin." In *Not Work Alone: A Cross-cultural View of Activities Superfluous to Survival*, ed. Jeremy Cherfas and Roger Lewin, 112–140. London: Temple Smith.

Universidad Mayor de San Andrés (UMSA), Capitanía del Alto y Bajo Isoso (CABI), Office de la recherche scientifique et technique outre-mer (ORSTOM). 1996. "Perfil de proyecto: Producción de la crema antifúngica 'Aguaratimi' sobre la base de guirakillo planta medicinal de la etnia isoceña guaraní." Unpublished manuscript.

Utley, Robert. 2004. "Introduction" to the 2nd ed. In *The Last Days of the Sioux Nation*, by Robert Utley, xi–xvi. New Haven, CT: Yale University Press.

Utley, Robert. 1963. *The Last Days of the Sioux Nation*. New Haven, CT: Yale University Press.

Venables, Robert. 1990. "Looking Back at Wounded Knee 1890." *Northeast Indian Quarterly* 7 (Spring): 36–37.

Vestal, Stanley. 1932. *Sitting Bull—Champion of the Sioux—A Biography*. Boston: Houghton Mifflin.

Vidal, Gore. 1977. "The Wizard of the Wizard" and "On Re-reading the Oz Books" *New York Review of Books*, September 29 and October 13.

Viveiros de Castro, Eduardo. 2002. *A inconstância da Alma Selvagem e outros ensaios de antropologia*. São Paulo: Cosac and Naify.

Viveiros de Castro, Eduardo. 1998. "Cosmological Deixis and Amerindian Perspectivism." *Journal of the Royal Anthropological Institute* 4 (3): 469–488.

Viveiros de Castro, Eduardo. 1992. *From the Enemy's Point of View: Humanity and Divinity in an Amazonian Society*. Trans. Catherine V. Howard. Chicago: University of Chicago Press.

Wagenknecht, Edward. 1929. *Utopia Americana*. Seattle: University of Washington Bookstore.

Walker, Harry. 2012. "Demonic Trade: Debt, Materiality, and Agency in Amazonia." *Journal of the Royal Anthropological Institute* 18 (1): 140–159.

Walker, Robert S., and Lincoln A. Ribeiro. 2011. "Bayesian Phylogeography of the Arawak Expansion in Lowland South America." *Proceedings of the Royal Society B: Biological Sciences* 278 (1718): 2562–2567.

Wallace, Anthony F.C. 1956. "Revitalization Movements." *American Anthropologist* 58 (2, April): 264–281.

Warner, Michael. 1999. *The Trouble with Normal: Sex, Politics, and the Ethics of Queer Life.* New York: Free Press.

Wallerstein, Immanuel. 1979. *The Capitalist World Economy.* Cambridge: Cambridge University Press.

Watson, Elmo Scott. 1943. "The Last Indian War, 1890–1891: A Study of Newspaper Jingoism." *Journalism Quarterly* 20 (3, September): 205–219.

Widdowson, Frances. 2008. *Disrobing the Aboriginal Industry: The Deception behind Indigenous Cultural Preservation.* Montreal: McGill-Queens University Press.

Wilbert, Johannes. 1991. *Encyclopedia of World Cultures: South America.* New Haven, CT: Yale University Press.

Wikler, Daniel. 1979. "Paternalism and the Mildly Retarded." *Philosophy and Public Affairs,* 8 (4): 377–392.

Wishart, David J. 2004. "Introduction." In *Encyclopedia of the Great Plains,* Lincoln: University of Nebraska Press.

Wood, Graeme. 2008. "Mennonites and Mammonites." *Weekly Standard* 13 (3, April 21). https://www.washingtonexaminer.com/weekly-standard/mennonites-and -mammonites.

Yasumoto, T., and C. Y. Kao. 1986. "Tetrodotoxin and the Haitian Zombie." *Toxicon* 24 (8): 747.

Young, Allan. 1980. "The Discourse on Stress and the Reproduction of Conventional Knowledge." *Social Science and Medicine, Part B: Medical Anthropology* 14 (3): 133–146.

Znamenski, Andrei. 2007. *The Beauty of the Primitive: Shamanism and the Western Imagination.* Oxford: Oxford University Press.

Zuidema, R. Tom. 1983. "Hierarchy and Space in Incaic Social Organization." *Ethnohistory* 30 (2): 49–75.

Zuidema, R. Tom. 1977. "The Inca Calendar." In *Native American Astronomy.* Vol. 1:221–259. Austin: University of Texas Press.

Zuidema, R. Tom. 1964. *The Ceque System of Cuzco: The Social Organization of the Capital of the Inca.* Trans. Eva M. Hooykaas. Archives Internationales d'Ethnographie 50. Leiden, Netherlands: Brill.

Index

Page numbers in italics indicate illustrations

Amerindians: Achuar of Ecuador, 165, 166–169; of American frontier, 149; and Amerindian myth, 167; and Amerindian shamanism, 80, 120, 141, 143–144; in contrast to Western societies, 9–10, 173; and dependency, 17, 18; and disability theory, 17; and genocide, 149; and genocide of Indians, 152; and the Ghost Dance, 70; and increase in claims of indigeneity, 14; and Lakota people, 62; literature about, 151–152; and Matilda Gage, 201n2; myths of, 164, 165; and Native American Church, 130; of North American Great Plains, 32; oral traditions of, 169; and Oz books, 165; past of, 130–131; and peyote use, 130; practices of, 130; and revitalization movements, 17; and status-oriented societies, 9; and status vs. contract societies, 169; and vulnerability, 7–8, 18, 77; and white Mormons, 62. *See also* North American Indians; North American Plains Indians; Sitting Bull

Anthropology: Amazonian anthropology, 80; Americanist anthropology, 173; and Amerindian myth, 165; and Andeanology, 21, 22; and Anne-Christine Taylor's work, 7–8, 106–107, 109; and arutam complex, 106–107, 166, 168, 169; and autonomy, 9, 10, 12, 15; and

claims of disability and indigeneity, 14–15; and dependency, 10–14, 15; and disability theory, 4, 6, 8–9, 10, 11, 12, 14–16, 75, 75–79, 76; and feminist theory, 4, 5, 10, 11–14; and fieldwork investigations, 4–5, 6, 10, 18; and interconnectedness, 193; and Islamic societies, 11–12; and Isoso, Bolivia, 175; and kinship, 5, 6, 14, 22–23, 107, 108; and LaBarre's work, 74, 116; lowland South American anthropology, 5, 7, 14, 166, 195–196n1; and masculinity, 107; and modernity, 17; and prophetic movements, 76–77; and revitalization movements, 74–75; and shamanism, 6–7; and status vs. contract societies, 9, 14–16; and study of Amerindians, 17, 74–75; and traditional medicine, 133; and universal human features, 10, 11–13; and village life, 145; and vulnerability, 10, 75, 77–78; and witchcraft, 115, 145. *See also* Ghost Dance movement; Isoso, Bolivia; Mooney, James; Schultes, Richard Evans; Znamenski, Andrei

Apiaguaki Tüpa, 63, 65; age of, 47, 62; and autonomy, 25; birth year of, 148; and Bolivian politics, 25; as the Chaco prophet, 148; as chief of Guaraní people, 38, 41, 57, 65; and Chiriguano peoples' testimony, 78; and disability theory, 75; fate of, 32, 59; father of,

63; and follower Juan Ayemoti, 31, 32, 34, 35, 36, 48, 57, 59, 63, 197n12; and Guaraní people, 45, 61, 185; image of, 25–26, *26*; indigenous following of, 170–171; and invulnerability to settlers' arms, 77; as a **kereimba** (a warrior), 25, 44; and Kuruyuki massacre, 27, 31, 41, 55, 58; and masculinity, 25, 26; mother of, 31–32, 35, 39; name of, 42–43, 63; Sanabria's biography of, 27–29, 34–39, 43, 45, 46, 63, 123; and shamanic arts, 34; as a Tunpa (superior being), 47; Wikipedia entry for, 196n10

Apiguaiqui Tumpa: Biography of the Chiriguano People and of their Last Leader (Sanabria), 27–29, 58–59

Baum, L. Frank: background of, 170; and capitalism, 153; children's and other literature of, 153, 154, 155; disablement in works of, 154–155, 156–157; and eulogy of Sitting Bull, 148–149; and falseness as a theme, 155, 156; and femininity, 157; and gender ambiguity, 153–154, 157; and genocide of Indians, 149–150, 162; and Indian vulnerability, 7; and love of home, 154, 155; and masculinity, 156; mother of, 201n2; Oz books of, 4, 7, 148, 150, 152, 153, 154–157, 170, 201n1; and religion, 153; and white power, 7; and Wounded Knee massacre, 7; as a young man, 153

Baynton, Douglas, 11, 15

Bolivar, Simon, 69

Bolivia: Amazonian region of, 182, 184; and Andean capital La Paz, 113; Andean indigenous people of, 38–39, 103; Andean region of, 25, 28, 31, 38–39, 69, 95, 96, 97, 104, 139; Arawak group in, 98, 99–100; Asamblea de Pueblos Guaraní (APG) in, 41; and border with Paraguay, 175; Catholic clergy in, 40–41; Chaco Indians of, 29, 45, 64; and Chaco War, 19, 40, 139, 175, 182, 183, 184, 185; and Chiriguano people (or Ava, "men"), 19, 28, 29, 139, 183, 184; and city of Santa Cruz de la Sierra, 18, *20*, 28, 104, 112, 136, 140, 145, 176, 183; ethnobotanical resources of, 81; and European imperialism, 69; and government in Sucre, 46, 55; government of, 46, 55, 139, 184; Guaraní language in, 84; and Guaraní people, 6, 19, 40–45, 96, 108, 184; and immigrants, 188–189; indigenous communities in, 113, 138–140, 184, 188;

Indigenous Universities in, 25; investigative laboratory science in, 81, 113; Isoseño people in, 44, 120, 129, 140, 142, 144, 147–148, 174, 175, 183, 184; and liberation theology, 41; Machareti in, *177*; and Mennonite colonization of the Chaco, 182; Mennonites as settlers in, 8, 24, 175, 177; and modernity, 8; NGO groups in, 136–138; and Parapeti River, *20*, 96; and Parque Nacional Kaa-Iya del Gran Chaco, 5, *20*, 136, 138, 139; and political engagement of indigenous peoples, 40–41, 96, 104; protected areas in, 129; and revitalization movements, 83–84; and Simón Bolívar, 69; and South American Gran Chaco, 5; and Standard Oil, 139; submission of indigenous groups in, 38; town of Charagua in, 176, 178; tumpa period in, 40, 42–43. *See also* Guaraní people; Isoso, Bolivia; Kuruyuki, Bolivia

Bonilla, Oiara, 14, 108

Cameron, Ewen, 125–126

Chané people, 44–45, 71, 96–99, 101, 104–105, 107, 175. *See also* Chiriguano people

Chavarria, Melchor, 56–57

Chiriguano people: and Apiaguaki Tüpa's influence, 78; Ava people, 41; and biography of Apiaguaki Tüpa, 27, 28–29, 32, 34, 38; and Chané peoples ("Chiriguano") as slaves, 107; character of, 55, 70; communities of, 98, 99; and "conquest by cows" of the Chaco, 172; and examples of "god-men," 28–29; and Franciscan mission at Ivo, 46–47; Guiariyu as important to, 34–35; harvest festival of (**Arete Guasu**), 48–49; horses and cattle of, 68; and intentions of indigenous people, 78–79; and **ipaye**, 199n6; and Kuruyuki massacre, 55–56, 71; and masculine warrior (**kereimba**), 139, 140; and masculinity, 26, 43, 44, 45, 104, 106; and Nuer society, 107; and photo of "Chiriguano" man, 32–34; and revolts against white people, 34, 35; and shamans, 38; and Simba people, 41; and slavery, 97; songs of, 58; and struggles with Spanish, 38–39; weapons of, 65. *See also* Apiaguaki Tüpa; *Apiguaiqui Tumpa: Biography of the Chiriguano People and of their Last Leader* (Sanabria); Chané people; Kuruyuki, Bolivia

Combès, Isabelle, 27, 33, 48, 71, 196n5, 196n7; work of, 197n14

Culver, Stuart, 156

Davis, Lennard, 151, 159, 161, 163, 164, 166

Davis, Wade, 116–121 *passim*, 122–126, 127, 129, 132, 133, 158, 170. *See also One River* (Davis)

DeMallie, Raymond J., 78

Dependency: and Amerindian myth, 165, 168; and the charismatic relationship, 73; and Guaraní people, 44, 45; and Kuruyuki massacre, 24; and *Love's Labour: Essays on Women, Equality, and Dependency* (Kittay), 4; and projects in Isoso, Bolivia, 137–138; and relational dependency status societies, 164–165; and responsibilities for children, 104; and shamans, 101; and Shulamith Firestone, 195n2; types of, 135, 191; and vulnerability, 147

Disability: and activist Harriet McBryde Johnson, 193; and Americans with Disabilities Act of 1990, 159; and Amerindians, 166–167, 169; and children's literature, 164; and contract societies, 158–160, 161, 162–164, 165, 191; and eugenics policies, 161; and faking disability, 159, 162, 163; and *Game of Thrones*, 201n4; and impairments of Charles II, 195n3; and indigenous peoples, 164; and the Law of Persons, 159–160; mental disability, 158, 160, 161, 164; and Oz books, 7, 164; physical disability, 158; and status vs. contract societies, 159–164

Don Jorge Romero: and Apolonia (wife), 85, 86–87, 101, 106, 107; as a consultant to medical care initiative, 136; and curing sessions, 85; death of, 87; and dominance as well as beauty, 93; and ethnobotanical "laboratory," 84; and **guirakillo** samples, 84; home of, 138; and kinship, 93–94, 106; livestock of, 106; marriage of, 105, 106; patient of, 101; and the **paye**, 85–86, 90, 91, 92, 115, 141; shamanic powers of, 169; and supernatural illnesses, 142; and traditional medicine, 82, 86; and witchcraft, 90, 129

Don Miguel Cuellar Vaca, *171*; apprenticeship of, 85, 141; children of, 88, 102, 104, 111, 139; as a consultant to medical care initiative, 136; and curing people, 92, 141; death of, 87, 104, 111, 140; and dominance as well as beauty, 93; and Don Jorge Romero, 82, 84, 85, 86, 87; and ethnobotanical "laboratory," 81, 106, 112,

113, 114–115; and gas pipeline, 138; grave site of, 139; healing powers of, 112; and kinship, 89, 93–94, 102, 174; livestock of, 106; marriages of, 105; masculinity of, 106; patient of, 101–102; and the **paye**, 90, 91–92, 115; and *Salamanca*, 111; shamanic powers of, 120, 169; and traditional medicine, 82, 113; violin of, 88, *103*; and wife Neli, 87–88, 102–104, 106, 107, 111; and witchcraft, 90, 142; wives of, 87–88, 106, 107; and women, 109

Duvalier, Papa Doc, 126, 127

Eastman, Charles, 64, 65, 67, 68, 69

Evans-Pritchard, Edward, 107

Ferguson, James, 14

Flesh of the Gods: The Ritual Use of Hallucinogens (Schultes, LaBarre), 131

Fraser, Nancy, 13–14

Freud, Sigmund, 10, 75, 76, 154

Gender, 9, 11, 143, 153–154, 157, 158, 160

Geronimo, 26, 32, 40, 58, 63

Ghost Dance movement: and American Indians, 17, 27, 62, 63–64, 68, 70, 71–72, 197n2; and demands for troops, 64; and dependency, 73; and disability theory, 75; and ethnic and racial identity, 70; and hallucinatory visions, 72; and intentions of indigenous people, 6, 64; and Kuruyuki massacre, 26; and LaBarre's work, 73–74, 76, 116; and Lakota people, 62, 64, 70, 78; and police suppression, 29; and religion, 70, 71, 73–74, 78; and revitalization movements, 73; and stressful circumstances, 72–74; and work of Anthony Wallace, 72–73; and Wounded Knee massacre, 24, 63–68, 80; Wovoka as prophet of, 30–31, 62, 63, 64. *See also Ghost-Dance Religion and the Sioux Outbreak of 1890, The* (Mooney)

Ghost-Dance Religion and the Sioux Outbreak of 1890, The (Mooney), 71

Ghost Dance: The Origins of Religion (LaBarre), 73–74

Gimenez, Alberto, 81

Gordon, Linda, 13–14

Green Medicine: The Search for Plants that Heal (Krieg), 132

Guaraní people: and Aireyu family, 28, 41–42; Arawakanness of, 97; and Asamblea de

Pueblos Guaraní (APG), 41, 43; Ava Guaraní people, 25, 28, 29, 41, 43, 96, 103, 185–186; Bolivian Guaraní people, 19, 29, 40–45, 61, 89, 94–96, 97, 98–99, 104, 139, 184, 186, 187, 197n15; and Catholic missions, 186; and Chané peoples ("Chiriguano"), 44, 96, 97, 98–99, 104–105; cultural revitalization of, 27; and displacement to Argentina, 40; and displacement to Paraguay, 40; and Don Miguel Cuellar Vaca, 106; and families' resources, 19; and Guaraní Aquifer, 172; and Guaraní Occidental, 184, 193; histories of, 6, 36, 38, 48, 97; and Indian sexuality, 31–32; and intentions of indigenous people, 6, 48–49; and Isoseño, 41; and Kuruyuki massacre, 6, 25; language of, 43, 44, 47, 88, 97; and linguist Bret Gustafson, 45; and masculinity, 6, 37–38, 43, 44, 45, 97, 101; and meaning of **karai** (white), 89; **Ñemboati Guasu** ("Grand Assembly") of, 81; and Paraguayan Chaco, 186; and the **paye**, 89; and politics, 6, 40, 41, 43–44, 45, 170; reasons for migration of, 44–45; and resurrection in Paraguay, 48; and revitalization movements, 45; and Simba people, 41; songs of, 31, 37–38; Tupí-Guaraní peoples, 45, 89, 94–96; and white European people, 174; and word **tumpa**, 196n5. *See also* Apiaguaki Tüpa; Isoso, Bolivia

Healing Forest, The (Schultes and Raffauf), 127, 128, 130, 132

Isoso, Bolivia: and animal remedies, 198n3; **Artete Guasu** festival in, 83, 198n2; Catholicism in, 83, 186; and Chaco War, 185, 186; and Chané peoples ("Chiriguano"), 19, 41, 45, 96, 97–98, 99, 107, 140, 175, 185, 198n3; and city of Santa Cruz de la Sierra, 87, 89; and contract societies, 147–148; in contrast to Western societies, 173, 192; development projects in, 3, 4, 5, 136–138; division of, 139–140; and ethnobotanical "laboratory" funding, 113–115; ethnobotanical research in, 135; and evangelical Christianity, 83, 84, 88; and fieldwork investigations, 18, 82, 83, 84, 85, 86, 90, 94, 99, 101, 138, 139, 142, 144, 145, 174, 185; and gas pipeline, 138–139; Guaraní as language of, 5, 18, 19, 82, 84, 85, 86, 94, 96, 175; and Guaraní Occidental community,

174; and Guaraní people, 19, 21, 94–96, 105, 106, 108; and Guirapembirenda or Rancho Viejo, 138, 139, 174–175, 185; health care in, 19, 142; history of, 175; hunting and fishing in, 19, 83, 98, 108; and Ibasiriri, 81–83, 84, 85, 86, 95, 99, 101, 106; and irrigated agriculture, 18, 83, 96, 145; and **karai** (white) settlers, 18–19, 83, 90, 113; and kinship, 93–94, 99–101, 174, 175; laboratory of traditional medicine in, 84, 111, 113–115, 136, 139; life in, 6, 79, 80, 83–84, 101, 145–146; matrilineal or patrilineal leadership in, 99–100; and meaning of **mbaekuaa** (witch), 89–90; medicinal plant use in, 82, 84, 115; Mennonite farms in, *20*; and Ñande Yari ("our grandmothers") area, 98–99; national park project in, 128, 129, 135, 138; **Ñemboati Guasu** ("Grand Assembly") of, 81; NGO groups in, 136–138; and Parapeti River, 5, 18, *20, 21*, 98, 138, 184; and Parque Nacional Kaa-Iya del Gran Chaco, 139; and plant **guirakillo**, 81; and politics, 175; prisoners of war from, 185; and religions, 19, 88, 145, 186; schools and education in, 19, 94; and settled agriculturalists, 84; shamanism in, 131, 141–142, 144; and shamans, 3, 5, 80–81, 85–92, 93, 94, 102, 106, 110, 111–112, 115, 139, 144, 169; social hierarchy of, 94, 96–97; and status vs. contract societies, *21*, 111; and surname **Iyambae** ("without owner"), 19, 21; and Swiss Red Cross, 136; and term **paye**, 90; and traditional medicine project, 128, 129, 135; and traditional remedies from animal sources, 133; villages of, 3, 5, 18, 19, *20, 21*, 81–82, 83, 85, 86, 88, 89, 91, 94, 95, 99, 138, 145–146, 174–175; and vulnerability, 143, 147; water supply of, 114; and witchcraft, 82, 83, 84, 86, 111, 129, 144–145, 147–148; women and children of, 3–4, 86; women's roles in, 108. *See also* Mennonites

Kittay, Eva Feder: and analogical thinking, 193; and community, 13; and dependency, 4, 8, 10, 13, 191; and human universals, 12–13; and *Love's Labour: Essays on Women, Equality, and Dependency*, 4

Kuruyuki, Bolivia: and Angelico Martarelli's account of events, 46–52, 53, 54, 55, 56; and Apiaguaki Tüpa, 26, 27, 47–48, 55, 56–57; "battle" of, 46–57, 58, 71; and dates of massacres, 60; and deaths of Ava Guaraní people, 25, 58; and escalation of hostilities, 49, 55; and intentions of indigenous people, 70, 79; and invulnerability, 77; and joint command of Gonzales and Frias, 53–57; and killing of Christians, 50–52, 56; and killing of Indians, 50, 51, 54, 55–56, 57; literature on, 61; massacre at, 6, 24, 25, 27, 31, 38, 41, 54–55, 56, 57, 58, 59, 60, 61, 69, 71, 148, 197n15; number of warriors at, 47–48, 50, 52, 53, 54; and parallels with Wounded Knee, 61; and Santa Rosa Mission, 46, 49, 50–51, 54, 55, 56, 57. *See also* Sanabria Fernández, Hernando

LaBarre, Weston, 74, 116, 130, 131, 132, 200n9
Last of the Mohicans, The (Cooper), 152, 196n8
Leary, Timothy, 122
Levi-Strauss, Claude, 34, 167, 173
Life of Sitting Bull and History of the Indian War (Johnson), 29–31
Love's Labour: Essays on Women, Equality, and Dependency (Kittay), 4

Maine, Henry Sumner, 9, 160, 180, 188
Massumi, Brian, 5
Mennonites: and agriculture, 8, 24; and Alberta, Canada, 176; American migrations of, 8; Bolivian Mennonites, 175, 176–177, 178, 182, 188–189; Canadian Mennonites, 179–180, 181, 182; Chaco Mennonites, 173, 176, 179; and Chaco War, 182; and contract vs. status societies, 192–193; and contract vs. status societies, 180, 190–191; emigration of, 188; European and Russian migrations of, 8, 178–179, 180, 182; and farming, 8, 24, 178, 182, 183; Filadelfian Mennonites, 176, *177*; and German language, 8, 179; and historian Peter Klassen, 182; and indigenous people of Paraguay, 183; and Menno Simons, 178, 201n5; and migration to Canada, 178, 179, 182; and modernity, 8, 174, 177–178, 179, 180; and pacifism, 179, 180, 182; Paraguayan Mennonites, 175, 178, 179–180, 182, 188, 189; and religion, 8, 24, 178, 179, 183; and Russian Revolution, 179; sale of Isoseño lands to, 139; and Second World War, 182–183; settler colonies of, 8, *20*, 24, 112, 173, 174, 178, 183, 186; and the Ukraine, 179, 180, 183. *See also* Paraguay
Metraux, Alfred, 28–29, 35, 40, 42

Mooney, James: and anthropological literature, 74; and events at Wounded Knee, 71; and Ghost Dance movement, 71–72; and government's "Indian policy," 30–31; and "Lost Bird" (Marguerite), 60–61; and Smithsonian Institution, 64; and Wovoka's life and prophecy, 62–63, 64. *See also Ghost-Dance Religion and the Sioux Outbreak of 1890, The* (Mooney)
Morales, Evo, 188

North American Great Plains: Apache people of, 26, 172; approximate boundaries of, *23*; and Canadian Prairies, 23; and cattle ranching, 172–173; and challenges to settlers, 23, 69; features of, 5, 23, 172; and government's policy, 173; and horses, 23, 172; and images of "wild Indians," 23; and independence, 172, 173; and large land holdings, 23–24, 173; and massacre at Wounded Knee, 6; and modernity, 69–70; Mormons on, 173; and Plains Indians, 6, 32, 172; and sign language, 195n1; Sioux people of, 26, 172; societies of, 23, 172, 173; and South American Chaco region, 23, 172–173, 176; and vulnerability, 6, 69–70
North American Indians: of American frontier, 64, 69–70; Arapaho Indians, 62; Big Foot, 66–67; and Cheyenne Agency, 66; Dakota people, 64, 65; and European colonization, 71; and Ghost Dance message, 62–64, 68, 70; killing by ambush of, 65, 69; Lakota people, 29, 61, 64, 67, 68, 70, 78; Navajo Indians, 62; Plains Indians, 62; prejudice against, 69–70; religious movements of, 71; and revitalization movements, 74–75; Sioux people, 64, 65, 70; Smohalla movement of, 63; and status vs. contract societies, 69; tomahawks of, 65. *See also* North American Plains Indians
North American Plains Indians: of American frontier, 29, 32, 40, 172; Apache people, 32, 33, 38, 172; and Ghost Dance message, 62, 63–64; and horses, 27; images of, 26; Lakota people, 29, 61, 63–64, 67, 68, 70, 78; and *The Last Days of the Sioux Nation* (Utley), 58–59; literature on, 6, 58–59; and parallels with Chaco Indians, 27; photos of, 25–26; Sanabria's interest in, 61; Sioux people, 30–31, 32, 58, 59, 70, 148–149, 150, 172, 196n2. *See also* Geronimo; Sitting Bull

One River (Davis), 120, 132, 200n3

Paraguay: and Alfredo Stroessner in power, 183, 186, 187, 188, 191; and Argentine Casado family, 173, 181; army of, 185, 186, 189–190; and Ava Guaraní people, 185–186; black market economy in, 175; and border with Bolivia, 175; Casado holdings in, 24, 173, 181; Catholic clergy in, 41; and Catholic missions, 186, 189; Chaco region of, 174, 181, 184–185, 187, 188; and Chaco War, 19, 40, 175, 182, 184, 185, 186, 187; and colonies in the Chaco, 182, 186; and contract societies, 189; displaced Guaranis in, 40; fieldwork in, 4, 185, 186; and Filadelfia, 186, 189, 191; government of, 185, 187, 188, 190, 191; Guaraní language in, 184, 186; and Guaraní Occidental community, 174, *177*, 183–188, 189, 190, 191; and Guaraní prophetic promise, 48–49; and immigrants, 180, 181; indigenous peoples of, 182, 183, 184, 186, 187, 188, 189–190, 191; Isoseño people in, 174, 185, 186, 187; Mennonites as settlers in, 8, 174, 179–180, 181, 182, 183, 185, 186, 187, 189, 190–191; and modernity, 8; and President Eusebio Ayala, 181; and Royal Dutch Shell, 139; and status vs. contract societies, 188; and War of the Triple Alliance, 180–181. *See also* Mennonites; South American Gran Chaco

Plotkin, Mark, 132, 133–134, 200–201n14

Race, 9, 11, 142, 143, 157, 158, 160
Rawls, John, 12
Rockefeller, Laurance S., 128

Saignes, Thierry, 26–27, 48
Sanabria Fernández, Hernando: and account of Kuruyuki attacks, 52, 54–55, 58, 61; approach of, 31, 36, 39–40, 42, 46, 58–59, 62; and Ayemoti's letter, 197n11; background of, 28; and biography of Apiaguaki Tüpa, 27–29, 31, 34, 35–39, 40–41, 42, 43, 45, 123, 148, 170; as connoisseur of Indian lore, 28, 29, 33, 38, 39; and events in the Chiriguania, 61; and Guaraní history, 6, 38–40, 45, 139, 196n3; and intentions of indigenous people, 48, 49; and photo of "Chiriguano" man, 32–34; and prophetic movement of Guaranis, 6; and Richard Schultes, 124; style of, 196n8, 196n9

Schultes, Richard Evans: and Afghan fieldwork, 123; and Amazonia, 131; and Amazonian Indians' use of ayahuasca, 130; background of, 124; and biographer Wade Davis, 116, 117, 118, 119, 121, 122, 123–124, 125, 126–127, 133, 199–200n2; and CIA's MKULTRA program, 122; and Columbian Kofan, 199n1; and Columbia trip, 118, 119, 122, 123, 129, 200n12; devotees of, 132, 133; and the environment, 127; and essay in *Flesh of the Gods: The Ritual Use of Hallucinogens*, 131; and ethnobotany, 7, 115–116, 120, 121, 134; fanbase of, 170; and friendship with LaBarre, 116; and Gold Medal for Conservation, 128; and hallucinogens, 130; and Harvard University, 121, 122, 123, 124, 134; and indigenous knowledge, 127; legacy of, 132; and medieval witches, 130; Mexico trip of, 121; and peyote use in Kiowa in Oklahoma, 130; and plant-derived psychoactive substances, 125, 130, 134–135; and plants, 122, 132, 134–135; and *Plants of the Gods*, 122; and religion, 135; and research on curare, 116–117, 118, 125, 126; and rubber collection and research, 118, 119; and shamanism, 134; and shamans, 120; and Timothy Plowman, 123. *See also Healing Forest, The* (Schultes and Raffauf)

Sexuality, 160, 161, 162, 163, 164
Shaman and the Jaguar, The (Reichel-Dolmatoff), 129–130

Shamanism, 144; Amerindian shamanism, 6, 80, 105, 108; and Apiaguaki Tüpa, 34; ayahuasca shamanism, 131; and Don Jorge Romero, 106; and ethnobotany, 7; ethnographic accounts of, 131; and fieldwork, 80, 90; and Guaraní ethos of defiance, 107; and hallucinogens, 131, 132, 141; and healing, 80, 85, 92, 132, 141; horizontal shamanism, 92; and hunting and predation, 80, 92, 108; and importance of wives and families, 7, 108; and indigenous knowledge, 120; and interconnectedness, 193; in Isoso, Bolivia, 131, 141–142; and Kayapo of Brazilian Amazon, 92–94; and kinship, 108; and laboratory of traditional medicine, 7; lowland South American shamanism, 108, 141, 144; and masculinity, 7, 93, 108, 109; and **mbaeruvi isi** ("mbaeruvi mother"), 141; and the **paye**, 85–86, 89–90, 141–142; and plant knowledge in South America, 134; and plants, 129–130, 134; as religion of hunter-gathering societies, 131; Schultean view of, 120, 129–130; and shamanic powers, 110–111, 144; and shamans, 174; and shaman's personality, 131; Siberian shamanism, 105–106; skepticism of, 144; and status societies, 120; study of, 84, 90, 108–109; and transition to pastoralism, 105; vertical shamanism, 92; and a visionary experience, 72–73; and witchcraft, 90, 141–142

Shamans: Amerindian shamans, 120, 141, 143–144; of ancient cults, 35; Apiaguaki Tüpa, 34, 35–36, 39, 62, 148, 170–171; and Cameron, 200n6; chants of, 109; and disease cures, 134; Don Jorge Romero, 82, 84–87, 90, 91, 92, 93–94, 97, 101, 105, 106, 107, 109, 115, 129, 136, 138, 141, 142, 169; Don Miguel Cuellar Vaca, 81, 82, 84, 85, 87–88, 89, 90, 91–94, 101–104, 105, 106, 107, 109, 111–113, 115, 120, 136, 138, 139, 140, 141, 142, 169, *171*, 174; Europeans' view of, 143–144; and Guaraní term *paye*, 46, 85–86, 89, 90, 91–92; Guirariyu, 34–36; in Ibasiriri, 82, 86; in Isoso, Bolivia, 3, 5, 6, 7, 80, 81–82, 85–88, 102, 110, 115, 139, 144, 169; the "Jaguar Shaman," 133; of a Kofan village in Columbia, 118; Kuarirenda, 86; and laboratory of traditional medicine, 5, 6, 7, 110; lowland South American shamans, 115, 120, 141–142; and Mark Plotkin, 133–134; and meaning of **mbaekuaa** (witch), 89–90; and medical doctors, 142, 144; as native environmental scientists, 144; as native priests, 144; and patients, 101–102, 141–143, 169, 170; and the **paye**, 199n5; and plant medicine, 115; and process of becoming one, 34, 35–36, 91–92; in Rancho Viejo, 174; in relation to medicine, 136; and religion, 144; and shamanic congress, 112; and shamanism, 129, 131; of South America, 7; and *tsunki* (river-dwelling underwater wives) dreams, 168–169; Tupí-Guaraní shamans, 36, 86, 89; and ventriloquism, 36; and vulnerability, 142–143, 169; and witchcraft, 144; women shamans, 112; Wovoka, 30–31, 62–63, 148, *170*, 171. *See also* Shamanism

Siebers, Tobin, 17, 75–76, 159, 163, 191–192

Sitting Bull: and Apiaguaki Tüpa, 63; and Battle of Little Bighorn, 29; as a "brave," 40; and Buffalo Bill Cody's Wild West Show, 66; death of, 29, 63, 66, 148; Johnson's account of, 29–31; and Kuruyuki massacre, 26, 58; as leader of Sioux, 30, 32, 65–66; quote from biography of, 29

Smoak, Gregory, 70, 71, 197n2

South American Chaco Indians: and horses, 27; and parallels with Plains Indians, 26, 29

South American Gran Chaco: and Amazonia, 21–22, 95; of Bolivia, 8, 18, 23, 24, 31, 44, 45, 69, 88, 129, 136, 139, 145, 182, 184, 186; and Bolivian tumpa of 1892, 29; boundaries of, 22; and cattle ranching, 172–173; and Chaco War, 40, 182; and Chané farms, 172; and colonialism, 31; and "conquest by cows" of the Chaco, 172; features of, 5, 18, 23, 88, 95, 114, 173; and feeding and protecting, 100; and Filadelfia, 176; and government's policy, 173; and Guaraní Aquifer, 172; and Guaraní people, 104–105; and horses, 23, 172; and hunting and predation, 100; and images of "wild Indians," 23; and independence, 172, 173; indigenous peoples of, 172, 176, 179, 181, 191; and irrigated agriculture, 96; and kinship, 100–101, 105; language of, 199n7; and large land holdings, 23–24, 173; and Mennonites, 173, 178, 182, 183; and modernity, 69–70; music of, 88, 111–112; and North American Great Plains, 23, 172–173; of Paraguay, 8, 23, 24, 174, 178, 185–186; and Parapeti River, 199n9; and Parque Nacional Kaa-Iya del Gran Chaco, 5, *20*; pre-Columbian settlement of, 31, 96; and prophetic movement of Guaranis, 6, 24; and relations of dependence, 173; settlers on, 23, 172; societies of, 22–23, 24, 45, 98, 172; and South American indigenous narratives, 7–8; and South American shamanism, 108; and vulnerability, 69–70, 174; and white European people, 174. *See also* Mennonites; South American Chaco Indians

Sumner, Colonel, 66

Tales of a Shaman's Apprentice: An Ethnobotanist Searches for New Medicines in the Amazon Rain Forest (Plotkin), 132

Taylor, Anne-Christine: and absence of certainty, 173–174; and the Achuar, 165, 166; and Achuar narratives, 166, 168; as an Amazonianist, 109, 165; and Amerindian myth, 164, 165–169; and analogical thinking,

193; and debility, 8; and introspection, 165; and Jivaroan culture, 106–107, 165, 168, 169; and power, 8; and South American indigenous narratives, 7–8

Tonton Macoutes, 126–127

Trouble With Normal, The (Warner), 161

United States: and American Sign Language, 11; and Americans with Disabilities Act of 1990, 15, 159; and Battle of Little Bighorn, 29; and Baum's Oz books, 150–151; and Baum's *The Woggle-Bug Book*, 157; and Bolivia, 129; and CIA's MKULTRA program, 121–122, 125, 200n5; and Civil War, 180–181, 202n4; Dakota territories of, 69; and dependency context for welfare, 14; and funding for Schultes, 119; and Ghost Dance movement, 71–72; and government's treatment of indigenous peoples, 64, 69–70, 149, 152; and increase in claims of disability, 14, 15; indigenous communities in, 62, 63–64; and LSD research, 122, 126; and massacre at Wounded Knee, 29, 64–68, 69; and Mennonites, 183; and mobilization of troops and press, 64–65, 69; Mormons in, 24; and Native American Church, 130; and Oz series for children, 7; and Paraguay, 188; and peyote use in Kiowa in Oklahoma, 130; Plains Indians of, 6, 11, 29; and relations with Sioux people, 30; and Richard King, 173; and Rockefeller family, 128; settler colonialism in, 130; and status vs. contract societies, 69; and support for Duvalier, 127; and U.S. Rubber, 122; and World Wide Fund for Nature-US, 128; and Wounded Knee massacre, 6, 17, 69

Utley, Robert, 58–59, 61; book of, 197n16; and intentions of indigenous people, 67, 78; and Sitting Bull's biography, 66; on Wounded Knee massacre, 67, 68, 197–198n3

Vidal, Gore, 150, 153, 157

Wallace, Anthony F.C., 72–73, 74, 198n5

Witch Doctor's Apprentice: Hunting for Medicinal Plants in the Amazon (Maxwell), 132–133

World Health Organization, 135

Wounded Knee: accounts of, 31, 58–59, 62, 63, 67–68, 197–198n3; and Baum's editorial, 149–150; and camp at Wounded Knee Creek, 66–67; and compensation for Lakota people, 68; and dates of massacres, 60; and encounter of whites and Indians, 80; and intentions of indigenous people, 66, 70, 78; and invulnerability, 77; and Kuruyuki massacre, 26, 58, 59, 60, 61; and literature on, 61, 72; and "Lost Bird" (Marguerite), 60–61; massacre at, 6, 7, 17, 24, 27, 29, 58, 60, 61, 66–68, 70, 148; numbers of soldiers and Indians killed at, 67–68; photographic record of, 61, 68; and projection and misdirection, 126; and settlers' sentiments about Indians, 69; and Sioux people, 30, 58; and vulnerability, 70; and Wovoka, 171. *See also* Ghost Dance movement; Mooney, James

Wovoka, *170*; age estimate for, 62; birth year of, 148; death of, 63, 171; as the Ghost Dance prophet, 30–31, 62, 63, 64, 75; parents of, 62; as the Plains prophet, 148; spiritual influences of, 63; and welcoming white Mormons, 62

Znamenski, Andrei, 105–106

www.ingramcontent.com/pod-product-compliance
Lightning Source LLC
Chambersburg PA
CBHW070922030426
42336CB00014BA/2497